# 70 YEARS OF
# RYE HOUSE
# SPEEDWAY

# 70 YEARS OF
# RYE HOUSE
# SPEEDWAY

## NORMAN JACOBS

*This book is dedicated to Len Silver for over fifty years service to speedway in general and Rye House in particular.*

First published 2007

STADIA is an imprint of
Tempus Publishing Limited
The Mill, Brimscombe Port,
Stroud, Gloucestershire, GL5 2QG
www.tempus-publishing.com

British Library Cataloguing in Publication Data.
A catalogue record for this book is available from the British Library.

ISBN 978-07524-4162-7

Typesetting and origination by Tempus Publishing Limited
Printed in Great Britain

# Contents

Introduction and Acknowledgments     7

Foreword     8

The 1930s     11

The 1940s     19

The 1950s     25

The 1960s     42

The 1970s     55

The 1980s     80

The 1990s     113

The 2000s     129

# INTRODUCTION AND ACKNOWLEDGMENTS

Rye House speedway first opened to the public on 27 May 1934 as an amateur track operated by the Rye Stortford Motor Cycle Club. Two years later, Harringay Speedway took it over and launched it on its career as a major training track for young riders; a role it still enjoys today. Although the winter training school no longer takes place, Rye House is still one of the few tracks which gives its youngsters proper second-half races to compete in. Amongst those who had some of their earliest experience of speedway at the Hoddesdon track are a number of World Championship finalists and internationals, including Mike Broadbank, Ron How, Split Waterman, Gerry Hussey, Cyril Maidment and George White. Others to have come through the school include riders of the calibre of Bobby Garrad, Karl Fiala, Marvyn Cox, Andrew Silver and Steve Boxall.

As well as its role as the country's leading training track, Rye House has had a long history of league speedway from the pre-war Sunday Amateur Dirt Track League, through the Southern Area League of the 1950s and on into the British League era, and now runs two teams in the Premier League and the Conference League. Between 1934 and 2004, Rye House has only missed eight years, being one of the few tracks in the country to remain open during the war years.

This is the story of Rye House, its successes and failures, its highs and lows, its riders and larger-than-life promoters and managers, such as George Kay, Mike Broadbank, Colin Pratt, Ronnie Russell and 'Leaping Len' Silver, who has been associated with the track as a rider, promoter, manager and owner for over fifty years.

I am indebted to a number of riders, staff and supporters who have given up much of their precious time to talk to me about their time at Rye House. It was very noticeable that everyone I spoke to recalled their time at Rye House with great affection. In particular, I would like to thank Len Silver, Mike Broadbank, Martin Goodwin, Tommy Sweetman and his son Chris, Bob Andrews, Pete Sampson, Stan Stevens, George Barclay, Gerry King, Steve Ribbons, John Hyam and John Chaplin.

I would like to say a special thank you to Tony Hurren for his help and for penning the foreword to this book, to Barry Stephenson for his help with the early years and also to John Sampford for his help with many of the statistics contained within the book.

I am very grateful to a number of people and organisations for their help with the photographs. In particular, to Ian Moultray and the Friends of Edinburgh Speedway, Retro-Speedway for the photograph of Brian Foote, Mike Kemp, whose Elsa May Smith collection has proved invaluable, and Steve Dixon and Ken Burnett for giving their permission to publish a number of their photographs. The front cover photograph of Kelvin Mullarkey and the photograph of Mullarkey and Ashley Pullen on page 73 are copyright Mike Patrick and are reproduced by kind permission.

All averages, unless otherwise stated, are calculated match averages (cmas) and include bonus points. Qualification for inclusion: six matches.

# FOREWORD

## THE LIGHTER SIDE OF RYE HOUSE

The first time I saw speedway at Rye House, I was absolutely petrified. It was soon after the Second World War, when I was nine or ten years old, that my father took me to the picturesque Hertfordshire raceway.

I had been used to watching speedway at West Ham's Custom House stadium and, although The Hammers were playing to crowds of more than 30,000 – intimidating for a youngster – we stood on the terraces a reasonable distance from our swashbuckling heroes.

At Rye House it was different. Our spot on the terraces seemed to bring us within touching distance of the riders and, as a young boy, it seemed to me that they might come through – or over – the fence at any given moment.

My father and I were West Ham supporters and also watched The Hammers at other London venues. We enjoyed our regular Tuesday nights at Custom House where, under floodlights, we saw the big names of the day such as Eric Chitty, Malcolm Craven, Jack Parker and his brother Norman, Vic Duggan, Ron Johnson, Bill Kitchen, Tommy Price and so on.

It was a different scenario when we went to Rye House. If the weather was decent, we would head for Hoddesdon with our sandwiches and other goodies. It was more of a day out, a picnic maybe, as opposed to an evening's racing at London's major speedway arenas.

Rye House was known, justifiably, as the training track of the stars. Youngsters – and some not so young – would be taught the art of sliding a bike and the more advanced trainees could expect, at the very least, a second-half outing after an official fixture had taken place.

It will be well documented elsewhere in this book that riders such as Gerry Hussey, Mike Broadbank (I still think he should be known as Broadbanks, because he always rode under that name), Colin Pratt, Brian Brett and countless others first cut their racing teeth at Rye House.

I saw those riders mature into top-flight professional speedway stars, but I would bet anyone a pound to a penny that Pratty and his contemporaries look back on their time at the training ground with a lot of affection and recall countless tales that would bring tears to their eyes.

The point I'm trying to make is that even when Rye House competed in the Southern Area League, nobody expected the presentation and the bill of fare to be up to Wembley standards. However, the riders performed as if their lives depended on it and the crowd was always entertained.

I seem to remember that the Lord's Day Observance Society was all-powerful in those days and it was against the laws of the land to open turnstiles on the Sabbath. The way round it was to sell 'one-day membership' tickets from a table near the entrance.

Former Harringay fanatic and Hackney Supporters' Club supremo Snowy Beattie was invariably in charge of ticket sales and used to guard the entrance with his life. However, Dingle Brown will tell you with a glint in his eye that he and his mates would often hoodwink Snowy and cross the River Lea to bunk in. Boys will be boys.

From the mid-1960s, I moved from being a Rye House terrace type to stand-in announcer for the legendary Ted Sear, ultimately becoming the regular mike man for the series of open meetings that were run at the time.

This book will concentrate on the more serious side of speedway at Rye, so I thought I would outline a few incidents that happened in the announcer's box that were serious to me at the time, but which I can now look back on with a wry (excuse the pun) grin on my face and which, hopefully, will amuse readers.

The first one concerns an individual meeting refereed by an ageing official whom, I believe, was a wartime squadron leader – or something like that.

In common with the situation at many tracks, the announcer and referee shared the same facility at Rye House. Before the meeting began, I introduced myself to the referee, but I was wasting my time. He didn't look so much at me as through me and never said a word.

After the first heat, I announced the result and gave the crowd the race time. The referee then said to me, 'I want you to announce that times given at this meeting are unofficial.' I asked him why that was and he growled, 'Simply do as I ask.' I duly informed the crowd.

A couple of races later, the official ludicrously excluded a rider for being the cause of the stoppage and my appropriate announcement brought the expected response from the crowd. It also prompted the excluded rider to march across the centre green, helmet tucked under his arm, through the gap by the starting gate and up the rickety stairs to the referee's box. A right old slanging match ensued, whereupon the ref told the rider he was fining him.

I was asked to tell the crowd of the referee's decision and that led to more abuse heading our way and, I seem to recall, an impromptu whip-round. It is astonishing how so many people in the crowd seem to put as much blame on the announcer as on the bloke who made the offending decision.

However, what had gone before was mild by comparison with what was to follow. It was the race prior to the interval and the riders were lined up at the starting gate – red on the inside, blue off gate two and so on. When the tapes went up, the riders in the red, blue and yellow helmet colours made an equal getaway, but the guy in white had missed it completely. As the riders went into the first bend the rider in red missed the turn and brought down the riders in blue and yellow. The rider in white simply rode round the mayhem.

In the pile-up, the rider in red – the obvious cause of the stoppage – lost his helmet colour to reveal a white helmet underneath. The referee – you've probably guessed it – instructed me to exclude the rider in white for being the primary cause of the stoppage. I was having none of that and attempted to explain the situation to the ref, who told me to carry out his instructions. I'd had enough, I said, 'If you want that announced, you announce it yourself. The rider in white is just below us on his way back to the pits.'

The ref suddenly realised that he might have misread the situation and the first civil words he uttered to me all afternoon were, 'Ask the clerk of the course to come to the telephone.' The clerk of the course confirmed my view of the incident and the referee instructed me to announce that the rider in red – or, at least, the rider who set out in red – was to be excluded.

The situation brought an element of détente to the relationship between the referee and myself. A couple of races later, he explained that he had asked me to announce that the race times were unofficial because official times could only be given by a timekeeper licensed by the Speedway Control Board.

I simply went to my coat pocket and, without saying a word, showed him my official pass. To my amazement, he said, 'You should have showed me that in the first place.' To add insult to injury, the referee then instructed me to inform the crowd that the times were, after all, official ones.

On another occasion I was working at Rye House with a referee – a nice man – who had only a short spell in the role. I don't think he was in the top category of referees and one of his major problems was that he appeared to lack communication skills.

Referees need to liaise with riders, team managers and other pit officials and it does help if one is articulate. On this occasion, the referee excluded a rider – correctly in my opinion – for being the cause of the race stoppage.

Here, again, the rider – helmet tucked under his arm – climbed the stairs to the referee/announcer's box and let forth a stream of expletives. The ref turned to the rider and said, 'If you talk to me like that I'll stick one on you.'

The rider believing, not surprisingly, that he was being threatened with violence, retorted, 'You bloody well try it.' The ref looked aghast, but I defused the situation by explaining to the rider that I felt sure the referee meant that the rider would incur a fine.

On another occasion, I was announcing at a team event at Rye House, after which there were the customary second-half races. Rye House general factotum Bill Mathieson – I'm not sure whether he was clerk of the course – telephoned me and said, 'An Italian trainee is going out in white, but we're having difficulty getting his name.'

I told Bill that the ref would want to know who it was and Bill said, 'For the moment call him Agostini.' I told the ref that the rider in white was Marco Agostini (or something like that) and he duly filled his programme in without questioning whether the guy was licensed or not.

There were young riders at Rye House trying hard to make the grade and secure places in league teams, plus a few old hands who simply wanted to flex their muscles, when they might have been better off in the armchair with their slippers on.

I said at the outset of this article that the book would contain copious words covering the serious side of the sport. My mission was to write something more light-hearted (but true) and I hope I haven't given the impression that Rye House in the 1960s was some kind of 'Carry on Speedway' arena.

However, it wasn't perhaps promoted in such a serious or professional manner as one would expect speedway to be today and I feel a comment made to me by arguably the best referee of all time, Arthur Humphrey, will bear testimony to this.

Arthur – whose brother Harold always accompanied him to meetings – said to me: 'I love coming here Tony. I run it as I would run any meeting, but I always feel the pressure is off me. It is an arena where, more than any other, I can relax and enjoy the racing.'

I think that adequately sums up Rye House during my time as the venue's announcer. It was a track where riders could learn their trade under 'Queensberry' rules, but where the rigidity of the rulebook was occasionally sacrificed.

And, as the saying goes, a great time was had by all!

Tony Hurren
Former Rye House Announcer

# The 1930s

## 1934/35

The first known proper dirt-track speedway meeting took place on 27 May 1934. It was run under the auspices of the Rye Stortford Motor Cycle Club, whose secretary was Mr T.H. Felstead of 21 Bell Lane, Sawbridgeworth. The meeting consisted of sixteen races in four individual events: the Standing Start trophy, the Rolling Start trophy, the Handicap event and a Special Match Race. Amongst the riders taking part were Tiger Hart and Ken Brett. Meetings continued on a fortnightly basis until 2 September.

The track, approximately 440 yards in length, was built on a piece of land, formerly a watercress field, next to the River Lea. There is a story that the track was originally built some six years previously by Mr Gerard Frogley for his two sons, Roger and Buster, to practice the new sport of dirt-track racing, recently imported from Australia. The Frogley family were well-known local aeronauts who founded the Herts and Essex Aero Club, operating out of an airstrip built, like the dirt track, on a piece of land belonging to the family near Broxbourne.

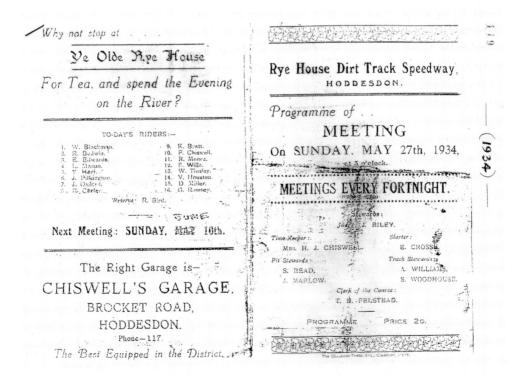

The programme cover from the first meeting ever held at Rye House on 27 May 1934.

The Frogley boys became pre-eminent in the new sport and were two of the leading British exponents in the early years, Roger becoming the first British Star Riders' Champion in 1929 and Buster captain of the famous Wembley team.

In 1935, both greyhound racing and further dirt-track racing were staged at Rye House. The racing in 1934 and 1935 was very much an amateur affair, with locals from the Rye Stortford Club trying out their hand at the new sport.

## 1936

A big change came in 1936 when Harringay speedway, under their dynamic promoter Tom Bradbury Pratt, decided to take a hand in the track's fortunes. In September 1935, Bradbury Pratt put in an application to the Auto Cycle Union (ACU), the governing body for the sport in Great Britain, to run a training track at Rye House. The idea was that a training school be set up and run by Harringay but under the overall control of the Speedway Control Board. Mr Singleton, the speedway manager at Harringay, explained:

> To our mind it is negligence that ambitious novices who have spent pounds on their equipment are not allowed to obtain all the facilities necessary for the making of speedway riders. One feature of our scheme is that these boys be registered, and that the School supply new riders to the Provincial League tracks at the discretion of the Control Board.

At the time, there was only one other recognised training track in the country, at High Beech. Youngsters who wanted to break in to speedway for the most part had to buy a bike, take it along to a National League track and ask for a trial. With hundreds of youngsters wishing to try their hand, it was very much pot luck who would get a trial and who wouldn't. It was this problem that Mr Bradbury Pratt wished to address. It is true that there were other non-league tracks for novices and juniors, such as Eastbourne and Barnet, but none of these provided any actual instruction for the youngsters.

In the spring of 1936 there was a big furore in the speedway press and amongst speedway supporters that two Americans, Jack and Cordy Milne, had been allowed to ride in this country by the ACU. Once again, the question of training up our own youngsters came to the fore. To try and encourage young riders, the Control Board came up with an alternative scheme to training tracks: they set up the Provincial League. In effect this was a second division, consisting of six tracks: Bristol, Cardiff, Liverpool, Nottingham, Plymouth and Southampton. This, they hoped, would encourage more young riders into the sport. Unfortunately, it did not turn out the way the Control Board hoped and the Provincial League very soon became a place where older, more experienced riders, who couldn't break into a National League team, went. As the *Speedway News* pithily explained at the time, it became a 'Home of Rest for Tired Riders'.

This turn of events, combined with the fact that the High Beech Training School closed down in June 1936, encouraged Harringay to pursue their case harder with the ACU, from whom they had received no reply since their original application in September 1935, some nine months earlier.

This time, Harringay got the answer they wanted and on 20 June, Messrs S.R. Singleton and G. Kay, who were to be the organisers of the training track on behalf of Harringay, announced that they had at last got the go-ahead:

> The track is a quarter-mile cinder circuit comparable with any of the provincial league speedways. Practice for riders with equipment will be held every Thursday evening from 5:30 onwards. The charge per evening is 3s 6d to cover full personal insurance. The opening meeting will be on Sunday June 21st, when the programme will consist of scratch races and a 9-heat 6-a-side team match. At present the management is in touch with other affiliated clubs operating Sunday meetings with a view to arranging home and away matches.

A general view
of Rye House in
1936.

Providing the others are interested there seems to be no reason why a league should not be run of the local affiliated clubs, and thus give the real novices a chance to participate in team racing. It is thought that riders may emerge from this type of racing who can quickly adapt themselves to team racing. In the event of any club member wishing to go to one of the big teams or a Provincial League team, the Rye House management feel that would be up to the A.C.U. to arrange things to ensure that he gets a square deal. No ex-contract rider of more than two years' service will be allowed to participate at these meetings without special permission from the Controlling Body. At present no rider is allowed on the track at Rye House unless covered by personal accident insurance identical with that of the major tracks. The management regret that at present they cannot cater for the novice with no equipment. To do so would be far too expensive.

The idea, therefore, was to run training sessions on Thursdays with meetings open to the public on Sundays. In contrast to most of the other non-league tracks of the time, such as Barnet and Smallford, which were mainly grass tracks with some cinders thrown down at the corners, Singleton and Kay made sure that Rye House was a 'proper' speedway track with cinders all the way round to give the youngsters a feel for the real thing.

The Sunday meetings got underway with a number of open meetings running scratch team matches and individual events. However, they pulled off something of a coup on 19 July when they staged one of Putt Mossman's 'Motor Rodeo and Circus' meetings. Putt Mossman's troupe was a world-renowned American group of riders who, at that time, were visiting National and Provincial League tracks around the country putting on their shows which included many 'death-defying' feats, such as crashing through solid wooden doors and riding through flaming walls of fire. In fact, when Mossman crashed through the solid wooden wall in the finale to his act at Rye House, it was even more dangerous than the crowd imagined, as Mossman was riding with a very bad injury he had sustained in Paris the previous Sunday.

On 2 August, Mr Bradbury Pratt felt it was time to show off his first-year trainees to the public and put up a cup, the T. Bradbury Pratt Cup, to be raced for by the best of his novices. The winner was F. Murray, who won all three of his heats. Hayhow was second, Dellow third and Fred Curtis fourth.

In the second half of the programme, some of the more experienced juniors took part. The winner of this event was Charlie Robinson, who had proved himself over the previous weeks to be the best of the bunch at Rye House, although he was pushed hard in one race by the twenty-one-year-old Archie Windmill.

In the following week's Taylor Walker Cup, Robinson once again came out on top. Although Robinson had it won from the gate, the final was an exciting race as behind him Rol Gower, Phil Lewry and Pip d'Allessandro had the crowd on their toes for all four laps as they passed and re-passed each other all the way round the track. Eventually, d'Allessandro just pipped Lewry and Gower respectively.

The following week, some of Rye House's leading riders made the short trip to Barnet to take part in the annual Inter-Club Championship. The final was between Robinson, Jim Boyd, Windmill and C. Traynor, with Robinson taking first place. So, in their first full year, Rye House had managed to find the 'amateur' champion of Great Britain. It was a great honour for Robinson to be presented with the cup by the great Vic Huxley.

On 6 September, a team representing Rye House took on the Putt Mossman team in a challenge match. It was a brilliant performance by the youngsters, but in the end they went down by 41 points to 28. Robinson captained the Rye House team and scored eight points, plus one fall when racing shoulder to shoulder with Mossman in heat eleven. Other members of the Rye House team that day included Reg Allen, who scored seven points, Les Trim with five and d'Allessandro with four.

Mr Bradbury Pratt put up another cup on 13 September, this time for the best Rye House junior. Along with the cup, Bradbury Pratt was also offering the winner and the runner-up the chance to appear at Harringay the following week. Robinson was the hot favourite to win, but, after winning two races easily, he fell while well in front in his third race. He recovered to win his last race in the fastest time of the day, 92.0 seconds, but his total of nine points from four rides was not enough for him to make either first or second place. Allen, Charlie Lish and Trim all scored 12 points. In the run-off, Allen led from start to finish with Lish in second place. The main event was followed by the 'Big Six' event for the top six riders of the day, to be ridden in two heats of three riders per heat, with the two winners meeting in a match-race final. Bradbury Pratt announced that the winner of this, unless it was Allen or Lish, would also have the opportunity to ride at Harringay the following week. The two finalists were Robinson and Allen. The final only got as far as the first bend before Allen came down and although Robinson was actually in front, Allen's bike somersaulted over him and caught Robinson in the rear, bringing him down too. Robinson won the rerun on borrowed machinery.

The following week at Harringay, Lish won the 'Nursery' event in the second half and then, for good measure, beat Robinson in a special Junior Match Race.

For the grand finale to the season, Rye House took on Dagenham, another training track that had started just after Rye House. Dagenham had already raced a number of inter-track matches; something Rye House had not really gone in for, preferring the individual trophy-style meeting. As well as having more experience of team racing, the Daggers were also unbeaten. However, the clash was eagerly looked forward to by the Rye House supporters and a large crowd turned out on 4 October to cheer their team on. Rye House had their strongest pairing out in heat one as Robinson and Allen got the team off to the perfect start with a 5-1 over the Dagenham captain, the brilliant Frank Hodgson, and his partner Aussie Powell. Unfortunately, neither of the Rye House riders finished in heat two as both Trim and Desmond fell while holding a 5-1. The Rye House team went further behind in heat three as Dagenham's Jim Boyd and Fred Quick took a 4-2 over Windmill and d'Allessandro. The match looked all

Charlie Robinson, winner of the 1936 Inter-Club Championship

over after heat four as the home team suffered a 5-1 reverse. The score was now Rye House 8 Dagenham 15. A 3-3 in the next heat was followed by the start of the Rye House comeback as, in heat six, Robinson and Allen struck with a 5-1. Once again, this was countered by a Dagenham 5-1 in the following heat, but in heat eight it was Rye House's turn to get a 5-0 as neither of the Dagenham riders finished. Heat nine saw another 4-2 for Dagenham, but it was heats ten and eleven that turned the match for Rye House as both ended in 5-1s for the home side. Heat eleven was something of a surprise as it matched d'Allessandro and Trim against the high-scoring Dagenham pair of Quick and Challis. However, some brilliant team riding by the Rye House duo at a critical time set the match up for a last-heat decider. Rye House needed to stop Dagenham getting a 5-1 to be sure of winning the match. With Robinson riding for Rye House there seemed little danger of that happening and, sure enough, Robinson completed his maximum with a fine victory to bring Rye House home 37-33 in their first proper Challenge match against another recognised club side. The Rye House scores were: Robinson 12, Allen 8+4, Windmill 6, d'Allessandro 6, Trim 5+1.

## 1937

Rye House was due to re-open for the 1937 season on 18 April but, unfortunately, heavy rain flooded the track and the new opening date was set for 2 May with a Challenge match against Dagenham. This was to be a return fixture as the Rye House team had already met and lost to the Daggers on the latter's home track by the embarrassing score of 54-17.

At the return on their own track, Rye House did not fare much better, going down 43-25. With the leading riders from the previous year - Robinson, Allen, Lewry and Windmill - all looking for team places with National or Provincial League teams, a new crop of youngsters were representing Rye House. Of the established 'stars' at Rye House, only Windmill eventually made the grade, later riding for Hackney, Wimbledon and Walthamstow. Robinson had a few outings at Wimbledon and Lewry at Wembley, but generally these riders were top grass-track stars and when they couldn't break through in to speedway in a big way, they decided to return to the grass tracks.

The best of the new crop in the matches against Dagenham were Basil 'Bumblebee' Bumstead, A. Stewart and J. Hamilton, but it was obvious they were not yet up to the standard of the previous year's juniors. Rye House's next team outing was another two-leg affair, against High Beech. Once again, they were on the losing end of two beatings.

Apart from losing to Dagenham and High Beech, Rye House had an unfortunate start to the season in another way as four out of their first seven fixtures were washed out by heavy rain.

However, things began to look up for Rye House as, firstly, the rain stopped and, secondly, they recorded their first victory of the season on 22 August against Eastbourne, 47-25. The Rye House scores were: Boyd 12, Tommy Allott 11, R. Lovell 9, W. Lowther 8, Robinson 5, Curtis 2. The return leg at Arlington on 4 September was an exciting affair, with Eastbourne gaining their revenge, 52-32, leaving Rye House the victors on aggregate, 79-77.

A significant event in the history of Rye House was announced on 18 September 1937, when Hackney skipper and Australian Test rider Dicky Case revealed that he was to retire and take over the coaching at Rye House. He bought the Rye House Residential Hotel, Hoddesdon, along with which went the Rye House track. He planned to continue the fine work started by Harringay Speedway and to co-operate with the ACU in providing instruction: 'such as a raw novice could not hope to get anywhere else.' With Case's involvement, oversight of the school switched from Harringay to Hackney.

His first proposal was aimed at giving juniors a proper feel for competitive racing by instituting a league for the training tracks such as Rye House, High Beech, Dagenham and any others that wished to come in with them. Along with the hotel and track came some sixty acres of ground, including five miles of River Lea frontage with boathouse and boats, football and cricket grounds, horse-riding stables and a fairground, for all of which he had great plans. He intended to develop leisure activities in the area so that speedway would be at the centre of a family day out and become a big draw for Londoners.

Naturally, though, it was on the speedway track that he concentrated his biggest efforts, taking three months to completely redesign and relay the track. He banked one corner, leaving the other flat in order to give novices a chance to learn all styles and conditions of riding. As soon as he was satisfied with his revamp, Case decided tried out the new track for himself. He borrowed a bike and without bothering to change into leathers got round the four laps in 84 seconds, six seconds faster than the official track record. He was so pleased with his effort that he decided not to retire after all but to combine his work at Rye House with a comeback for Wembley.

As well as improving the track, Case had a new safety fence built, in addition to a proper paddock and changing rooms for the riders and a stand for the public. The track could hold 6,000 spectators in total. Although it may have only been a training track, Case wanted to make sure that the facilities were first class for all concerned.

## 1938

At the beginning of April 1938, Case announced that his new school would be open on Monday and Wednesday afternoons and that each beginner had to provide his own equipment. Case's view was that before a rider can be any good he had to understand his own machine from A to Z. His hope was that he would discover a star of the future at Rye House: 'Who knows but that I may help by finding and training a really good novice at Rye House? After all, Frank Arthur found me; cannot I carry on his example?'

Dick Case's proposal for a training track league looked as though it was about to come to fruition at the start of 1938, when initially three tracks, Eastbourne, Smallford and Dagenham (with two teams, Dagenham and Romford), formed the Sunday Amateur Dirt-Track League. Although Case had been a strong advocate of the League, it wasn't until later in the season, in early June, that Rye House finally entered it as well.

Wimbledon rider Ron Howes demonstrates the art of leg trailing at Rye House in 1938.

Rye House opened its first league season on Easter Sunday with a special Easter Championship. Among those taking part were Malcolm Craven, Fred Curtis, Les Bowden and Steve Langton. The former Wembley star and pioneer rider Colin Watson made a guest appearance, setting up a new official track record of 88.8 seconds. For half-time entertainment, a motor ball match was laid on between North Hants and Hackney Wick.

The next meeting, on 15 May, was a Rye House versus The Rest Challenge match. Les Trim was appointed team captain of the newly named Cubs. Along with Trim, the team consisted of d'Allessandro, Dellow, Morris, Jock Hamilton, Ken John, Johnny Myson and Jack Milross.

Trim won the next big event at the track, the Rye House Amateur Championship. The cup was due to be presented by none other than 1936 World Champion Lionel Van Praag, but owing to injuries sustained in the Test match at Belle Vue he was unable to appear, so Les Trim had to be content with Mrs Case presenting the cup instead. Trim led the final from start to finish, beating off a late challenge from Jack Hyland on the last bend. He received a great ovation from those hardy souls who had braved a distinctly wintry afternoon.

Rye House met High Beech in a challenge on 5 June, losing 49-34, then, on 19 June they took on Smallford, with the Cubs this time proving triumphant in front of their home supporters, running out as victors, 44-39.

Rye House's first ever league fixture took place away at Eastbourne on the 10 July. It was an unfortunate start to their league career as they were hammered 56-27. Things didn't get much better in the return fixture back at Hoddesdon on 17 July, as the home side were once again obliterated, this time by a score of 52-29. The Cubs' first league victory came the following week when Rye House managed to put one over Romford at the latter's track, running out victors by 56 points to 26, the first of many victories Rye House were to score over the next seventy or so years. Unfortunately, Rye House were back to losing ways the following week, going down 46-37 at home to Smallford. It was at this point that the Sunday Amateur Dirt-Track League seemed to collapse. Dagenham closed down for a while at the beginning of August, which meant their match against Rye House, scheduled for 7 August, never took place and, although Dagenham did re-open later in the season, neither they nor Romford raced any more league matches. Rye House had just one more league match, on 18 September, when they lost yet again to Eastbourne, 46-36. Rye House scorers in this match were: J. Hamilton 9, Milross 9, Vic Weir 8, Myson 4, R. Hall 4, Andy Menzies 2.

In all, Rye House managed just five league matches in the season out of a possible 16, as all teams were due to meet each other four times, twice each home and away. With just two points to show for their efforts, they were well behind Eastbourne, who had 20 points, but who had managed to fulfil 12 of their fixtures.

For the remainder of the season, Rye House returned to individual trophies and Challenge matches. On 28 August, Putt Mossman returned with his 'American motor-cycle circus and rodeo of men and girl riders.' Presented for the first time in England, Mossman demonstrated his famous 'Leap for Life!' Riding a motorcycle, he rode up an inclined board and jumped over two ships in the River Lea – a total leap of sixty feet. There were also the usual double-board wall crashes and other stunts, as well as midget car racing, 'featuring some of the world's finest midget drivers.'

On 11 September, Rye House took on the Hackney Wick Cubs under their captain and former Rye House rider Archie Windmill, while on 25 September, following a challenge match against High Beech, the newly crowned world champion, Bluey Wilkinson, raced in the second half in a donkey race. As the season came towards its end, Case announced that for the 1939 season, following in the tradition of the recently opened Butlins Holiday Camps at Skegness and Clacton-on-Sea, he intended to turn his sixty-acre estate into a speedway supporters' camp with every sort of amusement thrown in. 'It would,' he said, 'be a great place for speedway fans to spend a holiday.'

The final meeting of the season, on 9 October, saw both the Jack Hey Cup and the Mossman Cup being competed for. After the meeting, an au revoir dance was held in the Rye House ballroom.

*1938 Sunday Amateur Dirt Track League*

| Date | H/A | Opponent | W/L | Score |
|------|-----|----------|-----|-------|
| 10 July | A | Eastbourne | L | 27-56 |
| 17 July | H | Eastbourne | L | 29-52 |
| 24 July | A | Romford | W | 56-26 |
| 31 July | H | Smallford | L | 37-46 |
| 18 September | A | Eastbourne | L | 27-56 |

P5 W1 D0 L4
For 176 Against 236
No final position; league not completed

# 1939

At the start of the 1939 season, Case finally announced his retirement as a rider, saying he wished to concentrate on his Rye House activities. He also had a change of heart regarding equipment for juniors and said he was prepared to loan machines and all the kit necessary at 'very low rates.'

The season commenced on Easter Sunday, 9 April, with the Easter Cup. The rest of the season took on the now familiar form of individual trophies and Challenge matches. Although also riding for second division Crystal Palace, Les Trim continued as club captain and two young promising Hackney juniors, Stan Dell and Nobby Stock, were signed up. Other team members included Jack Milross, Vic Weir, Paddy Stynes, Bob Hall, Johnny Myson, J. Milton and Mat Hall. Dell proved to be the star rider of the season, top scoring with 10 points in the Cubs' 49-35 victory over High Beech on 14 May and then winning the Rye House Championship on 25 June.

Les Trim won the following trophy meeting while a Challenge match between Rye House and Jim Baylais' team saw the home side triumph 47-37. Hackney's Jim Baylais got some revenge the following meeting when he won the Wimbledon Trophy at Rye House. In between those two meetings, Rye House had sent a team to race against Dagenham at the latter's track. In a very exciting meeting, the two teams drew 40-40, Baylais top scoring for Rye House with a maximum 12 points. Vic Weir scored eight for the Cubs and Mat Hall five.

With such close ties between Hackney and Rye House, the juniors were now swapping regularly between the two teams, in particular, Stan Dell, Nobby Stock, Jim Baylais and Vic Weir. Weir, in particular, improved so much during the season that in August he was given a trial for First Division Wimbledon.

Rye House's last meeting of the 1939 season took place on 20 August when yet another challenge match between Rye House and Jim Baylais' team ended in defeat for the home side, 47-35.

In common with all other speedway tracks across the country, racing ceased on 3 September when war was declared. In fact, Rye House was the first track to suffer from the suspension of speedway as they were due to meet Dagenham on that very day at 3.45p.m.

# The 1940s

## 1940

Unlike practically every other track in the country (with the honourable exception of Belle Vue), this was not the end of speedway at Hoddesdon until the cessation of hostilities, as racing returned on 12 May 1940 with the running of the Harringay Speedway Supporters' Club Trophy. Although Dicky Case still owned Rye House, the Harringay Speedway Motor Cycle and Light Car Club, under the management of George Kay, returned to promote speedway at the track. This first wartime meeting saw a number of favourites turn out, including Doug Wells, Vic Weir and Jack Milross. An even older favourite, Archie Windmill, proved to be the best rider of the afternoon, scoring a 12-point maximum but, unfortunately, in the final of the event he 'conked' and the meeting was won by Ron Clarke from Milross.

The second meeting, on 2 June, was a challenge match against Hackney Wick. Rye House had a guest captain for the afternoon, none other than West Ham's Canadian star, Eric Chitty, who, unsurprisingly, sailed through the meeting undefeated to lead Rye House to a 51-32 victory. Ron Clarke scored ten for the home team and Benny King nine.

Rye House versus Norwich wartime programme cover, 24 August 1941.

With hardly any other speedway taking place in the rest of the country, Rye House became a Mecca for speedway riders looking for some racing and the next match was a challenge against New Cross. This time, Wembley's George Wilks captained Rye House, while Bill Longley captained the New Cross side. Another good 40-30 win for Rye House was spearheaded by their temporary captain with a maximum 12 points, ably backed-up by Windmill, 11, and Clarke, 10.

The following meeting saw a change of name for the venue as Rye House Speedway became 'Dick Case's Speedway', a title it was to retain until the end of the war. This meeting, on 30 June, took the form of a Challenge match between Rye House and Eric Chitty's team. In a very exciting match, the home side lost by just two points, 37-35, with captain Ron Clarke scoring 10. The rest of the team was Roy Uden, Roy Duke, Cyril Anderson, Jack Milross, Bob Hall, Geo Gower and J.L. White.

The 1940 Rye House Individual Track Championship was next on the agenda on 14 July. This was won by Clarke, who not only scored maximum points in the rounds but also won the final, beating Roy Craighead into second place. Five more meetings followed, with further challenge matches and individual trophies, with the final meeting taking place on 1 September, a Challenge match between Ron Clarke's team and Roy Craighead's team.

# 1941

With most tracks now closed, Rye House's achievement in putting on ten meetings during 1940 was quite a triumph, but they surpassed themselves in 1941 by managing to stage thirteen meetings, with one rained off.

Still known as Dick Case's Speedway and run under the auspices of Harringay Speedway, the season kicked off with a three-team tournament between Ron Clarke's team, Roy Craighead's team and Bob Harris's team. As well as these three, Geo Gower, Doug Wells, Jack Milross, Benny King and Roy Uden all turned out, with Harris's team winning out.

At this opening meeting, George Kay said it was his hope to run meetings every week, but that it would be difficult to plan too far ahead as the availability of riders would be a problem with some now in the armed forces and some working shifts on vital war work.

The following week, Kay said that Rye House had been criticised in certain quarters for continuing to run speedway meetings and 'wasting petrol'. He said he wanted to make it quite clear that speedway machines did not use petrol 'but wood alcohol which is made entirely in this country and which cannot be used for road purposes.' He urged supporters to remember this if criticised themselves for continuing to follow the sport. All the usual suspects turned up at the second meeting, Clarke, Craighead, Gower, Milross, Hall, King and Uden amongst them, but a special treat was announced for the third meeting when it was revealed that Archie Windmill would be home on leave and taking part as a guest rider. Along with Windmill, the regulars turned out with Milross, winning the big event of the afternoon, the Spitfire Scratch Race final.

The next meeting, on 22 June, was to be the first in a series of meetings held during the season, the Trophy Handicap. The idea was that it would be run in a 'Grand Prix' style with the rider gaining the most points at the end of the season declared the winner. The first round proved to be a most exciting affair, as two scratch riders, Ron Clarke and Jack Harris, dead-heated for first place in the final. In spite of this exciting start, nothing more was heard of this particular trophy during the rest of the season. A team event took place the following week between Clarke's team and Doug Wells' team. Although Roy Craighead proved to be the hero of the afternoon by scoring a nine-point maximum for Clarke's team, it was Wells' team that won, 28-25.

Racing continued in this vein for the rest of the season with individual and team meetings. The Rye House regulars were able to turn out for most of the meetings. During the season, Craighead began to show himself as the best of the bunch and he capped some fine performances by winning the Rye House Individual Championship on 3 August.

The following week, Rye House took on a strong Norwich team consisting of Dick Wise, Syd Hipperson, Bert Spencer and Syd Littlewood. The Rye House team was Ron Clarke, captain, Jack Harris, Roy Craighead and Benny King. Only four heats long, this meeting proved to be an appetiser for a full-scale meeting between the two teams on 24 August, when more or less the full Norwich team paid a visit to Hoddesdon. The Rye House team for this encounter was Clarke, captain, Harris, Craighead, Ron Howes, Dicky Harris and Milross, with Hall and Gower as reserves. Archie Windmill guested for the Stars. The local lads did Rye House proud, thumping their second division opponents by the magnificent score of 54-28. Craighead scored nine points from three rides but unfortunately suffered engine failure in his other ride.

The last meeting of the season, on 31 August, featured the 'Au Revoir' Cup and was won by Roy Uden from Ron Clarke. A sign of the times was that a collection was held for the Prisoners of War Parcel Fund.

## 1942-1945

Racing returned the following year with at least six more meetings being staged. Owing to the exigencies of war, some of the Rye House riders could no longer ride regularly at the track, including Clarke and Jack Harris, but others managed to put in a number of appearances, with Craighead and Windmill tending to dominate proceedings. As well as the Rye House riders, a number of the Norwich team made regular appearances at Hoddesdon, including Syd Hipperson, Syd Littlewood and Bert Hutson. Interestingly, Paddy Mills was also a regular visitor to the track. Mills had been a Sheffield rider before the War but was to join Norwich once hostilities ceased.

A similar story in 1943 saw four more meetings being staged, but it was becoming increasingly difficult to find enough riders to fulfil the fixtures and racing ceased after the meeting on 2 August until the VE Trophy was held on 5 August 1945. This was won, appropriately enough, by Roy Craighead with a 12-point maximum. Others to take part in this meeting included Charlie Dugard, Syd Hipperson and Geo Gower. Although not starting until August, Rye House managed to stage ten meetings that season, finishing on 30 September.

Although Rye House was now back open to the public, it was what was going on behind the scenes that was probably to have a more lasting effect on British speedway. While Harringay, under George Kay, was still promoting the meetings, Dick Case offered his training school facilities to the North London tracks so that they would be able to train up their own juniors. Harringay, West Ham and Wembley, therefore, all had their training days once a week.

Dick Case instructs juniors in the art of speedway while the Wembley manager, Alec Jackson, looks on.

Harringay's day was overseen by Wal Phillips, with help from former Rye House junior Nobby Stock and Joe Bowkis, but it was Wembley manager Alec Jackson who made the most of the facilities on offer and even injected £4,000 cash into Rye House to improve those facilities.

He took a personal interest in the training and it certainly paid dividends as he unearthed a number of riders who were to form the backbone of possibly the greatest team of all time, a team which won the National League every year from 1946 to 1953, with the exception of 1948, when they were forced to race their home matches at Wimbledon due to the Olympic Games being held at Wembley.

## 1946

Because there had been no league racing for six years owing to the war, it was felt the fairest thing to do in 1946 on the recommencement of league speedway was to allow all teams to keep two riders from their pre-war team and then choose a further five from a pool consisting of all the riders not retained in that way. Wembley chose to keep Tommy Price and George Wilks from their pre-war line up and then drew Bill Kitchen and Bob Wells from the pool. At this point, Jackson withdrew from the pool saying he would fill the remaining places with juniors he had discovered at Rye House. One of these was Roy Craighead, who had come on by leaps and bounds during the war years. The other three were Bill Gilbert, Alf Bottoms and Bronco Wilson.

At the start of the 1946 season, Jackson announced he had found two more juniors, products of Rye House, who he wished to sign up for his famous Wembley Lions. These were Driver Bill Kemp and Corporal Walter Waterman of REME. Both had had to return to the army and were not due to be demobbed until September. Jackson began lobbying the War Office to obtain their early release.

Of the six riders unearthed at Rye House by Jackson, five of them were to go on to establish reasonable careers in speedway with one in particular having a very distinguished career. The star amongst them, of course, was Corporal Walter Waterman, known universally as 'Split'. Waterman, who became one of Britain's leading riders and characters in the late 1940s, '50s and early '60s, twice finishing runner-up in the World Championship. Gilbert finished fourth in the 1948 Speedway Riders' Final (the immediate post-war equivalent of the World Championship), while Craighead, Bottoms and Kemp all went on to ride with some success in league speedway. Bronco Wilson was tragically killed in a crash at Harringay in 1947, just as he too was beginning to show much promise.

During the 1946 season, Rye House put on a number of meetings, both individual trophies and Challenge matches against other non-league sides, such as Eastbourne. In fact, it was former Rye House captain, now an Eastbourne rider, Ron Clarke, who broke the track record, winning his race in a time of 86.2 seconds, while another former captain, Les Trim, won the prestigious Victory Cup on 9 June. Total attendance for the year stood at 55,393.

## 1947

The 1947 season started badly for Dicky Case as not only the track but also his pub was flooded when the River Lea overflowed. However, the season itself continued successfully, with more open meetings and more juniors beginning to find their feet in British speedway. A full programme of seventeen meetings was held, while training also continued at Case's school. Amongst the riders taking part in the public meetings were Arthur Flack, who captained the Rye House team that year, Jack Milross, Benny King, Johnny Myson, George Bason, Dennis Gray, Peter Robinson and a youngster from the training school by the name of Wally Green, who was to become a top rider with West Ham and finish second in the 1950 World Championship.

Jack Maddern leads Bill Thatcher
at Rye House in 1948.

# 1948

The 1948 season started with the Easter Championship and included a mixture of old established Rye House hands such as Milross and Gower, together with some of the best young riders from the training school. The meeting was won by Jimmy Grant, a first-year junior discovered by Wal Phillips. Although still only a novice, Grant was given the honour of captaining his own team in Rye House's next meeting – Jimmy Grant's Team versus Arthur Flack's Team. Not only that, but he led his team to victory by 53 points to 38, with a magnificent paid maximum from five rides. His early season form was nothing short of sensational and he was pressed into service with Harringay for their first league match. Although the strong Wembley side were the visitors, Grant scored eight points. He continued as a member of the Harringay side until 1950. Another first-year youngster to make an appearance at the Easter Trophy was Alf Viccary, who also found a team place with Harringay before being loaned out to Oxford.

A new name, that of Stan Bedford, appeared for the first time on the Rye House programme for the next meeting on 25 April, the Novice Knock-Out Championships. Bedford was to be associated with Rye House for the next decade, although he had an inauspicious start, coming last in his one and only race that afternoon.

Rye House took on league opposition in their next meeting when they raced against third division Yarmouth. Captained by Flack, the team rode brilliantly to record a 49-33 victory. In what was a good all-round team effort, the scores were: Arthur Flack 9, Joe Bowkis 9, Alan Briggs 8, Geo Gower, 7, Fred Pawson 6 and Stan Clark 6. Frank Bettis and Stan Bedford were non-riding reserves.

The season continued with its diet of individual meetings and Challenge matches, while the team also filled one away fixture against old rivals Eastbourne on 11 July. This was the first meeting of the two teams in a decade, as they had not met since the ill-fated Sunday Amateur Dirt-Track League days. The Eastbourne team kept their 100 per cent record over Rye House with a narrow 42-40 victory.

On 10 October, a special Challenge match against 'The Rest' was held. Another newcomer by the name of Reg Fearman was blooded in the Rye House team. The fifteen-year-old Fearman rose to the occasion, scoring nine points in Rye House's 49-35 victory. The following year, practically on his sixteenth birthday, he was to make his debut for West Ham.

# 1949

With the new discoveries now coming to the fore, the older brigade were beginning to drop out of contention at Rye House. Of the pre-war and early wartime days only Milross and Gower started off the season. Names like Flack, Fearman, Viccary, Briggs, Bedford, Stan Clark, Gray, Robinson and yet another couple of young discoveries in Pat Flanagan and Allan Kidd were taking over as the regular Rye House performers, and by mid-season both Gower and Milross had dropped out of the picture. A couple of juniors on Norwich's books, Fred Brand, who went on to appear in the 1954 World Championship final, and Bill Codling, were also regulars at Rye House during the year. An interesting rider in Harold Bull, an Australian and nephew of the great Vic Duggan, turned out on several occasions.

Most of the meetings in 1949 were either for individual trophies or were 'made-up' Challenge matches between Rye House's own riders. The big meeting of the year, the Rye House Championship, was won by Jack Wright.

# The 1950s

## 1950

By the 1950s, the Rye House track had become acknowledged as the best training track in the country, with many clubs, including Wembley, Harringay, Walthamstow and Rayleigh, taking full advantage of its facilities. Case himself organised two full-day training sessions, on Tuesdays and Thursdays, for any youngster who wished to come along and try out. The day consisted of a morning session, during which Case put them through their paces, a pub lunch and an afternoon session similar to the morning. Each day was limited to thirty juniors. The other clubs hired the track for half-days for their own training. During the winter, Swedish teams would also come over for practice, while individual riders such as the 1949 World Champion, Tommy Price, also hired the track to try out new engines or just to give themselves a few practice laps.

As well as being the best training track around, Rye House was also pulling in large crowds for its Sunday meetings. Many London supporters made the trip by train or bus, while the Harringay Supporters' Club used to send a regular contingent of forty fans, under the leadership of their secretary, Snowy Beattie, on bicycles. As in the pre-war days, a trip to see Rye House speedway was just one part of a pleasant Sunday out for Londoners. As well as the racing, there were the river boats, the fair and the peacocks walking around the large pub gardens to add to the attraction. Having so many supporters from different clubs made the area around the track very colourful as all of them sported their own team's colours.

The 1950 season started with the greatly improved Stan Bedford winning the Easter Cup. A number of the 1949 juniors had moved on permanently to league teams, including Fearman to West Ham and Flanagan to Aldershot. Others were combining league appearances with Sunday afternoon appearances at Hoddesdon, for example Viccary at Harringay, Brand at Yarmouth and Kidd at Poole.

Two new juniors graduated to team racing in 1950: the first was Geoff Woodger, who was to remain with Rye House through their Southern Area League days and the other was one of the greatest finds ever to come out of Rye House, Ron How. How had written to Harringay in the autumn of 1949 asking for a trial and was advised by Wal Phillips to go along to the Rye House training school. It didn't take Phillips long to realise that here was a youngster with enormous potential, and he signed him up for Harringay, giving him a few second-half try-outs. How soon made the Harringay Junior team and then the first team as reserve. He continued to combine his team appearances with outings at Rye House in 1950 and '51, before becoming a fully-fledged member of the Harringay squad. After Harringay closed in 1954, he moved on to Wimbledon, where he played a major role in arguably the greatest team of all time – a team which won the National League every year from 1954 to 1961, with the sole exception of 1957. Apart from his team credentials, How qualified for the World Championship final no less than nine times, finishing fifth in 1964. Also in 1950, on 2 July, a young junior by the name of Vic Ridgeon put in an appearance at Rye House as a member of Ron Barrett's team in a Challenge match against Alf Viccary's team. Like Bedford two years previously, it was a very inauspicious start for a rider destined to become Rye House's captain and leading rider through most of the 1950s as he too scored no points from his two rides.

One of Alec Jackson's discoveries at Rye House, Corporal Walter 'Split' Waterman, who went on to become one of the country's leading riders and characters.

The Rye House Championship that year was won by Viccary, who beat George Flower and Ron How in the final. How got his revenge in the final meeting of the season, winning the Au Revoir Trophy on 22 October and setting the seal on the year that had seen the remarkable rise of this young rider from mere novice to accomplished star of tomorrow.

## 1951

As usual, the 1951 season started with the Easter Trophy, this year won by D. Cross. The nucleus of the team that was later to form the Southern Area League team, Bedford, Woodger and Ridgeon all put in a number of appearances during the season in the usual individual and team challenge meetings. Norwich rider Bill Codling proved to be the best at the Rye House circuit that year as he walked off with the Whitsun Challenge Trophy and the June Championship, though Cross came back at the end of the year to take the September Championship.

Once again, there were a number of new discoveries who were to go on to better things. Foremost amongst these were Cyril Maidment, another member of the all-powerful Wimbledon team, and later Belle Vue, who qualified for two World Championship finals, and Ronnie Genz, who rode for New Cross, Oxford and Poole, amongst others. Both Maidment and Genz went on to become internationals, representing England in Test matches. Another discovery that year was Bobby Croombs, son of the former West Ham star Tommy Croombs. Bobby was also to play a part in the Rye House Southern Area League team of later years before moving on to New Cross in 1960.

At the end of the season, the authoritative *Stenner's Annual* dubbed Rye House the 'novice centre' of speedway in Britain.

Rye House discovery Gerry Hussey. Hussey
went on to appear in the 1958 world final.
His career was tragically cut short by a fatal
accident the following year.

## 1952

1952 saw more of the same at Rye House. Vic Ridgeon became a permanent fixture, while Stan
Bedford at last achieved his potential by winning the Rye House Championship, though probably
the most consistent rider at Hoddesdon that year was Derek Clarke, who won both the May
Championship and the July Championship. This year's crop of discoveries included two more riders
who went on to ride for the peerless Wimbledon team of the 1950s, Alf Hagon and Jim Tebby.

## 1953

1953 was a vintage year for new discoveries at Rye House. Amongst those appearing for the
first time in public was Mike Broadbank. Broadbank had been around Rye House ever since
anyone could remember. As a young boy, he had been a pusher-off and was known, for obvious
reasons, as the boy with a red flag. After leaving school at the age of fourteen, he had gone to
work full-time for Dicky Case, preparing the track and doing many other odd jobs around
the stadium, all for the princely sum of £3 10s. In the meantime, he had helped form the
Hoddesdon Kangaroos, a cycle speedway team for whom he designed the colours based on
Case's Australian international colours. Through his work on the track, and through his cycle
speedway exploits, he got to know many of the riders at Rye House and they encouraged him
to go into speedway, not that he needed much encouragement! In particular, he got to know
the Harringay rider Steve Ison very well and eventually worked for him, cleaning his leathers
and bike and anything else that needed to be done. Through him, he got to know the Harringay
team. One day, the great Vic Duggan, Harringay's Australian captain, visited Rye House and
Broadbank decided to try and impress him with a special long, sweeping broadside at the front
of the stadium just as Duggan was arriving. Duggan was so impressed that he gave Broadbank

*2s 6d* and an ice cream as a reward. Broadbank was an overnight sensation, equalling the track record on 19 April in one of his first appearances in public. Races at the 440-yard Rye House track were then run over three laps instead of the normal four. Broadbank's time of 62.6 seconds equalled Stan Clark's record set up two weeks previously.

Other discoveries that year included Gerry Hussey, George White, Dave Slater, Gil Goldfinch, Len Silver, Derek Timms and Eric Hockaday, all of whom were later to go on to greater things. In fact, so great was the competition now from the young up-and-coming stars and the already established men that the prestigious Rye House Championship had to be run over three meetings, with two qualifying rounds and a final. In the end, it was won by Gerry Hussey from Alf Hagon in second place, with Dave Slater third. Hussey, a true overnight sensation, went on to ride for West Ham, Norwich and Leicester. He qualified for the 1958 World Championship final and rode several times for England in internationals. Tragically, he died at the very young age of twenty-six following a crash while driving in a midget car race in Australia in March 1959.

Recalling his debut year at Rye House, Len Silver remembered that George Kay had his own unique way of paying the riders at the end of the afternoon's racing. All the riders would line up outside the pay box, while Kay paid them their earnings with the two shilling and half crown pieces collected from the day's takings.

There was a thrill for the Rye House faithful on 5 July when, as part of the afternoon's racing, two special match races were laid on between two of the biggest names in speedway, Norwich's Aub Lawson and West Ham's Wally Green. Apart from the war years, this was the first time that names of this calibre had appeared at Rye House in competition. Lawson beat Green by two races to nil. It says something for the standard of the juniors at Rye House that Lawson's winning times were 63.2 and 67.8, both outside the track record.

A special Coronation Shield event was held to celebrate Queen Elizabeth II's coronation that year. Like the Rye House Championship, this too was run over three meetings, with two qualifying rounds and a final. This time the winner was George White, who beat St Austell's Denis Newton and Rye House's own Bill Simpson into second and third place.

A Rye House Select versus The Rest Challenge match on 11 October was to herald the end of an era at Rye House, as in 1954 Rye House was to take part in a formalised league structure for the first time since the abortive Sunday Amateur Dirt-Track League in 1938.

# 1954

Rye House's return to league racing was mooted at the end of 1953 when a new league for amateur tracks was proposed, to be called, uninspiringly, the Amateur League. As the start of the 1954 season approached, the name was changed to the Metropolitan League. Six teams entered the league, Rye House, Eastbourne, Ringwood, Brafield, California and Aldershot, though Aldershot withdrew midway through the season.

Rye House's team was to be called the Roosters and consisted initially of former Yarmouth rider and now Rye House stalwart Vic Ridgeon as captain, with Stan Bedford, Derek Clark, Bill Simpson, Dave Slater, Geoff Woodger, Tommy Worrall and Dave Murray. The first match was away to Eastbourne on 25 April and resulted in a win for the newly formed Roosters, 49-34. It was a real team effort with Ridgeon, Bedford, Clark and Simpson all scoring eight points, while Slater and Woodger added seven each.

Rye House's first match in front of their own supporters came on 2 May, when the Roosters took on and beat California 47-37. Once again, it was a good all-round team effort, though Ridgeon proved to be the undoubted star of the afternoon with 11 points.

The next home match was one of the best meetings ever seen at Rye House as Aldershot took them to a last-heat decider. But, with Woodger and Ridgeon scoring a 4-2, it was enough to give the Roosters their third straight victory.

After this match, the name of the league was changed again, this time to the Southern Area Training League, as it was felt this reflected its make-up more accurately than Metropolitan League.

However, this too was soon changed, with the word Training being dropped. So, for the rest of the season the league was known simply as the Southern Area League.

Rye House's first reverse of the season came in their next match, an away fixture against Brafield, which they lost 46-37. Ridgeon was on good form again, scoring 11 points, but this time did not receive the backing of the rest of his team.

A new rider came into the team on 29 May, when Jack (Jim) Heard took his place at reserve. His debut, at Aldershot, was rather unpromising as he only scored two points. But, the following day, on his own track against Brafield, he turned in an amazing performance, scoring a maximum 12 points from the reserve position in only his second outing in public. In his next match, against Eastbourne, he had three rides and won them all and then followed this up with 10 points against California. The captain, Vic Ridgeon, was also continuing to carry all before him, and with these two now proving almost unbeatable together, with the excellent backing of riders like Dave Slater and Stan Bedford, Rye House were beginning to be viewed as potential champions of the new Southern Area League.

A brief halt to the Roosters' success came on 4 July when Ringwood scored an impressive 50-33 victory. Even then, Ridgeon, described by many as the Jack Young of the Southern Area League because of his armchair style, recorded a maximum.

Rye House bounced back in great style, winning their next two league matches. Then, in August, they more or less made sure they would win the title by signing up track specialist Al Sparrey. In his first match, against Brafield, he partnered Ridgeon. The pair recorded three 5-1s in their three heats together and Sparrey also won his other heat. The result was a smashing 53-31 victory as Heard weighed in with 10 paid 11 as well.

Although Rye House were favourites to take the league, they weren't having things all their own way and behind them there was a terrific tussle taking place between California, Ringwood and Brafield. By winning their last match at home, 50-34 over Ringwood, the Roosters made sure of the title, in spite of losing their last two away matches. It had been a close-run thing, however, as Rye House finished the league on 20 points, while the others all finished on 18. The fifth team, Eastbourne, managed just six points from three wins out of 16 matches.

At the end-of-season Southern Area League Riders' Championship, held at Rye House, Vic Ridgeon finished in third place behind Ringwood's Alby Golden and Ernie Lessiter. Dave Slater was fourth equal. Although he did not quite make first place in the Riders' Championship, Ridgeon did win a number of other individual trophies at Rye House that year, including the Whitsun Trophy, the August Trophy and the Hertfordshire Chase.

As well as winning a number of individual events and coming third in the SAL Riders' Championship, Ridgeon was also third highest scorer in the league behind California's Gil Goldfinch and Ringwood's Ernie Lessiter. There is no doubt that the Rye House captain was one of the stars and first successes of the new league.

Unlike the Sunday Amateur Dirt-Track League, this new amateur league had proved to be very successful. Respected speedway journalist Jim Stenner summed up the season and the hopes for the future by saying:

> The Southern Area contest is now very much a watertight affair and staffed almost entirely by the stars of tomorrow. The type of racing served up is real sport – full blooded devil-may-care stuff on which the cinder game strives. Everyone's happy – riders, promoting clubs and the fans – and what great fun it is.
>
> Before very long, I expect to see a chain of week-end leagues across the country…That it can pay off one day is always possible as happened in the case of West Ham star Gerald Hussey, winner of the Rye House track championship a year ago.

At the end of the 1954 season, Harringay closed and therefore no longer operated Rye House. George Kay himself took over the rights to the speedway racing at the stadium and continued to promote in his own name with Fred Peachey as his assistant and team manager.

The 1954 team that won the inaugural Southern Area League title. From left to right: Vic Ridgeon (captain), Derek Clark, Geo Kay (promoter), Jim Heard, Stan Bedford (on bike), Geoff Woodger, Dave Slater, Vernon Brown, Dave Still.

## 1954 Southern Area League

| Date | H/A | Opponent | W/L | Score |
|------|-----|----------|-----|-------|
| 25 April | A | Eastbourne | W | 49-34 |
| 2 May | H | California | W | 47-37 |
| 16 May | H | Aldershot | W | 44-39 |
| 23 May | A | Brafield | L | 37-46 |
| 29 May | A | Aldershot | L | 33-48 |
| 30 May | H | Brafield | W | 49-34 |
| 13 June | H | Eastbourne | W | 60-22 |
| 20 June | A | California | W | 46-38 |
| 27 June | H | Ringwood | W | 51-33 |
| 4 July | A | Ringwood | L | 33-50 |
| 11 July | H | Eastbourne | W | 54-30 |
| 18 July | A | Eastbourne | W | 43-38 |
| 8 August | H | California | L | 41-43 |
| 22 August | H | Brafield | W | 53-31 |
| 29 August | A | Brafield | L | 31-46 |
| 5 September | H | Ringwood | W | 50-34 |
| 12 September | A | Ringwood | L | 34-50 |
| 26 September | A | California | L | 28-55 |

P16 W10 D0 L6

For 712 Against 621

Position: first (out of five)

## 1954 Southern Area League

| Name | M | R | Pts | BP | Total | CMA |
|------|------|------|------|------|------|------|
| Vic Ridgeon | 18 | 72 | 153 | 9 | 161 | 8.94 |
| Derek Clark | 12 | 47 | 69 | 16 | 85 | 7.23 |
| Bill Simpson | 17 | 68 | 108 | 13 | 121 | 7.12 |
| Jack Heard | 14 | 53 | 87 | 7 | 94 | 7.09 |
| Stan Bedford | 13 | 45 | 63 | 15 | 78 | 6.93 |
| Geoff Woodger | 14 | 50 | 74.5 | 9.5 | 84 | 6.72 |
| Dave Slater | 18 | 69 | 112 | 3 | 115 | 6.67 |
| Vernon Brown | 10 | 27 | 34 | 5 | 39 | 5.78 |
| Dave Still | 12 | 34 | 40.5 | 8.5 | 49 | 5.76 |

# 1955

Although Ridgeon had proved himself to be a star of the new league, even he was eclipsed in 1955 by the return of Mike Broadbank from National Service. Broady, as he was known, had been unable to take part in the 1954 campaign, but he made up for it with a vengeance in 1955. His first outing was in Rye House's opening meeting, the Easter Championship. Although he came second to Al Sparrey, it was his riding that caught the eye. He showed that he had lost none of his skill during his year away.

The Roosters' first league match was away to Brafield. It proved to be one of the best meetings ever seen in the new league, thanks in large part to Broadbank, who found difficulty in getting away from the gate. His dashes from the back kept the crowd on their toes all afternoon and resulted in a 12-point maximum and an away win for Rye House.

During the course of the season, Broadbank won four individual trophies at Rye House, the Silver Trophy, the Crutcher Trophy, the August Trophy and then, on 25 September, the big one, the Southern Area League Riders' Championship, beating his captain, Vic Ridgeon, into second place in spite of starting off the day ill in bed with a temperature well into the 100s. By the end of his last race, he was so ill that he had to be helped off his bike as he no longer had the strength to dismount himself. Following this victory, leading speedway journalist and *Speedway Star* editor John Hyam commented, 'Without a doubt, Broady is a champion in every meaning of the word and is destined, I am convinced, for the highest honours that speedway has to offer.' He also finished up top of the *Speedway Star* SAL rankings for the year and was the league's leading points scorer with 124 at a cma of 9.73. During the year, he received second-half bookings from a number of first division clubs including Norwich, West Ham and Wembley.

It was a good year for the team too. They started off with five straight victories, including two crushing defeats over Ringwood, 57-24 and 61-22, and a stunning 55-27 win over Brafield. In all three of these matches, Ridgeon led his team from the front, scoring 12-point maximums. As well as Ridgeon and Broadbank, the team consisted of Al Sparrey, Jack Heard, Stan Bedford, Dave Slater and Bill Simpson. Geoff Woodger had retired at the end of the previous season but was called into the squad at various times during the year as a replacement for injured riders. Vernon Brown and another new discovery, sixteen-year-old Gerry King, also rode in six matches each. Of these ten riders, only Sparrey had not come through Dick Case's training school. He was a former grass-tracker who had learned his speedway at Rayleigh.

The result of these early victories, which saw Rye House topping the league table by early June, was an increase in crowd numbers. The regular gate at this Sunday afternoon amateur track was normally somewhere between 2,000 and 3,000. For the SAL Riders' Championship, the gate reached an official figure of 6,000, though Case always maintained that at least 10,000 had witnessed the event.

The Roosters' first defeat came on 25 June, when they went down 50-33 away to California. They soon made up for this defeat, however, when they crushed Eastbourne 67-17 in their next home encounter. The Eastbourne team was so poor that it was said at the time that if there was a second division in the Southern Area League then Eastbourne would be in the third! Ridgeon, Broadbank, Simpson and Slater all recorded paid maximums.

Two more victories followed, home to Brafield and away at Eastbourne, and then another humiliating defeat for Eastbourne, 61-23. Home and away defeats of California came next, with Sparrey top-scoring both times.

The final league match was another home defeat of California, this time by the overwhelming margin of 62-22. It was such a runaway victory that it was considered to be the worst match of the season. One spectator is supposed to have said, 'Rather Eastbourne were here, at least they have a go!'

With just two losses all season, Rye House romped away with the league title, retaining it for the second year running. It shows the dominance they had over the rest of the league when it is realised that the runners-up were California. Although Broadbank was the league's top scorer, the rest of the team also put in outstanding performances. The other two heat leaders, Ridgeon and Sparrey, recorded cmas of 9.65 and 9.54 respectively, while Heard and Woodger both had 8-plus averages. Even eighth man in the averages Bill Simpson recorded 7.40.

Inevitably, Rye House lost Broadbank at the end of the season as he went off to try his luck with Wembley for the 1956 season. Some time before this, he had already been earmarked as a possible Wembley rider by their captain Tommy Price. Price used to visit Rye House regularly, talent spotting for his team. He was so impressed with Broadbank that he told his manager, Alec Jackson, to sign him up before anyone else got him. He told Jackson, 'Broadbank may be only a young whippersnapper, but I think he can beat me round Rye House.' In 1957, on Wembley's closure, he moved to Swindon to become part of the only other team to top the National League during Wimbledon's dominance. He became a regular in the England Test team and went on to qualify for five World Championship finals plus two more as reserve.

## 1955 Southern Area League

| Date | H/A | Opponent | W/L | Score |
|---|---|---|---|---|
| 17 April | A | Brafield | W | 44-40 |
| 24 April | H | Ringwood | W | 57-24★ |
| 15 May | A | Eastbourne | W | 47-33 |
| 22 May | H | Brafield | W | 55-27 |
| 29 May | H | Ringwood | W | 61-22★ |
| 5 June | H | California | W | 47-36 |
| 12 June | A | California | L | 34-50 |
| 19 June | H | Eastbourne | W | 67-17 |
| 3 July | H | Brafield | W | 44-40 |
| 10 July | A | Eastbourne | W | 47-36 |
| 24 July | A | Brafield | L | 29-55 |
| 28 August | H | Eastbourne | W | 49-35 |
| 18 September | A | California | W | 45-38 |
| 9 October | H | California | W | 62-22 |

★ Ringwood withdrew mid-season; results deleted from the final table

P12 W10 D0 L2

For 581 Against 416

Position: first (out of four)

*1955 Southern Area League (cma with bonus points)*

| Name | M | R | Pts | BP | Total | CMA |
|------|---|---|-----|----|----|-----|
| Mike Broadbank | 13 | 51 | 120 | 4 | 124 | 9.73 |
| Al Sparrey | 12 | 46 | 97 | 14 | 111 | 9.65 |
| Vic Ridgeon | 13 | 52 | 119 | 5 | 124 | 9.54 |
| Jack Heard | 12 | 42 | 84 | 9 | 93 | 8.86 |
| Geoff Woodger | 7 | 15 | 27 | 3 | 30 | 8.00 |
| Stan Bedford | 13 | 50 | 75 | 19 | 94 | 7.52 |
| Dave Slater | 12 | 46 | 74 | 12 | 86 | 7.48 |
| Bill Simpson | 9 | 33 | 53 | 8 | 61 | 7.40 |
| Vernon Brown | 6 | 15 | 12 | 4 | 16 | 4.23 |
| Gerry King | 6 | 12 | 8 | 0 | 8 | 2.67 |

# 1956

It looked, at one time, as though there would be no Southern Area League in 1956 as only three teams, Rye House, Eastbourne and California, entered and it was felt, therefore, that it would not be viable. But a new team, the Southern Rovers, under the management of Les King, put in an application. Although, as the name implied, the team had no home base, they were prepared to run their home matches at the tracks of the other league teams. With the acceptance of this novel idea, the Southern Area League was once again up and running.

The backbone of the team was Ridgeon, Sparrey and Slater. Two long-standing members, Bedford and Simpson, left, and with Broadbank also leaving, three new riders were brought in to the team. King was promoted from reserve, while former Rye House discovery Bobby Croombs came in, along with the latest training school discovery, seventeen-year-old Brian Brett. Jimmy Chalkley came in as reserve.

Three of Rye House's leading riders from their Southern Area League days. From left to right: Bobby Croombs, Vic Ridgeon, Brian Brett.

The Roosters started off the season where they'd left off, with a 52-32 victory over California. But this was followed by a very close home match against Southern Rovers. With one heat to go, the Rovers were leading 40-38. Sparrey took off from the gate, but Ridgeon was left floundering at the back. A 3-3 and a home loss looked inevitable until Ridgeon suddenly found some speed and, on the last bend of the second lap, drove right round the outside, passing Neil Roberts on the back straight. He maintained his position until the chequered flag, giving Rye House a 4-2 lead and levelling the match at 42-42. It was only the second time in three years that Rye House had failed to win a home match in the league. A loss in their next match away to California put a severe dent in their title aspirations, but confidence was restored with a 54-30 victory over a resurgent Eastbourne, currently top of the table. When the Roosters completed the double over Eastbourne by a score of 54-29 in their next match, they began to think of winning the title again. Ridgeon had once again been in top form and was ranked at number one in the *Speedway Star*'s May rankings, with Sparrey at number two.

Results generally continued to go Rye House's way and by mid-season they had risen to the top of the table, but then the whole league ran in to trouble with the Lord's Day Observance Society. For some reason, although all three tracks were running on a Sunday, the Society threatened to take only Eastbourne and California to court, not Rye House. However, to be on the safe side, the Speedway Control Board and the ACU advised Rye House not to operate a gate. California got round the problem of charging admission by giving free admission but doubling the cost of the programme and holding a collection in the interval. Eastbourne switched their race day to Saturday.

George Kay said he thought that the Lord's Day Observance Society had left Rye House alone because they had agreed with the local council many years before not to open before 4p.m. and to make sure the meetings finished before 6p.m. if at all possible, so that people would have time to go to church in the morning and the evening. They had also agreed not to play records during the meeting and that once a month the vicar of Hoddesdon and Turnford would be able to broadcast a message to the crowd during the interval. It was also because of the restrictive Sunday trading laws that Rye House were not actually allowed to charge for admission to the meetings as such. Instead of a turnstile, as most speedway clubs had, Rye House just had a gate through which spectators passed. Inside the gate was a long table at which Kay and his helpers sat taking money off the punters. The money was not for admission but was to join the supporters' club for the afternoon. To meet the strict terms of the law, the racing was thrown in for free!

With the threat to the Southern Area League overcome, racing continued as before. A new name, that of Ernie Baker, came into the Rye House set-up and made people sit up and take notice. His debut came in the second leg of the SAL Cup final. Rye House had lost the first leg away at California 61.5-45.5 and needed a big win if they were to carry off the cup. Looking for a new rider to help out at reserve, they found him with the help of John Hyam, who recalls:

> I contacted Dicky Case and told him that Ernie Baker had impressed me after I had seen him ride in practice sessions at both Wimbledon and Eastbourne. Ernie at the time was too inexperienced to get in to the team of all talents at Plough Lane, while for some obscure reason, Charlie Dugard seemed reluctant to give Ernie a chance at Arlington. I decided that Dicky Case was a man to give a rider a chance if he came well recommended and reckoned that Speedway Star headed notepaper and the fact the editor was writing on his behalf would get Ernie a chance at Rye House and it seemed to work.

When Baker arrived at Rye House just before the match, George Kay and Rye House manager Fred Peachey arranged for him to have a couple of practice laps to get him used to the track. In both runs, Baker fell. It was with some trepidation that Peachey put him in to the team. However, when the match started, he completely out-rode the California reserves, scoring a reserve's paid maximum, helping to win the match 70-38 for Rye House. Ridgeon also played his normal captain's part, scoring an 18-point maximum. Rye House won the cup 115.5-99.5 on aggregate.

The young Ivan Mauger put in a few appearances for Rye House in 1957. Behind him is Tommy Sweetman and on the right is Ronnie Rolfe.

By July, Rye House were well on the way to taking the league title as well as the cup. Their three heat leaders were ranked numbers one, two and three in the Southern Area League, with Ridgeon at one, Croombs at two and Sparrey at three.

With Ridgeon now going so well, it looked inevitable that he would follow Broadbank's example and sign for a National League team. Indeed, the inevitable happened when, on 18 August, Ridgeon signed on with Southampton. But there was worse news to follow for Rye House as Sparrey signed up for Swindon and Croombs for Wembley. It looked as though the Roosters would have to start almost from scratch for 1957.

In the meantime, there was a season to finish and a league to win. By the time of their last fixture on 14 October, the Roosters were heading the league with 15 points, but just behind them was Eastbourne on 13. As it happened, the last match of the season was between these two rivals for league honours. But there were no problems for the Rye House lads as they thumped the Eagles by 56 points to 28 to take the Southern Area League title for the third year in succession.

The last major trophy of the season was the Southern Area League Riders' Championship. As usual, heats had been held on all the tracks to find the sixteen riders for the final. Vic Ridgeon headed the qualifiers with 28 points out of a possible 30, but then the Control Board dropped a bombshell by announcing that he was ineligible to ride in the final as he had signed for Southampton. Kay and Peachey immediately slapped in a protest, arguing that, although Ridgeon had signed for Southampton, he was still the Rye House captain and still competing regularly in the Southern Area League and therefore he should still be eligible for the Southern Area League Riders' Championship. Common sense eventually prevailed and Ridgeon was allowed to take his place in the final.

It was felt by many that Ridgeon's form at Rye House that year – as well as being almost unbeatable round the circuit, he had also lowered the track record to 61.6 seconds – made him a certainty to take the title. Sadly for him, it was not to be. In his first race, an oiled-up plug prevented him from even starting. He won his second and third races, but a faulty clutch again put him out before he even started his fourth. For his final race, he borrowed Bobby Croombs' machine and promptly blew it up. The title was won by Eastbourne's Leo McAuliffe, who scored 14 points. His only defeat of the day came at the hands of Rye House's teenager, Gerry King, in the most exciting race of the afternoon. McAuliffe got away from the tapes but was chased hard by King, who just managed to squeeze past McAuliffe as they crossed the finishing line. Rye House's highest-placed rider was Dave Slater, universally known as 'Slater the Gater' for his very fast starting technique, who finished third.

Apart from the slip-up with the SAL Riders' Championship, it had been yet another good year for Rye House and the individual team members, with a hat-trick of league successes for the team, while Ridgeon was ranked as top rider in the league as well as being easily the league's top point-scorer. Slater was second highest in the league.

Rye House had plenty more reasons to be proud, from the training school, which was still turning out riders of the highest calibre, to the facilities at the stadium itself. Discussing why the SAL Riders' Championship was being held at Rye House again, John Hyam made the point that this 'is ample proof of the splendid presentation and showmanship that the promoters of Rye House have put in to the past two finals. Attempts have been made to stage the final on other circuits, but when the final moment of decision has arrived the SAL management have voted "en bloc" Rye House.' He went on to say that the whole league should extend 'special thanks to George Kay, Fred Peachey, Dicky Case and their sterling helpers for the hard work they have put in behind the scenes to make the Championship the "showpiece" of the year in the SAL.'

At the end of 1956, Dicky Case sold the pub and the track and went back home to Australia. It was the end of a long and fruitful association with the track, going back thirty years.

## 1956 Southern Area League

| Date | H/A | Opponent | W/L | Score |
|---|---|---|---|---|
| 15 April | H | California | W | 52-32 |
| 29 April | H | Southern Rovers | D | 42-42 |
| 6 May | A | California | L | 36-47 |
| 20 May | H | Eastbourne | W | 54-30 |
| 27 May | A | Eastbourne | W | 54-29 |
| 24 June | H | California | W | 56-26 |
| 14 July | A | Eastbourne | L | 37-40 |
| 22 July | H | Southern Rovers | W | 49-35 |
| 16 September | A | California | L | 39-43 |
| 23 September | A | Southern Rovers | W | 52-32★ |
| 14 October | H | Eastbourne | W | 56-28 |

★ Raced at Rye House for double points
P12 W8 D1 L3
For 527 Against 384
Position: first (out of four)

## Southern Cup

First Round
| Date | H/A | Opponent | W/L | Score |
|---|---|---|---|---|
| 10 June | H | Southern Rovers | W | 58-50 |

Final
| Date | H/A | Opponent | W/L | Score |
|---|---|---|---|---|
| 1 July | A | California | L | 45.5-1.5 |
| 8 July | H | California | W | 70-38 |

Rye House won the cup 115.5-99.5 on aggregate

## 1956 Southern Area League (cma no bonus points)

| Name | M | R | Pts | CMA |
|---|---|---|---|---|
| Vic Ridgeon | 11 | 44 | 113 | 10.27 |
| Al Sparrey | 8 | 32 | 80 | 10.00 |
| Dave Slater | 11 | 44 | 93 | 8.45 |
| Bobby Croombes | 9 | 34 | 61 | 7.18 |
| Gerry King | 11 | 42 | 72 | 6.86 |
| Brian Brett | 10 | 32 | 37 | 4.63 |
| Jim Chalkley | 11 | 36 | 36 | 4.00 |

The 1957 SAL Riders' Championship final line-up. From left to right, back row: Ron Walton, Maury Conway, Tommy Sweetman, Allen Lunn (Rye House), Pat Flanaghan, Brian Meredith, Pete Mould, Les Searle, Brian Brett (Rye House). Front row: Ross Gilbertson, Leo McAuliffe, Noel Conway, Bobby Croombs (Rye House), Dave Still (Rye House), Ronnie Rolfe (Rye House), Jim Heard.

## 1957

During the close season, Ridgeon travelled to South Africa, where he became the only current Southern Area League rider ever to ride in a full Test match when he rode for England in the seventh Test between South Africa and England at Durban on 23 February 1957. He scored one point.

On his return to England, Ridgeon decided not to move to Southampton after all. There was talk during the winter of his going into motor racing with Jimmy Chalkley as his mechanic, but both of them turned out for Rye House's first meeting of the season, the Easter Cup. This was won by Gerry King. Two more individual meetings followed: the Brian Crutcher Trophy and the Thompson Trophy, both won by Ridgeon.

The team itself began the season with a Challenge match at home to California, which they duly won 46-37. The Southern Area League once again consisted of four teams, though this year the Rovers had found a permanent home at Rayleigh.

With Ridgeon and Croombs back in the team after all, backed up by Slater, King, Brett and Chalkley, there were high hopes of retaining the league title for the fourth year. Newcomers to the team included Allen Lunn, Dave Still and Ronnie Rolfe.

The first league match of the year was away at Rayleigh. It was not the start the Roosters were looking for as they went down 58-26.

It was at this point that both Vic Ridgeon and Jimmy Chalkley decided to hang up their leathers. It left the team in a desperate state and several more heavy away losses – 51-32 and 59-23 to Aldershot (who had taken California's place in the league), and 51-32 to Eastbourne – meant that there was no chance they were going to retain their league title. Fortunately, their home form remained good and included victories over Eastbourne, 66-17, and Aldershot, 52-29, giving the home fans some hope, but a loss to Rayleigh, 42-40, consigned Rye House to the indignity of bottom place in the league for the first time in their history.

Gerry King was appointed captain and tried valiantly to step into Ridgeon's shoes. His 86 points from nine matches was a good effort for the youngster but, as a captain, he lacked Ridgeon's personality and was not able to inspire either the fans or his team in the same way.

Croombs tried his best and managed two maximums during the year, but beyond these two there was little support. Slater had a very disappointing year, scoring just 49 points from 10 outings, and that included one 12-point maximum. Brett was also a little disappointing. In a year when he was expected to reach the top, he managed just 37 points from 10 matches.

Two youngsters were drafted into the team. The first was Ernie Baker, who had made such a spectacular debut the year before. He had an all-action style that kept the crowd enthralled, but he received very little reward for his efforts, managing just eight points from three matches. The other youngster went by the name of Ivan Mauger. He was plagued by machine problems and, after scoring just five points from three matches, he was dropped.

There was no consolation in the Southern Area League Riders' Championship either. Bobby Croombs was Rye House's highest-placed rider, but he could only manage joint seventh place.

With King and Croombs both being signed up by Wimbledon at the end of the season, things did not look too good for 1958.

## 1957 Southern Area League

| Date | H/A | Opponent | W/L | Score |
|---|---|---|---|---|
| 16 June | H | Eastbourne | W | 66-17 |
| 23 June | A | Eastbourne | L | 32-51 |
| 30 June | H | Southern Rovers | L | 40-42★ |
| 13 July | A | Aldershot | L | 32-51 |
| 14 July | H | Aldershot | W | 52-29 |
| 27 July | A | Rayleigh Rovers | L | 26-58★ |
| 7 September | A | Aldershot | L | 23-60 |
| 8 September | H | Aldershot | W | 48-35 |
| 22 September | H | Rayleigh Rovers | W | 51-32★† |
| 6 October | A | Eastbourne | L | 36-46† |

★ Southern Rovers became Rayleigh Rovers on 2 July

† Raced for double points

P12 W5 D0 L7

For 406 Against 420

Position: fourth (out of four)

## 1957 Southern Area League (actual match average)

| Name | M | Pts | CMA |
|---|---|---|---|
| Gerry King | 9 | 86 | 9.56 |
| Bobby Croombs | 9 | 76 | 8.44 |
| Vic Ridgeon | 6 | 35 | 5.83 |
| Dave Slater | 10 | 49 | 4.90 |
| Dave Still | 7 | 34 | 4.86 |
| Allen Lunn | 8 | 37 | 4.63 |
| Brian Brett | 9 | 30 | 3.33 |
| Ronnie Rolfe | 6 | 18 | 3.00 |
| Jim Chalkley | 6 | 14 | 2.33 |

# 1958

As things turned out, Rye House did not have to worry about the 1958 league season as it was abandoned for the year. With the withdrawal of Rayleigh from the league, it was felt to be no longer viable. There was talk at the beginning of the season of the three remaining teams joining together with Exeter, Yarmouth and junior teams from First Division tracks Swindon and Norwich to form a junior league, but Rye House, along with Aldershot and Eastbourne, soon withdrew from the talks as they considered the pay rates for the new league too high. As it happened, it was probably as well that Rye House were not in the league as their season did not get under way until August.

The new owner, Les Lawrence, who had taken over at the beginning of the previous season, was really only interested in the greyhound racing, which he saw as a more lucrative enterprise than speedway. As a result, he decided to expand the facilities available for the greyhounds, intending at first to close the speedway down and build a new club room over part of the track. However, a number of Rye House supporters got together and contacted their former hero, Mike Broadbank, to ask him if he would speak to Mr Lawrence about retaining speedway at Rye House. Broadbank agreed and approached Lawrence saying that, if he could give him a piece of land elsewhere within the Rye House grounds, he would be prepared to build a new track himself at no cost to the new owner. Lawrence showed Broadbank a very marshy field at the back of the greyhound track and said he was prepared to give it to him for nothing if he felt he could make something of it. Broadbank, together with his father Alf, looked at the field and agreed to take it. They then set about marking out a new track. They first put a post in the middle of the field so they could work out the size and where the track would go exactly. They then got a Ferguson tractor with a blade on the back and rode it round and round the intended track to mark it out. A nearby power station supplied enough cinders free of charge to make the track. The cinders were brought in by a continuous stream of lorries and dumped in two piles in the centre. From there, they were hand-raked onto the track and spread round. The starter's box was made out of wood with a tin roof and a wooden safety fence was made out of two by four planks with 4ft-high corrugated tin attached. They obtained the old Harringay starting gate and put new magnets on. Many of the past and current Rye House riders came down to give a helping hand as none of them wished to see Rye House die. It was a labour of love for the Broadbanks and the riders and supporters who helped out. They put in many long hours unpaid, but at last the new track was ready. Although the new track was only 325 yards long, races were still held initially over three laps.

With Mike Broadbank now in charge at the track, it meant the time had come for George Kay to retire, thus severing his connection with Rye House, which went back to 1936. Fred Peachey remained as team manager for the time being.

A new track record of 53.2 seconds was set up by Brian Meredith at the first meeting on 3 August. Meredith also won this first meeting, the August Trophy. New signing Clive Hitch was involved in the most exciting race of the afternoon when, after four laps of wheel-to-wheel action with former California rider Tommy Sweetman, the pair dead-heated. After this race, Sweetman was also signed up, although it was a very makeshift team and only came together for the three home and one away challenge matches held that year. Others to turn out for the team that year included Baker, Rolfe, Brett and two new training school discoveries, Stan Stevens and Pete Sampson, both of whom were to go on and make a name for themselves in senior racing.

Because of the shortness of the track, it was soon decided to change to the more usual form of four-lap races. Sweetman set up the first track record on 17 August with a time of 70.0 seconds. This was lowered on 21 September by Brian Brett to 69.4. Brett also won the end-of-season Rye House Championship.

In all, only six meetings were held in 1958 as Rye House prepared themselves for more league action in 1959.

## 1959

The Southern Area League returned in 1959 with five teams: Rye House, Eastbourne, Aldershot, Ipswich and Yarmouth. The Rye House team was Croombs, Sweetman, Hitch, Baker, Rolfe, Stevens and Sampson, all of whom had put in at least one appearance during the short non-league 1958 season. The season started with two rained off meetings, but the third meeting saw them pull off a 41-31 win over Eastbourne in a Challenge match. Sweetman and Croombs both rode well.

The following week, Coventry's Brian Meredith won the Rye House Trophy thanks to a last-heat victory when he came from last to first place, overtaking Sweetman, Gil Goldfinch and Bob Thomas on the way.

Things in the league started off well, with a handsome 43-26 victory over Yarmouth in the first match of the season. Sweetman scored ten points, while Croombs and Rolfe both contributed nine each. In his first ever league match, Stevens scored four points from the reserve position. In the second half, Sweetman won the Silver Sash from Yarmouth's Ivor Brown.

In the first few meetings, dust had caused problems at the new track and spectators complained about getting covered in the stuff. Mr Lawrence's answer to this was to buy a fire pump, which proved beneficial all round and kept the dust to a minimum.

Rye House suffered their first reverse on 24 May when they lost at home, 38-33, to Eastbourne. Colin Gooddy scored a maximum for the visitors, while only Sweetman came good for the Roosters, scoring 11 points. An away defeat to the same team by the same score followed. Victory over Ipswich by 47-30 was, however, followed by another home defeat to Yarmouth, 37-35. In order to strengthen the team, Rye House had signed up Brian Meredith and, although he and Baker rode well against Yarmouth, Sweetman had a nightmare of an afternoon plagued with mechanical troubles and only managed six points. With the arrival of Meredith in the team, Stevens was left out, but Yarmouth arrived a man short so he was drafted into the Bloaters line-up for the afternoon. Ironically, he scored six points from his two rides, a reserves' maximum. He then went on to win his three second-half races. It was the culmination of a great week for Stevens as had also just won the Essex round of the National Individual Cycle Speedway Championship.

Thanks to his performance for Yarmouth, Stevens was immediately drafted into the Rye House line-up for the following week's match against Aldershot. Riding at number one, he scored eight points from three rides before suffering from engine failure in his last.

A 44-28 victory over Aldershot gave Rye House a fifty per cent home record, and, with only winning one match away, over Ipswich, 37-35, it meant their dreams of a fourth Southern Area League title had to remain unfulfilled. In the end, they finished fourth with just six points.

It had been a disappointing year for the Roosters as there is no doubt that, on paper, they looked capable of much better things. The captain, Tommy Sweetman, was the undoubted star. He scored double points in most matches and when he didn't it was usually only because of engine trouble. In the league as a whole, he finished up as the third highest point-scorer behind Eastbourne's Colin Gooddy and Yarmouth's Ivor Brown. Croombs also suffered from machine troubles and was unable to show his true form. Rolfe was inconsistent, one week he would record a high score, the next week he was struggling. Baker was a great asset at home, but away he was little better than a reserve. Thirty-one of his total of 40 points came at home. He did not seem to be able to get to grips with away tracks and lost most of his points through falls. In Stevens, however, Rye House had found the junior of the year. By the end of the year, he was being spoken of as a Rye House discovery in the same mould as Broadbank and Brett, with equally as bright a future.

Towards the end of the season, there was talk of Rye House joining a much bigger league the following year. Up in the North and Midlands, a man by the name of Mike Parker had opened up several defunct tracks and was running them outside the jurisdiction of the Speedway Control Board. In spite of this, he was having no difficulty in finding riders for his teams and they were proving hugely popular with speedway supporters, who had been deprived of their speedway for too long. Parker wanted to get together with the Southern Area League teams to form a national league for 1960, but the SAL promoters were reluctant to operate outside the official umbrella of the Speedway Control Board. A number of meetings were held between Parker, the SAL promoters and representatives of the riders with a view to resolving the issue and putting a plan to the Speedway Control Board for a new league.

Colin Gooddy, winner of the first Gerry Hussey
Memorial Trophy in 1959.

In November 1959, a meeting was held between representatives of the proposed new league
and the Control Board at which agreement was reached to form a new official league within
the orbit of the Speedway Control Board for 1960 to be called the Provincial League. All
the Southern Area League tracks applied to join but Rye House, along with Aldershot and
Eastbourne were turned down. The reasons given were that their tracks were not up to standard
and they raced on Sundays. Rye House appealed against the decision but were unsuccessful.

## 1959 Southern Area League

| Date | H/A | Opponent | W/L | Score |
|---|---|---|---|---|
| 24 May | H | Eastbourne | L | 33-38 |
| 7 June | H | Ipswich | W | 47-30 |
| 14 June | A | Eastbourne | L | 33-38 |
| 14 July | A | Yarmouth | L | 28-44 |
| 19 July | H | Yarmouth | L | 35-37 |
| 30 July | A | Ipswich | W | 37-35 |
| 2 August | H | Aldershot | W | 44-28 |
| 22 August | A | Aldershot | L | 32-37 |

P8 W3 D0 L5
For 283 Against 287
Position: fourth (out of five)

## 1959 Southern Area League (actual match average)

| Name | M | Pts | CMA |
|---|---|---|---|
| Tom Sweetman | 8 | 68 | 8.50 |
| Ronnie Rolfe | 7 | 47 | 6.71 |
| Ernie Baker | 7 | 40 | 5.71 |
| Clive Hitch | 8 | 36 | 4.50 |
| Bobby Croombes | 6 | 31 | 5.17 |
| Stan Stevens | 6 | 29 | 4.83 |
| Pete Sampson | 7 | 16 | 2.29 |

# The 1960s

## 1960

With Yarmouth being accepted into the new league and Ipswich moving straight up to the National League, the idea of a Southern Area League proved once again untenable, so, for 1960, it was back to non-league status and a season of open meetings.

At the end of 1959, Lawrence sold the speedway track to an organisation who wished to use the area for a go-kart track, but he had been so impressed with the work put in by Broadbank and the level of support the speedway was bringing in that he asked Broadbank if he would like to move the track back to the main stadium, only inside rather than outside the greyhound track. Mike and Alf Broadbank were only too happy to agree to this as the second track had never been satisfactory; being built on a marshy field, it had always had drainage problems and, of course, the facilities for the supporters were much better round the greyhound track with proper stands and clubrooms. And so, once again, the Broadbanks, with the help of former riders Sampson, Pratt and Stan Pepper, set about building the new track. The starting gate was brought over from the other track and a new one purchased just in case there were any problems with the original. Being inside the greyhound circuit, the new track was no longer the long, wide, open 440-yard track the original had been, but was reduced to 325 yards, the same as the second track had been, though, because of the restriction of the dog track, it was narrower. A new pit area was built with hot showers laid on for the riders for the first time. Before this, the riders had just been provided with buckets of cold water. Mike Broadbank also bought a caravan which he installed as a new speedway office.

Rye House captain at that time Tommy Sweetman recalls:

> The greyhound track was in front of the clubrooms. In 1959 it was decided to move the track back in front of the clubrooms but inside the greyhound track; this enabled the speedway patrons to use the facilities, clubrooms, etc. The safety fence was now wire so greyhound patrons could see the dog racing. The track was 325 yards. Access was often difficult as the running wire for the 'hare' on the dog track went across the access gates. On a Saturday and Sunday you had to wait until the morning dog trials were finished before you could get access to the speedway track. The River Lea, which runs next to the track, was the water source for watering it. Basically a truck with a large tank on the back was filled with river water by pump and driven around the track. Often the water tap would get blocked up due to river weed. Mike Broadbank ran the training school and Mike used the workshop facilities as his workshop to prepare his own bike.

Rye House ran the first part of the 1960 season on the old track while the new one was being built. The team itself also underwent some major changes as, firstly, Broadbank became the new promoter, secondly, a new manager, Freddie Millward, was brought in and, thirdly, the name of the team was changed from the Roosters to the Red Devils in honour of Broadbank himself, who was known as the Red Devil because he wore red leathers at a time when black leathers were the almost universally accepted norm.

*Above:* Rye House versus Eastbourne. The second meeting at the new track on 4 September 1960.

*Right:* Clive Hitch first rode for Rye House in 1958, was named captain in 1965 and even rode in the 1974 British League Division Two team.

   With so many team places now available to riders through both the National League and the Provincial League, Rye House no longer had exclusive call on most of its team, so the team line-up was never the same two weeks running. A number of the 1959 team did continue to turn out for Rye House, including Sweetman, Hitch, Stevens and Sampson, and a number of others came and went during the season, including Colin Pratt, Geoff Mudge, Jim Gleed, Bill Wainwright and Sandy McGillivray.
   The new season opened on 17 April 1960 with a best pairs event won by Sweetman and Joe Neath. Home and away challenge matches against Eastbourne followed, both of which were two of the most entertaining and thrilling meetings seen at the respective tracks for a long time. The score at Hoddesdon was 41-41, while at Arlington, Rye House went down by a single point, 36-35. Two further home victories in Challenge matches against Aldershot, 49-23, and Ipswich B, 39-32, followed.

The new track opened on 28 August in front of a record attendance with a special best-of-three match race series between Broadbank and world champion Ronnie Moore, with Moore winning 2-1. This was followed by the All Star Trophy, donated by Moore, which was won by Sweetman, with a faultless 15-point maximum, from Stevens and Hitch.

Further successes against Eastbourne, 39-31, including maximums by Sweetman and Mudge, and Ipswich B, 46-26, followed and the season concluded with the Rye House Championship won, not surprisingly, by Tommy Sweetman, who had proved himself once again to be the master of Rye House, both the old and the new circuits. He also ended the season as joint track record holder with Geoff Mudge with a time of 71.4. (Broadbank had won the first of the three match races on 28 August in a time of 70.4, but this was discounted for official record purposes).

# 1961

Although still only running Challenge matches with a team made up from week to week, Millward was pleased to announce at the start of the season that Vic Ridgeon had decided on a comeback and had been signed up by Provincial League Wolverhampton. He hoped to persuade the ever-popular former captain to turn out for his old club now and again during the season.

The season itself got under way on 2 April, with Tommy Sweetman winning the Easter Trophy. A Best Pairs event followed, on a rain-sodden track, which became more a battle for mere survival than a race meeting. This was won by Geoff Mudge, who scored a maximum 12 points, and Barrie Smith, a training-school novice. This was how the Best Pairs meetings were structured at this time – a top rider with a novice, to give the novices experience of riding with the better riders.

Rye House's first team match of the season came on 30 April, away to Eastbourne in a two-legged challenge. The Red Devils team for this encounter was Sweetman, Ridgeon, Mudge, Pratt, Roy Trigg and Ken Vale. Ridgeon only managed to finish one ride thanks to mechanical problems and the team went down 41-31. In the second leg at Rye House the following week, Ridgeon, who was welcomed back with loud cheers by the Rye House faithful, showed what he could do if he was free from engine failures and top-scored for his old team. But the victory, 38-34, was not enough to pull back the deficit and Eastbourne won the challenge 75-69 on aggregate.

The next two individual meetings were both won by Geoff Mudge, while the next team match was a four-team tournament against Eastbourne, New Cross and The Rest. New Cross, with three Rye House riders in their team, Sweetman, Trigg and Vale, along with Bill Wainwright, won the meeting with 33 points. Rye House, with Mudge, Hitch, Pratt and Giddings, came second with 22. The high point of the afternoon for Rye House fans was that Mudge equalled the track record of 69.6 seconds in the opening heat and then went on to score a 12-point maximum. Mudge was definitely proving himself the man of the season at Hoddesdon.

Three more former Rye House riders turned out for the Red Devils in the next home match – Stan Stevens, who scored nine, Pete Sampson, seven, and Sandy McGillivray, four – in an easy victory over Ipswich B, 56-28. Hitch scored a 12-point maximum, while Trigg scored a paid maximum.

Four more team matches followed during the season with a number of new riders coming into the team from the training school, including Terry Keats, John Bishop, and Tyburn Gallows. In all, Rye House rode eight team matches during the year, six at home and two at Eastbourne. Top scorer for the year was Trigg, who scored 46 points from six matches. Pratt scored 30 from five, Sweetman 29 from five, Mudge 24 from four and Hitch 22 from three. Sampson, Vale and Keats also rode in three matches. Sadly, Ridgeon's commitments to Wolverhampton only allowed him to ride in two matches during the season.

The 1961 Rye House team. From left to right, back row: Colin Pratt, Pete Sampson, Bill Wainwright, Ronnie Rolfe, Stan Stevens, Freddie Millward (manager), Jim Gleed. Front row: Clive Hitch, Tommy Sweetman (captain on bike), Sandy McGillivray.

On 24 September, the Mike Broadbank Training School Plaque was raced for by the best of that year's juniors and was won by Tyburn Gallows from John Mills. One rider who got no further than the first round was Alan Cowland. The final meeting of the season was the Rye House Championship, won this year by Stoke's Pete Jarman from Pratt and Sweetman.

Although a non-league club, Millward's combination of showmanship and organisation brought large crowds through the turnstiles, turning 1961 into probably Rye House's best-supported year since the late 1940s.

## 1962

Big changes took place before the 1962 season started. Gerry Bailey and Jack Carter took over promotion of the club with John Bailey the new manager. Mike Broadbank continued in his role as chief instructor. One unusual find he made over the close season was the sixteen-year-old Ray Cousins. He decided to model his style on one of the most exciting and spectacular riders the sport had ever seen, 'Cyclone' Billy Lamont, and took to leg-trailing, a style that had by now completely died out. Although this proved to be popular with spectators, it gave Broadbank a bit of a problem as he was a unsure how to teach leg-trailing.

Another of the Rye House juniors was also in the news as the Speedway Control Board ruled that their prospect from 1961, Tyburn Gallows, would no longer be allowed to use that name and had to ride under his real name of Raymond Humphries. His CND race jacket was also banned. They felt that both were bringing speedway into disrepute. Humphries later got round the ban by the simple expedient of changing his name officially by deed poll, so there was nothing the Control Board could do about it.

The leg-trailing Ray Cousins who gave Mike Broadbank a problem in how to teach him.

Rye House had the honour of starting the 1962 speedway season in Great Britain with an individual trophy meeting on 25 March. This was won by former Rye House Southern Area League rider Jim Heard. But the most remarkable thing about this meeting was that it marked the sensational debut of one of the winter training school products, Norman Hunter. He scored 11 points from four rides to finish third. In his last ride, he even managed to sweep past Rye House track expert Tommy Sweetman on the final turn. He had only been practising for four months. After this incredible debut, Hunter was signed up by Provincial League Leicester where, in his first season in speedway, he became the team's top scorer. He went on to become one of England's leading riders and to take his place in the English international side on many occasions.

Several more individual meetings took place with Geoff Mudge winning two, Sweetman one, Jarman one and Ipswich's Ron Bagley one. The first team meeting was against Provincial League Wolverhampton on 1 July, which the Red Devils won 49-27. Another four-team tournament was held on 12 August, with Stoke, Poole and Wolverhampton providing the opposition. The Rye House team of Sampson, Wanwright, Buster Brown, Bob Thomas and Dave Hemus finished third. Stoke, with three Rye House track specialists in Colin Pratt, Pete Jarman and Jim Heard in their team, were the winners. Other old Rye House favourites Roy Trigg and Geoff Mudge turned out for Poole, while Vic Ridgeon was the star of the Wolverhampton team.

A two-leg challenge match against the old enemy, Eastbourne, took place on 26 August and 2 September, with the first leg at home. The Rye House team for this meeting was Pratt, who scored a 12-point maximum, Brown, Sweetman, Sampson, Hemus, Keats and Cousins. The score was 43-34 to the Red Devils. The return match at Arlington turned out to be a most thrilling affair. Mudge and Trigg came in for Pratt and Brown, with the others remaining the same. Although they were ten points down after heat six, Rye House fought back to level the final score at 39-39 and win the challenge 82-73 on aggregate.

Rye House's ever-changing line-up saw Pete Jarman, Terry Stone and Geoff Penniket line up alongside Sweetman, Hemus, Sampson and Keats for the match against Weymouth on 23 September. With 12-point maximums from Sweetman and Jarman, and a further 12 from five rides from Stone, the Red Devils ran out easy victors, 50-33.

For the second year running, Jarman took the Rye House Championship, this time from Geoff Mudge and Tim Bungay, while the Training School Championship Trophy for first-year juniors was won by Mike Keen from Brian Leonard and Mike Garry. In a special Champions Match Race, Keen defeated the 1961 champion, Tyburn Gallows.

*Above Left:* Overnight sensation and Rye House discovery Norman Hunter went on to become Leicester's top scorer in his first season in speedway.
*Above Right:* Gerry Bailey, who took over the promotion of Rye House in 1962 with Jack Carter.

## 1963

Over the winter, Mike Broadbank travelled to Australia to race. His place as instructor at the training school was taken by his father, with the help of former Rye House discovery and now his Swindon teammate Brian Brett.

Terry Stone won the first meeting of the season, the Skol Lager Trophy, on 14 April, with Pete Jarman winning the Ace of Herts Trophy two weeks later. The first team match was away at Eastbourne, the first part of the normal two-leg challenge. The Red Devils team for this encounter was Sweetman, Sampson, Peter Jackson, Kid Bodie, Mike Keen, Alan Jackson and Kevin Torpie. Of the 29 points Rye House scored that afternoon, 20 came from Sweetman and Sampson. In the return leg, the same two accounted for 19 points, but this time they had Jarman leading them. With his 13 points, Rye House were able to just defeat the Eagles 40-38, but they lost the tie on aggregate 86-69.

It was just after this match that the Control Board announced that in future no contracted Provincial League or National League rider, other than Provincial League reserves and the lowest-scoring team man from Provincial League teams, would be allowed to ride at Rye House and Eastbourne. The theory behind this move was to give more opportunities to the genuine juniors to ride. However, Mike Broadbank, on behalf of the Rye House management, said that it could mean the end for Rye House. The view of both Rye House and Eastbourne was that the theory was all very well but they had to make their respective tracks into going concerns and they did not feel that the paying public would come to the tracks if all they could see week in, week out were juniors. For Rye House, it would mean no more Geoff Mudge, a man who had become something of an idol at Hoddesdon, no more Tommy Sweetman, Pete Jarman, Colin Pratt, Norman Hunter and many others who the crowds came to see. If the crowds didn't come, the track would have to close down and then there would be no opportunities at all for the juniors. Broadbank also made the point that it was important for the youngsters to ride against a better class of rider if they were to improve.

Broadbank gained the support of the Speedway Riders' Association (SRA) who were 'horrified' at the ruling, partly for the reasons already cited but also because it meant less rides for their members at Rye House and Eastbourne. The chairman of the association, Danny Dunton, wrote to the Control Board in very stark terms drawing their attention to the fact that it seemed likely that both tracks were now on the verge of closure.

After further three-way discussions between the tracks, the Control Board and the SRA, the Control Board eventually rescinded their decision and Rye House returned to action on 26 May with a challenge match against New Cross B. Tommy Sweetman captained Rye House to a 50-27 victory with a 12-point maximum. Pete Sampson backed him up with 10 paid 11.

Further individual meetings followed, won by Roy Trigg, Jim Heard and Colin Pratt, and then four Challenge matches, against Hackney B, Stoke B and Weymouth at home, all of which the Red Devils won, 46-44, 41-36 and 45-33 respectively, and Weymouth away, also won by Rye House, 41-37. For the most part, the team consisted of Pete Sampson, Mike Keen, Kevin Torpie, Tyburn Gallows (still at this time riding under his real name of Raymond Humphries), Peter Jackson, Alan Jackson and Terry Keats.

The final match of the season turned out to be another challenge match against an almost full strength Poole team. For this match, Rye House brought back three of their former stars, Pete Jarman, Tommy Sweetman and Jim Heard, to join Pete Sampson, Geoff Penniket, Mike Keen and Brian Davies. Even though Jarman scored a 12-point maximum, it wasn't quite enough to defeat a Poole team led by another Rye House favourite, Geoff Mudge, and they went down by the narrow score of 40-38.

This was not due to be the last match of the season, but two attempted stagings of the Rye House Championship, on 6 October and 20 October, were both rained off. So the season fizzled out to a rather damp end, but at least Rye House was still intact and still operating in front of large crowds after the scare they had received earlier in the season.

# 1964

While the training school was continuing its job over the winter of turning out future stars – two of this winter's discoveries were Ted Ede and Malcolm Brown, both later to find places in league teams – the rest of the British speedway world split into two warring factions. With the closure of Southampton, the National League were down to six teams. The Control Board did not think this was viable and so they put two alternatives to the Provincial League promoters. The first was that the league champions, Wolverhampton, be promoted to the National League. If this was not acceptable, then they proposed running one league consisting of sixteen teams. Both of these options were rejected by the Provincial League promoters. They did not like the handicapping which was then a feature of the National League and which it was proposed would continue, and they sided with the SRA over the restriction of foreign riders, which the Control Board rejected. The Provincial League promoters said they would continue to run their own league with or without official sanction from the Control Board and they asked the Royal Automobile Club (RAC) to launch an inquiry into the organisation of speedway in this country. As the season grew nearer, no agreement was reached and the Control Board threatened the Provincial League riders with suspension if they rode in an unofficial league. Coventry promoter Charles Ochiltree then announced that he was reopening West Ham to run in the National League, and with a viable league once more, the Control Board called on the Provincial League promoters to throw in their lot with them and either join the National League or form a second division. The Provincial League promoters were still unhappy with the way the sport was being run and they stuck together declaring they were prepared to run outside the Control Board's jurisdiction. The crunch came on 16 March with the first Provincial League match of the season, Exeter versus Cradley Heath. With the successful running of this meeting, the gap between the two sides widened and it was obvious there was to be no reconciliation in time for the 1964 season.

A Rye House stalwart throughout the 1960s, Tyburn Gallows.

All Provincial League riders had their licences suspended and were therefore unable to take part in international events such as the World Championship, but very few of their riders jumped ship and the Provincial League remained as strong as it had been in 1963.

The division was clear cut between the National League and the Provincial League teams. What was not so clear cut was the position of the five non-league tracks operating in 1964. These were Rye House, Eastbourne, Ipswich, Rayleigh and Weymouth. The latter four eventually opted to join a new league, the Metropolitan League, run within the orbit of the Provincial League, which also included riders from that league in two further teams, Exeter B and Newpool, a joint Newport and Poole junior team.

Rye House, on the other hand, opted to stay official and threw in its lot with the Control Board and the National League. The reason for doing so was explained by Broadbank, who said that it would be unfair to the youngsters they were training if they were to start their career by being 'outlawed'. Once they had reached a sufficient standard to get into a league team, it would be up to them to decide what they wanted to do. But Bailey added a cautionary note that he hoped the National League promoters might help them out and allow their riders to ride at open meetings during the season. He felt that as Rye House had stuck its neck out for the National League, the least they could do was to help Rye House. With that backing, it meant that Rye House would get to see some top-class riders during 1964, but would miss many of their stalwarts, such as Tommy Sweetman, Geoff Mudge, Pete Jarman and Jim Heard, all of whom had decided to stay with their Provincial League teams.

The first meeting was held on 12 April, the Skol Lager Trophy, and was won by former Rye House discovery Norman Hunter, now a heat leader with West Ham.

With the loss of the other non-league teams to the Provincial League sphere of influence, it meant that challenge matches were few and far between. In fact, there were only three all season and only two of those were as a Rye House team: the first was against a National League Select, the second against Young Coventry and the third was Stan Stevens' team against Norman Hunter's team. For the two matches as Rye House, Mike Keen captained the side.

Two Rye House captains,
Clive Hitch (left) and Tommy
Sweetman.

Other riders included Alan Stapleton, David Crane, Bob Warner, Eddie Reeves, Keith Whipp, Ian Champion and Geoff Hughes. Both matches were close-run affairs; against the National League select, the Red Devils ran out victors by two points, 40-38, while against Young Coventry, Rye House lost by two points, 43-41.

It was in the many individual meetings held that year that the supporters got to see some of the bigger names in the sport. The Gerry Hussey Memorial Trophy, for example, was won by Bob Andrews from Jimmy Gooch in second place. Both of these were World Championship finalists; Andrews had been joint fifth as recently as 1961 and 1962 and was to qualify again that year, 1964, while Gooch was to qualify the following year. Andrews also won the Ronnie Moore Trophy on 30 August. Others in the line-up included Gooch, Hunter, Sandor Levai, Martin Ashby, Teo Teodorowicz and Reg Luckhurst. The Rye House Championship was won by Gooch, with Ronnie Genz, a former Rye House discovery and now a top rider with Oxford, appearing in the line-up.

Rye House's biggest meeting that season, however, was a first-round qualifier for the World Championship held on 21 June; the first time Rye House had ever been awarded the honour of holding a round of the World Championship. Amongst those taking part were Levai, former world number three, Jack Biggs, Bob Kilby, Malcolm Simmons, Roy Bowers and former Rye House discoveries Stan Stevens and Ernie Baker. The winner was Coventry's Les Owen from Norwich's Tich Read.

## 1965

At the end of 1964, Broadbank decided to end his association with the club. Although they were still getting good crowds at the Sunday meetings, he didn't seem to be making any money. He always made sure that he paid all the riders and staff, of which there were about fifty, before the end of the afternoon. Out of the rest, he paid his rent to Carter and Bailey. This should have left him with some money for himself, but invariably there was nothing. He had his suspicions that there was at least one unscrupulous member of his staff who was pocketing more than his share but he never pursued the matter, deciding instead that he had no alternative but to get out. He had not wanted to leave and recalls that he was:

> very hurt when I had to leave, but there was no future there for me; people were ripping me off. Rye House was my life. I had spent all my spare time working on the track, raking it, maintaining the white line and so on. I put hours and hours into it. I am very proud

of the number of trainees who passed through my hands who went on to become top riders, names like Norman Hunter, Colin Pratt, Roy Trigg, Stan Stevens, Alan Cowland, Brian Leonard, James Bond, Mike Keen, Bob Thomas and Dave Hemus. I also gave riders from overseas their first taste of English speedway by allowing them to train at Rye House. Sandor Levai was one who spent many hours at Rye House when he first came over from Hungary and you could guarantee that most Australians who came over would make for Rye House first. The one thing I am glad of now is that Rye House is still open for speedway and very pleased that Len [Silver] is the promoter. He is a great showman and the best thing that could have happened for the club and the track.

The new promoting team that took over the running of Rye House for 1965 was WBS. promotions, consisting of Bill Wainwright, John Bailey and Tommy Sweetman, while the training school was taken over by two former Rye House discoveries, Pete Sampson and Terry Keats, who were cousins. Former announcer Ernie Hancock was installed as team manager. A new price structure for spectators was introduced with the price of admission being set at 3s 6d including a programme, which meant 3d saved on the 1964 cost, which had been 3s admission plus 9d for a programme. The cost for children and old-age pensioners was reduced from 2s to 1s 6d. Rye House continued to race on a Sunday. The main reason was to attract London-based Speedway supporters to Rye House for a Sunday out with a day by the river, an afternoon's racing and the traditional after-meeting social and dance at the clubrooms. In addition, none of the major league tracks raced on Sundays, so this gave the promoters a chance to invite contracted team riders from other clubs for a Sunday meeting. Because they were racing on a Sunday, the problem with the Lord's Day Observance Society still reared its head from time to time. To try and steer clear of trouble, the new management team continued to invite the local Church minister to give a short sermon at the Easter meeting and also gave a regular donation to the Church Restoration Fund.

A 1965 programme cover for the match against Poole on 22 August.

Even though peace had broken out nationally and a new league, the British League, comprising all the former National and Provincial League teams, had been formed, the new consortium promised to continue booking top-class riders for the Rye House faithful to watch. They promised at least ten changes of rider from open meeting to open meeting to give the regulars as many new faces to watch as possible. Clive Hitch was named as captain of the Red Devils and the season got underway on 18 April with Roy Trigg winning the Skol Lager Trophy.

For the first match of the season, against a London Select side on 25 April, the new promotion managed to put together a team with some real old favourites in it. As well as Hitch, the Red Devils included Vic Ridgeon, Stan Stevens, Pete Sampson and Tyburn Gallows, along with Ken Vale, Eddie Reeves and Tony Clarke. The London Select team had a familiar look about it too as it included a number of former Rye House riders and Rye House discoveries: Ted Ede, Brian Davies, Peter Jackson, Jim Tebby, Sandy McGillivray and Malcolm Brown. With a paid maximum, Hitch led his team to a 47-36 win.

Before the next meeting, a challenge match against Newport, major alterations were made to the track, which was shortened to 284 yards. The reason for this was that Rye House was still basically a training track and it was felt that the corners, as they stood, were too narrow and difficult to negotiate. The track was therefore shortened by reducing the white line distance, but, by keeping the fence in its original position, it gave the new layout wide sweeping corners which were easier for novices to get round. At the same time, the watering system was upgraded to reduce the overwhelming dust problem. The surface was shale, not the black cinders of the past, and the track location next to the river meant that the track either drained extremely well, creating dust, or flooded when the river level rose higher than normal.

Two new riders, Ken Adams and Peter Smith, featured in the Red Devils' line-up. Adams recorded a new track record of 67.4 and Rye House won the match 43-35.

The following meeting saw Bob Andrews put in a truly breathtaking performance to retain the Gerry Hussey Memorial Trophy with a faultless 15-point maximum, beating Rye House's own Pete Sampson into second place on 14. In every one of his five heats, Andrews managed to beat the track record set up only the week before, with heat four being the quickest – an incredible 63.0 seconds, shattering Ken Adams' time by an astonishing 4.4 seconds.

The next meeting was also an exciting affair as the Red Devils took on Hackney. At one time it looked as though the match would have to be abandoned following persistent rain, but not only did the new track cope with the water, it also provided a meeting full of close racing between two evenly matched teams. The Rye House team was Hitch, Sampson, Peter Jackson, Clarke, Leonard, Ede and Gallows, while the Hackney team included Roy Trigg, Brian Davies, Sandy McGillivray and Malcolm Brown. In a nail-bitingly tense finish, the Hackney pairing of Trigg and McGillivray took a 5-1 in the last heat to make the final score 39-39. Trigg scored a maximum for Hackney.

Rye House retained their unbeaten record on 22 August when they defeated Poole 45-33. This time, Roy Trigg scored a maximum for Rye House and was well supported by Malcolm Simmons with nine.

A number of individual meetings followed, with Malcolm Simmons winning two of them, while, fittingly, Clive Hitch won the Rye House Championship on 17 October. A return match against Hackney was pencilled in for 31 October to complete the season, but was rained off.


## 1966

The opening meeting of the new season was, as usual, the Skol Lager Trophy, won this year by another Training School discovery, Pete Seaton, who beat Eddie Reeves and Tony Clarke into second and third places. Old favourites Ridgeon, Gallows and Peter Jackson also took part in the meeting.

Before the next meeting, the first team match of the year, 36,000 gallons of water had to be cleared from the track which, in spite of this, still resembled a mud bath when racing finally got underway. In the most appalling conditions, the Rye House team, consisting of Hitch as captain, Simmons, Reeves, Seaton, Jackson, Ian Champion and Peter Thorn, put on a courageous display to win 46-30. Strangely enough, the Hackney team looked as much like a Rye House team as the home team did, tracking as they did Malcolm Brown, Tyburn Gallows, Sandy McGillivray, Vic Ridgeon and Pete Sampson.

The rain before this meeting gave a hint of what was in store for Rye House in 1966. The next meeting was rained off altogether as were four more during the season. Fortunately, the Red Devils did manage to get in four more team matches. The first was against a London Select, which Rye House lost 41-37. The team was almost entirely different to the one that had taken on Hackney. Hitch was injured and had to be content as a spectator in the pits. His place as captain was taken by Pete Jarman. Other members of the team were Don Smith, Peter Jackson, Pete Smith, George Marsh, Tyburn Gallows and Nev Slee. It was a matter of some comment at the meeting that Don Smith was mounted on an ESO machine and not a JAP.

With no Bob Andrews to defend his title, there was a new winner of the Gerry Hussey Memorial Trophy, Alan Cowland, who took the title from Hitch and a young up-and-coming British rider by the name of Ray Wilson. Clive Hitch and Pete Smith both scored maximums in the Red Devils' 40-34 victory over West Ham B on 3 July. They were supported by Tyburn Gallows, Tony Clarke, Peter Jackson, Nev Slee and a former discovery who had not been back to his old track for many years, Pat Flanagan. His lack of practice on the track showed as he fell three times in four races.

Rye House then won a four-team tournament against Hackney, West Ham and the Rest. All four, Hitch, Cowland, Gallows and Smith, rode well to come out on top with 41 points. West Ham were second with just 28. A new training school discovery by the name of Gary Everett turned out for the Rest team.

The next match was a real thriller as the Red Devils just managed to get the better of King's Lynn, 39-38. The final team match of the season was against Poole B, which proved to be another close match, with Rye House taking the spoils, 41-37. In scoring 11 points for the Red Devils, Alan Cowland recorded the two fastest times of the season, 65.4 and 65.8 (still over two seconds outside Bob Andrews' remarkable time). Another new name appeared in the Rye House line-up, that of Greg Kentwell.

The rest of the season was badly affected by rain but Ray Cousins managed to win the BSSC Championship Trophy for junior riders.

At the end of the season, the promoting team of Bailey, Wainwright and Sweetman decided it was time to pull the plug on public meetings. The weather had not helped during the season and there had been a marked decline in crowd numbers. It was to be three years before open meetings returned to the Hoddesdon Raceway.

## 1967/68

In the meantime, the training school continued under the guidance of Bill Mathieson, who had taken over from Sampson and Keats, although Sampson continued to look after the track machines. The charge was £2 for a rider with his own equipment and £3 10s for those without to cover the cost of the loan. The bikes for trainees were kept in bike sheds at the track. No one under the age of sixteen was allowed to hire a machine, nor was anyone who had had no previous experience of riding a motorbike. All riders were given a stipulated number of laps they were allowed and once they were done they had to return straightaway to the pits. There was to be no hanging about on the centre green or anywhere else. Although there was no hanging about after practice, one trainee of the time, George Barclay, recalls that there was sometimes plenty of waiting around before practice. On his first visit to Rye House, Mathieson's daughter, Valerie, who was in charge of scheduling the rides, made him wait for four hours because, as he

*Above:* Because Rye House ran on Sundays in the 1950s and '60s, entry was for members only, so every time you went you had to join the Supporters' Club and be given your ticket.

*Left:* Wimbledon rider Bob Andrews was a regular visitor to Rye House in the 1960s, twice winning the Gerry Hussey Memorial Trophy and smashing the track record by 4.4 seconds in 1965

says, he was the 'new boy'. After that, however, things improved for Barclay, though he was a bit put off when Mathieson started to teach him how to start properly as he could never get out of the gate quicker than his mentor. Of course, that was only to be expected, but what really threw George was when Mathieson did it side saddle and was still faster.

Once Mathieson had seen enough of a youngster to believe he might have the makings, he would get two, three or four of them together and hold informal races to see how they got on in competition. A number of promoters, such as Hackney's Len Silver and King's Lynn's Cyril Crane were regular visitors to the track, looking for the best of the youngsters to give trials to and possibly, just possibly, if they showed real signs of having what it took, sign up for team action.

## 1969

It was former promoters John Bailey and Jack Carter, trading as Carter & Bailey Ltd, who brought public meetings back to Rye House in 1969. Keeping Ernie Hancock on as team manager, they decided that the best way to keep the public interest alive was to create a contracted Rye House team that did not have to rely on borrowed riders so that the fans would see a consistent team every time and not, as had been the case, a rider ride for the Red Devils one week and then the opposing team the next. The first rider to be pencilled in was junior Steve Collins. The first meeting of the comeback season was a challenge match against King's Lynn Starlets. The team that afternoon consisted of Nigel Rackett, who was appointed team captain for the year, Collins, Ray Cousins, Ron Edwards, Barrie Smith, Ray Boughtflower and John Drew. Although it was their own team, it was a very weak one and they went down 54-24 to the Starlets.

This heavy defeat made the promoting team rethink their strategy of a Rye House only line-up and for the next match against Crayford they included two guests, Peter Seaton and Martyn Piddock. Seaton scored a maximum 12 and Piddock 11, but the Red Devils still went down to defeat, 41-36. A sensational new teenager, the seventeen-year-old Dave Jessup, won the Gerry Hussey Memorial Trophy on 13 July and Rye House managed to win the last two matches, 49-29 against Ipswich and 39-36 against Canterbury.

# The 1970s

## 1970

Although Carter and Bailey Ltd still owned the track, the promotion was taken over by Bill Mathieson and Johnny Guilfoyle.

Dave Jessup proved himself the rising star of British speedway yet again by winning the Skol Lager Trophy on 3 May. The field included a number of youngsters who were later to make a name for themselves in speedway, including Barry Thomas and Gordon Kennett, as well as current and former Rye House riders Nigel Rackett, Tyburn Gallows, Fred Sweet, Alan Jackson and John Drew. Fittingly, the next individual trophy meeting was won by the Rye House skipper Nigel Rackett, when he took the Lea Valley Park Trophy from Barry Thomas on 31 May in what was an excellent afternoon's racing. Even the referee, Mr G.R. Allan, made a special point of complimenting the Rye House management on their 'very good general presentation and the keenness of the racing.'

The first challenge match came on 12 July, when the Red Devils took on and lost to Ipswich in a thrillingly close encounter, 40-38. Brian Foote, winner of the Gerry Hussey Memorial Trophy two weeks previously, scored a maximum 12 points for Rye House, supported by Barry Thomas with nine and Nigel Racket with six. But it wasn't quite enough as the Ipswich team, led by newcomer John Louis, just managed to pip the Red Devils. The other members of the Rye House team were John Hibben, Fred Sweet, Mike Letch and Alan Sage. This was the only team challenge held during the season as the four-team tournament against Canterbury, Romford and Eastbourne was rained off.

Sadly, the match against Ipswich was the first and last time young discovery Mike Letch was to ride for the Red Devils. In the Ace of Herts Trophy held on 16 August, and won by Nigel Rackett, the junior was badly injured in one of the worst crashes ever seen at Rye House. In a three-man pile-up, he came off by far the worst, suffering a fractured spine. At the end of the season, a special Mike Letch Trophy meeting was held with proceeds going to the youngster. It was won by John Louis from Brian Foote and Barry Thomas.

## 1971

A number of improvements were made to the track and stadium during the winter. A new safety fence was erected, brought in from Guilfoyle's old training track at Chadwell St Mary, and the car park was extended and resurfaced. Former team member and training school instructor Pete Sampson, who now owned a fleet of coaches, proposed running a regular match-day service from Stoke Newington via Tottenham, Edmonton, Enfield, and Cheshunt to enable supporters from North London to get to the track without having to wait for the trains.

After the two short comeback seasons with only eight meetings each year, a slightly longer season of ten meetings was planned with several challenge matches pencilled in. The first was held on 2 May as the Red Devils took on Rayleigh after the traditional opener, the Skol Lager Trophy, won that year by Romford rider Kevin Holden.

Rye House scored a convincing 48-30 win over Rayleigh, followed two weeks later by a victory over Romford, 41-37. The Rye House team for both of these matches looked more like an Ipswich team with John Louis, Tony Davey and Pete Bailey all turning out for them. Tyburn Gallows made a comeback to Red Devils colours with Tony Childs and Tiger Beech also putting in appearances.

Rye House were unable to put out the three Ipswich stars in their next match as it was against Ipswich. However, they managed to get together another very strong team consisting of Tony Childs, Alan Emmett, Malcolm Ballard, Bob Young, Nigel Rackett, Peter Scanlon and Laurie Guilfoyle. It was too strong for Ipswich, who they defeated 45-33, in spite of a maximum 12 points from John Louis.

The last challenge of the season was against Canterbury on 5 September and was a much closer affair. With Tony Davey back in the squad, along with Emmett, Young, Gallows, Geoff Maloney, Steve Collins and Paul Mason, the scores were level at 36-36 going in to the last heat. Emmett shot off into the lead, followed by Canterbury's Ted Hubbard and Trevor Barnwell, but Barnwell fell, leaving Young to take the third spot and turn what looked like a certain draw into a narrow 40-38 victory for the Red Devils.

Brian Foote took the Gerry Hussey Memorial Trophy to finish off a season which, despite having seen some good racing and having brought a lot of success to the Red Devils team, had not seen any increase in crowd numbers. It was, therefore, decided to drop the number of meetings in 1972 down to seven.


## 1972

Unusually, the season started with a World Championship qualifying round, only the second time Rye House had been honoured with such a fixture. This took place on 16 April and was won by Dave Kennett. One of the riders who took part in this meeting was former Rye House discovery Ronnie Genz, now in the twilight of his career.

The normal opener, the Skol Lager Trophy, followed a month later on 14 May and was won for the second year running by Kevin Holden from Bruce Forrester. Alan Emmett won the Lea Valley Park Trophy, while the Gerry Hussey Memorial Trophy had to be abandoned after heat seven due to torrential rain.

The only challenge match held that year was against Rayleigh on 20 August. In a close match in front of a large crowd, the Red Devils put up a good fight but went down 41-37. Gordon Kennett scored a maximum 15 points for Rye House, while old favourite Stan Stevens gave him strong support with 10.

Kennett returned for the next meeting, the Ronnie Moore Trophy, and scored another 15-point maximum to take the prize. Pete Wigley came second after a run-off with Tony Childs, both having scored 13 points.

With only six matches being run, and only one of them a team match, it was not a great year for the Red Devils and 1973 was to prove even worse.


## 1973

Once again, only six meetings were scheduled for the season with the only team outing for the Red Devils being in a four-team tournament against King's Lynn, Rayleigh and Reading. With two attempts at running the Skol Lager Trophy rained off, the season eventually came down to just four meetings, starting with the Lea Valley Park Trophy on 17 June which was won by Barney Kennett. The next meeting wasn't until 16 September, when Stan Stevens won the Ace of Herts Trophy with a 15-point maximum from Brian Clark and Jack Walker.

The twenty-third of September saw the only team racing at Hoddesdon that year as Rye House won the four-team meeting. Led by Rye House's favourite son, Mike Broadbank, the

Red Devils scored 39 points with Reading on 29, Rayleigh on 14 and King's Lynn on 13. The rest of the Rye House team were, Peter Claridge, 10, Charlie Benham, 9, Stan Stevens, 8, and Peter Austin (reserve), 1. Broady's only defeat came at the hands of Reading's maximum man, Richard Greer.

The short season finished with the Rye House Championship for the Ronnie Moore Trophy, won this year by Lou Sansom, on his first visit to the track, from Malcolm Bedkober, with Peter Claridge third.

As the season finished, the future for Rye House was a little uncertain. The number of completed meetings had been falling and it wasn't clear whether there would be any meetings open to the public the following year, although the training school would continue. However, not only did Rye House continue but it was about to see the biggest change in its forty-year history.

## 1974

At the end of the 1973 season, Rayleigh was forced to close down as the site was to be redeveloped. The Rayleigh promoter, Len Silver, immediately began to look round for another track so the Rockets could continue. At first, he thought he had found the answer at Crayford, a track which had closed in 1970. However, there were planning problems and Silver was forced to continue the search. It occurred to him that maybe Rye House could prove to be the ideal spot. There was already a track in existence and it was used to running at the weekend, which was Silver's preferred option. After explaining the position to Bill Mathieson, Mathieson agreed to pass over the speedway rights to Silver for nothing in order to keep the Rockets alive. Mathieson himself stayed on as training school instructor, and as part of the new management set-up. Peter Thorogood was installed as the manager and Rye House made an application to take over Rayleigh's licence and run in the British League Second Division. For the first time ever, Rye House was about to become a senior league team.

Brian Foote, Rye House's leading rider in their first two seasons in the British League Second Division.

Some alterations were made to the track as the bends were shortened and banked, as well as to the stadium to try and bring it up to league standard. Terracing was installed on the back straight, a new office was built, a brand new public address system was introduced and new pits were created on the other side of the track with new dressing rooms for the riders.

At the beginning of April, the new Rye House team, who had taken the Rayleigh team name, the Rockets, with them, was named as Bob Young, captain, Brian Foote, Red Ott, Pete Wigley, Trevor Barnwell, John Gibbons, Steve Clarke and Peter Cairns. It was hoped that two injured Rockets, Peter Moore and Alan Emmett, would be able to join the side after recovering from injury. This was almost the same side as the Rayleigh team that had finished bottom of the league in 1973, with the exception of Tiger Beech who had retired. Silver was hoping that several of the riders, notably Foote and Clarke, would show improvement over their 1973 form and that when Moore and Emmett returned they would have a team worthy of a much higher position. For the Rye House supporters, it was a big change in their status and they looked forward to the new season as a fully-fledged league team, although there were some misgivings over the fact that they had imported a team that had finished stone last the season before.

The season began on 6 April with an away fixture at Canterbury for the first leg of the Johnnie Hoskins' Birthday Cup. It proved to be a stunning debut into the new world which they had entered as they flattened Canterbury 44-33, with Brian Foote scoring 10 paid 11 to top score.

Rye House's first home match in the new era took place on Sunday 21 April when the Rockets beat Canterbury 41-36 in the second leg, in front of a crowd of 3,500, to win the Cup 85-69 on aggregate. This time, Steve Clarke top scored with 13, while Foote again contributed 10 paid 11. Silver's hopes for Foote and Clarke looked as though they were about to come to fruition, and it seemed to the fans that their misgivings might have been misplaced.

In the league, too, things started well for the Rockets and they won their first two matches, the first at home to Ellesmere Port, 48-30, with Brian Foote this time turning in a maximum, and the second away, against Sunderland, 39-38. Though, for the Rockets' supporters who had made the long trip up north, there were some heart-stopping moments before the one-point victory was achieved. By heat seven, Rye House led by nine points, but then two 5-1s and a 4-2 in the next three heats put Sunderland in the lead by a single point. With just one heat to go, the score was Sunderland 36 Rye House 35, but thanks to a 4-2 from Trevor Barnwell and Peter Moore, who had returned after his injury lay-off, the Rockets just squeaked through by a single point.

Including the two challenge matches, the new Rye House's record was raced four, won four, including two away matches. With Foote and Clarke going so well and wily veteran Peter Moore back in the line-up, things were definitely looking good for the league newcomers. However, their next match saw their first defeat as they went down 46-32 to Berwick at Berwick. Once again, Foote turned in an impressive performance with 13 points, but Clarke failed to score any, while Moore only managed four.

Next up for Rye House was the home leg of the Division Two Knock-Out Cup second round tie against Peterborough (they had received a bye in the first round). Foote once again led the way with 11 points, but it was another defeat and the team's first home defeat as they went down 42-36. They also lost the services of Red Ott in this match following a fall in heat one in which he broke his collar bone. The flying start seemed to have come to a juddering halt. However, a stunning 50-28 victory over Bradford the following week restored some confidence as Foote and Barnwell top scored with 11 and 9 respectively.

Two more defeats followed as the Rockets were bundled out of the Cup, losing 52-26 in the second leg at Peterborough and then, worse still, losing by 21 points, 49-28, at home to old rivals Eastbourne. But even that wasn't the worst of it, as it was during this match, held on Whit Monday in front of the largest crowd of the season, that Steve Clarke suffered some horrific injuries in heat four. Clarke was involved in a three-man pile-up as Eastbourne's Bobby McNeil drifted into Brian Foote as they were coming out of the last bend on the final lap. Foote lost control and drifted out to the fence; as he did so, Clarke, who was bringing up the rear, crashed into him. Both machines and Clarke went flying up into the air. It was later discovered that he had fractured his skull and received severe back injuries.

It was still only May, and Rye House had already lost Clarke and Ott. Moore was also having difficulty in his comeback. He was nothing like the rider he had once been. On the plus side, Foote was still going well and Barnwell was also giving strong support, but there was no third heat leader now to back them up.

The one good aspect was that crowds were still holding up well and a new 300-seater grandstand was built.

The Rockets bounced back on 16 June with a 50-28 victory over Weymouth. This match saw the first appearance of Kelvin Mullarkey at Hoddesdon as he top scored for Weymouth with 12 points. This wasn't the last time Mullarkey was to be top scorer at Rye House.

Trevor Barnwell then shocked the Rye House management by putting in a transfer request. However, he agreed to stay on and continued to put in some useful scores. Rye House were now finding themselves on the losing end more often than not. Apart from their first victory over Sunderland, they had not won any more away matches and a defeat at home to Birmingham, 46-31, was their fourth home defeat. In an attempt to shore up the team, the manager, Peter Thorogood, signed up former Rye House captain Clive Hitch. In the next home match to Sunderland, Hitch weighed in with 14 points to lead the Rockets to a 42-35 victory. Because Hitch proved something of a success riding on his old stamping ground, Thorogood began to look around at other former Rye House riders and signed up Stan Stevens and George Barclay. Neither was quite as successful as Hitch, but Barclay in particular did well enough. One youngster was also signed up, Bob Cooper from Leicester. He didn't score many points but showed enough promise to give hope of better things to come the following season.

Rye House had a break for two weeks in July and, during that period, Thorogood made more improvements to the track, widening the straights by two yards. Combined with the banking that was completed before the season started, he hoped this would bring a big improvement in the racing and would especially help the home team. There were also improvements to the safety fence as the solid posts were removed except for the area around the starting gate. The rest of the fence was suspended off posts which were now moved back about four feet behind. This improvement made Rye House one of the safest tracks in the country.

Hugh Saunders rode for Rye House from 1975 to 1979 and then became team manager.

Although Rye House did reasonably well at home for the rest of the season, including a 50-28 win over Berwick, they had no further successes away from home and finished up losing every one of their away matches apart from that first. At home, Foote, Gibbons and Barnwell all rode well, as did Hitch, but none of them really shone on away tracks and, in the end, it was this that let them down in the final reckoning.

Nevertheless, the crowds were coming in bigger numbers than when Rye House was a non-league track. The club was also attracting more media attention, with a thirty-minute-long programme about speedway being made at the track and broadcast on the radio, including interviews with Silver, Thorogood, Foote and Bob Young as well as referee Arthur Humphrey.

The eighteenth of August saw the return to Hoddesdon of one of Rye House's favourite sons, when Mike Broadbank visited as part of the Stoke team. He showed he had lost little of his flair around the track as he notched up 13 points. Interestingly, the teacher managed to prevent one of his best pupils from scoring a maximum when he defeated Hitch in heat five. Broadbank apart, however, Stoke offered little in the way of resistance to the Rockets, who won the match 47-31, with Foote, Hitch and Barnwell gaining scores of 10, 10 and 9 respectively.

Towards the end of the season, Barnwell broke his wrist and missed a few meetings, though, by then, Young had at last got to grips with the track and put in a few good scores.

In the end, the team finished sixteenth out of nineteen teams, not a great league debut, but at least the Rockets had got themselves out of bottom place. Foote finished the season top of the Rye House averages with 7.93, followed by Hitch on 6.89 and Barnwell on 6.71. Other regular team members, Young, Gibbons, Cooper and Pete Wigley, could only manage averages of four and five. The Rockets needed improvement in all departments if they were to have any hope of getting out of the bottom half of the league in 1975, but with the hoped-for return of Steve Clarke and Alan Emmett there was still some optimism around.

The end of the season had been marred by a number of matches being rained off or run in wet conditions. The management realised they needed to completely overhaul the drainage system and, under the direction of Jim Stevens, the clerk of the course, the work was carried out over the close season.

## 1974 British League Division Two

| Date | H/A | Opponent | W/L | Score |
| --- | --- | --- | --- | --- |
| 28 April | H | Ellesmere Port | W | 48-30 |
| 3 May | A | Sunderland | W | 39-38 |
| 4 May | A | Berwick | L | 32-46 |
| 12 May | H | Coatbridge | W | 41-36 |
| 19 May | H | Bradford | W | 50-28 |
| 27 May | H | Eastbourne | L | 28-49 |
| 4 June | A | Barrow | L | 21-56 |
| 5 June | A | Bradford | L | 28-50 |
| 9 June | H | Workington | L | 38-40 |
| 14 June | A | Peterborough | L | 23-55 |
| 16 June | H | Weymouth | W | 50-28 |
| 23 June | H | Birmingham | L | 31-46 |
| 29 June | A | Weymouth | L | 27-50 |
| 2 July | A | Ellesmere Port | L | 22-56 |
| 7 July | H | Sunderland | W | 42-35 |
| 14 July | H | Scunthorpe | W | 47-30 |
| 15 July | A | Scunthorpe | L | 25-52 |
| 21 July | H | Berwick | W | 50-28 |
| 29 July | H | Boston | W | 40-38 |
| 4 August | H | Barrow | W | 42-36 |
| 12 August | A | Birmingham | L | 21-57 |

| 18 August | H | Stoke | W | 47-31 |
|---|---|---|---|---|
| 22 August | A | Teesside | L | 34-44 |
| 24 August | A | Canterbury | L | 30-48 |
| 26 August | H | Teesside | L | 37-41 |
| 8 September | H | Long Eaton | W | 40-38 |
| 12 September | A | Long Eaton | L | 26-52 |
| 13 September | A | Workington | L | 33-45 |
| 22 September | A | Eastbourne | L | 19-59 |
| 29 September | H | Crewe | L | 37-40 |
| 30 September | A | Crewe | L | 30-48 |
| 6 October | H | Canterbury | W | 44-33 |
| 10 October | A | Stoke | L | 27-50 |
| 11 October | A | Coatbridge | L | 19-59 |
| 13 September | H | Peterborough | L | 33-44 |
| 20 September | A | Boston | L | 28-50 |

P36 W13 D0 L23
For 1,229 Against 1,566
Position: sixteenth (out of nineteen)

## Knock-Out Cup

First Round Bye
Second Round

| Date | H/A | Opponent | W/L | Score |
|---|---|---|---|---|
| 5 May | H | Peterborough | L | 36-42 |
| 24 May | A | Peterborough | L | 26-52 |

Lost 62-94 on aggregate

## 1974 British League Division Two and Knock-Out Cup

| Name | M | R | Pts | BP | Total | CMA |
|---|---|---|---|---|---|---|
| Brian Foote | 38 | 138 | 352 | 11 | 363 | 7.93 |
| Steve Clarke | 8 | 29 | 43 | 11 | 54 | 7.45 |
| Clive Hitch | 13 | 61 | 92 | 13 | 105 | 6.89 |
| Trevor Barnwell | 24 | 96 | 147 | 14 | 161 | 6.70 |
| George Barclay | 10 | 48 | 65 | 2 | 67 | 5.58 |
| Peter Moore | 15 | 49 | 58 | 8 | 66 | 5.39 |
| Bob Young | 38 | 147 | 163 | 32 | 195 | 5.31 |
| John Gibbons | 34 | 127 | 149 | 19 | 168 | 5.29 |
| Bob Cooper | 27 | 82 | 78 | 20 | 98 | 4.78 |
| Pete Wigley | 37 | 122 | 115 | 18 | 133 | 4.36 |
| Stan Stevens | 12 | 27 | 17 | 4 | 21 | 3.11 |

# 1975

Management changes took place before the start of the 1975 season with Thorogood leaving to reopen Crayford and his place as general manager being taken by former Rye House rider Colin Pratt. The Supporters' Club also played its part during the winter as they raised enough money to buy a track spare for the Rockets.

As well as a change in management, there were also some substantial changes to the team as Clive Hitch, Trevor Barnwell, George Barclay, Peter Moore, Pete Wigley and Stan Stevens all left. To take their places, Tiger Beech and Dingle Brown were signed up. In addition, Rye House hoped to sign up Weymouth's number one, Kelvin Mullarkey, but Boston also wanted him and a tremendous battle took place between the two clubs to win his signature. Although Rye House finally won the battle, it was only after the first few weeks of the season had gone by, leaving the Rockets to start with a team no better, if not worse, than the one that had come sixteenth the season before. Brian Foote was named as team captain after Bob Young relinquished the position, feeling that he would regain his old form if he was relieved of the pressure of captaincy after his fairly indifferent 1974 season.

The installation of the new drainage system meant that the Rye House team were unable to get any practice in before the season started, though most of them were able to use the Hackney track, where Len Silver was also promoter and Foote took himself off to King's Lynn to put in some practice under Olle Nygren's expert eye.

The season got off to a disastrous start as Rye House lost at home to Stoke 46-32. Foote was top scorer with eight, but behind him only Steve Clarke came out with any real credit, scoring three points from the reserve position after a fall in this his comeback outing.

Mullarkey finally made the team only to break his collarbone and, after six matches, the Rockets were bottom of the league with just a single point gained from a home draw, 39-39, with Crayford. Once again, Foote was the top scorer and was more or less carrying the team. At this point, Pratt decided to bring in the best of the Rye House winter trainees, Karl Fiala.

Although a very promising rider, Fiala was never going to be the answer the Rockets needed. But Pratt's next move did go some way to alleviating the team's problems as he managed to talk former Hackney rider, Hughie Saunders, out of retirement. Saunders immediately slotted in as the team's number two behind Foote and was able to give him the sort of consistent support the team needed. Bob Cooper was also fast improving and a stunning 53-25 victory over Crewe on 1 June, in which Cooper scored his first paid maximum, at last saw the beginnings of a revival in the team's fortunes.

Further good home wins followed, for example, 47-31 over Peterborough, with Foote scoring a maximum, Saunders ten and Cooper eight, and 47-30 over Ellesmere Port, in which Mullarkey scored 11 paid 14 in spite of riding with a chipped ankle bone. In a tremendous heat nine, Mullarkey went from last to first in a breathtaking ride – the first of many the Rye House fans were to see over the next fifteen years. A double-header on 22 June saw two further victories for the Rockets, 44-34 over Scunthorpe and 44-33 over Weymouth and for the rest of the season Rye House could be relied on to win in front of their home fans.

But it was away from home that Rye House were still unable to break their duck and they suffered some heavy losses during the season: 52-26 at Birmingham, 54-24 at Bradford, 52-26 at Eastbourne and, worst of all, 58-20 at Crewe, the team that Rye House had beaten 53-25 at home. The Rockets managed just one away point all season, a 39-39 draw at Mildenhall.

The revival in their home form was enough to take them off the bottom during the season and, in the end, the Rockets slightly improved on their 1974 league position by finishing in fourteenth place out of twenty teams. But it was obvious that big changes were needed for 1976 if the team was to stand any chance of challenging for honours. Foote and Saunders had carried off their heat-leader roles reasonably well. Cooper was much improved and his 6.75 average was up two points over 1974, but the problem for Rye House was that this made him their third heat leader and he was just not good enough for that position.

Mullarkey had come in with a 6.25 average and had been plagued by injury during the year. In spite of giving up the captaincy, Bob Young never regained his old form. Tiger Beech had a reasonable year while, for a first year rider, Karl Fiala did well enough, finishing with an average of 4.58. Poor Steve Clarke never really got going after his promising return in the first match and he only rode in ten matches.

For 1976, Rye House needed at least one new heat leader and needed to see improvements in Mullarkey, Cooper and Fiala.

Bob Cooper rode for
Rye House from 1974
to 1979.

## 1975 New National League

| Date | H/A | Opponent | W/L | Score |
|---|---|---|---|---|
| 13 April | H | Stoke | L | 32–46 |
| 21 April | A | Scunthorpe | L | 34–43 |
| 22 April | A | Crayford | L | 32–46 |
| 4 May | H | Crayford | D | 39–39 |
| 25 May | A | Eastbourne | L | 26–52 |
| 26 May | H | Eastbourne | L | 31–45 |
| 30 May | A | Peterborough | L | 31–47 |
| 1 June | H | Crewe | W | 53–25 |
| 8 June | H | Workington | W | 45–32 |
| 9 June | A | Newcastle | L | 26–52 |
| 15 June | H | Peterborough | W | 47–31 |
| 22 June | H | Scunthorpe | W | 44–34 |
| 22 June | H | Weymouth | W | 44–33 |
| 26 June | A | Teesside | L | 30–48 |
| 27 June | A | Coatbridge | L | 34–43 |
| 28 June | A | Paisley | L | 29–48 |
| 29 June | H | Ellesmere Port | W | 47–30 |
| 5 July | A | Canterbury | L | 34–44 |
| 6 July | H | Bradford | W | 49–29 |
| 12 July | A | Boston | L | 38–39 |
| 13 July | H | Boston | L | 38–39 |
| 19 July | A | Berwick | L | 31–47 |
| 20 July | H | Canterbury | W | 39–38 |
| 20 July | H | Mildenhall | W | 47–30 |
| 23 July | A | Mildenhall | D | 39–39 |
| 27 July | H | Paisley | W | 49–28 |
| 27 July | H | Coatbridge | W | 46–32 |
| 3 August | H | Teesside | W | 48–29 |
| 10 August | H | Berwick | W | 46–32 |
| 12 August | A | Ellesmere Port | L | 27–51 |

| 13 August | A | Bradford | L | 24-54 |
| 4 September | A | Stoke | L | 34-44 |
| 5 September | A | Workington | L | 24-54 |
| 9 September | A | Weymouth | L | 35-43 |
| 15 September | A | Crewe | L | 20-58 |
| 21 September | H | Newcastle | L | 36-42 |
| 28 September | H | Birmingham | L | 33-45 |
| 29 September | A | Birmingham | L | 26-52 |

P38 W13 D2 L23
For 1,387 Against 1,563
Position: fourteenth (out of twenty)

## Knock-Out Cup

First Round
Bye
Second Round

| Date | H/A | Opponent | W/L | Score |
|---|---|---|---|---|
| 5 May | A | Birmingham | L | 18-60 |
| 11 May | H | Birmingham | L | 31-46 |

Lost 49-106 on aggregate

### *1975 New National League and Knock Out Cup*

| Name | M | R | Pts | BP | T | CMA |
|---|---|---|---|---|---|---|
| Brian Foote | 40 | 185 | 371 | 17 | 388 | 8.39 |
| Hugh Saunders | 24 | 97 | 161 | 20 | 181 | 7.46 |
| Bob Cooper | 39 | 166 | 240 | 40 | 280 | 6.75 |
| Kelvin Mullarkey | 32 | 126 | 176 | 21 | 197 | 6.25 |
| Tiger Beech | 36 | 128 | 164 | 18 | 182 | 5.69 |
| John Gibbons | 10 | 32 | 36 | 6 | 42 | 5.25 |
| Bob Young | 19 | 60 | 56 | 15 | 71 | 4.73 |
| Dingle Brown | 27 | 84 | 83 | 14 | 97 | 4.62 |
| Karl Fiala | 30 | 96 | 92 | 18 | 110 | 4.58 |
| Steve Clarke | 10 | 31 | 25 | 5 | 30 | 3.87 |

# 1976

More management changes took place over the winter as Pratt became co-director with Silver of Rye House Speedway Ltd. Further alterations were also made to the stadium itself as a new covered pits area was built.

The promotion quickly got their new heat leader as Hackney's Ted Hubbard asked for a transfer from Hackney so that he could return to the second division, renamed the National League. With a team now consisting of three recognised heat leaders in Hubbard, Foote and Saunders, supported by Beech and the ever-improving trio of Mullarkey, Cooper and Fiala, there was real hope at Hoddesdon that at last the Rockets could make an impression on the league.

But the first match ended in disaster as Ellesmere Port came to Rye House on 11 April and left with the two points, winning 39-36. It was a controversial heat nine that did for the Rockets. Hubbard was excluded after pulling a locker, causing Ellesmere Port's Gerald Smitherman to crash into him and fall. In the rerun, Turner and Smitherman led for the Gunners. Mullarkey was close behind Smitherman and on the third lap managed to get past. As he did so, Smitherman fell. The referee, Lew Stripp, allowed the race to continue but excluded Mullarkey, resulting in a 3-0 for Ellesmere Port. Both managers protested, Ellesmere Port because they said if Mullarkey was excluded for bringing down Smitherman then Smitherman should have been awarded two points. Pratt strongly protested on Mullarkey's behalf for what he called a 'diabolical decision'. But the referee was unmoved and 3-0 remained the final result.

After this match, Beech decided he'd had enough and retired. Into his place came a junior who had impressed everyone who'd seen him in second-half and after-meeting rides at Rye House, Hackney and Mildenhall the previous season. In fact, Mildenhall had already used Garrad in their Fen Tigers' Cubs team and were after his signature full time, but, fortunately for Rye House, he decided to sign up with them instead. Only sixteen years old and still at school, Bobby Garrad was more or less thrown in at the deep end as a result of Beech's sudden retirement, but it was one of the best decisions Silver and Pratt ever made as Garrad was to become, with Mullarkey and Fiala, the backbone of the Rockets team over the next five years.

His first match saw him riding away at Eastbourne, where he scored two points from the reserve position in Rye House's 45-33 defeat. He was unlucky not to score more as, in the rerun of heat two, Eastbourne's Steve Naylor fell and Garrad laid his machine down to avoid him. Naylor remounted to take second place, while Garrad was unable to get back up in time. In spite of the pleas of Colin Pratt, the referee refused to award him a point.

The following day, the Eagles paid a return visit to Rye House in a match that was to prove the Rockets' first win of the season by a score of 44-33. All three heat leaders came good as Saunders scored 10 paid 11, Hubbard 10 and Foote 8 paid 9, while the rest of the team - Fiala, Mullarkey, Cooper and Garrad - all gave good support.

Unfortunately, there then followed a run of three away matches in as many days on a tour of the north against Stoke, Workington and Paisley, all of which resulted in defeats. Although the results were disappointing, there was much encouragement from the form of the second strings and reserves. Garrad scored eight points at Stoke, which included his first two wins for the club, and Mullarkey scored 10 paid 13 at Paisley.

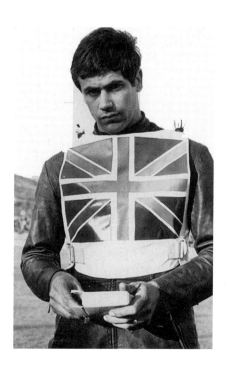

Former Rye House rider Colin Pratt returned as co-director and manager from 1975 to 1979.

Back at home, on 9 May, the Rockets really came good as they trounced Peterborough 53-25. Top scorer for Rye House was Garrad, who chimed in with 12 paid 13. Hubbard scored a 12-point maximum and the pair of them were presented with fifty cigarettes and five cigars by a Rockets supporter for their efforts (those were the days)! A second-half regular, the twenty-year-old Ashley Pullen made his debut for Rye House in this match as a replacement for Bob Cooper, who had decided to take a rest from speedway for a while. Out in heat two, Pullen won his very first race for the Rockets, beating his teammate Garrad and the Panthers' Ian Clark and Alan Cowland.

Rye House now began to pull out some big home victories: 53-25 over Scunthorpe, 55-23 over Workington, 59-19 over Berwick and 50-28 over Teesside. Unfortunately, at this point, Brian Foote suffered a bad foot injury and had to pull out of the team, missing the whole of the rest of the season. Until Cooper returned, towards the end of August, Rye House relied on rider replacement to cover his loss.

Although things were going well at home, as in previous years, they were still not finding any success away from home. A draw away at Oxford on 10 June saw them gain their only point until finally a 45-32 victory over Teesside on 5 August gave them two points for the first time away from home.

Four days before this victory, the Rockets had had a magnificent win over Paisley at home by 59-19. No less than four Rye House riders had scored maximums or paid maximums, with Hubbard and Mullarkey scoring 12, Fiala 11+1 and Saunders 10+5.

Two more away wins followed. The first was against Weymouth, 43-34. The second victory came after the Scunthorpe riders walked out of their match against the Rockets after heat five, claiming their own track was unraceable. At the time, the score was 16-14 to Rye House and the match and the two points were awarded to them. This wasn't good enough for Pratt, however. He claimed that, although it had been raining earlier, the track was getting better and was certainly in a better state at the point at which Scunthorpe had walked out than it was when the match started. He wanted more than two points. Firstly, he wanted compensation for the 100 Rye House supporters who had travelled to the match and, secondly, he wanted to be awarded maximum race points for the meeting as he felt that these could be crucial in deciding final league positions. However, he had to be satisfied with the two match points and the final score went down as 14-16.

With a better season at home and a few successes away, the Rockets' league position at the end of the year showed a great improvement on their first two seasons as they finished in fifth place.

They also put on a slightly better showing in the Knock-Out Cup. In 1974 and 1975 they had failed to win a single tie. This year, they knocked Canterbury out in the second round, 79-76, having been given a bye in the first round. Their run came to an end in the third round, however, as they went down 89-66 to Ellesmere Port.

It was a much better all-round team performance in 1976 as Hubbard topped the score chart with a 9.25 average. Saunders and Foote contributed plus seven averages and, when Foote was forced to withdraw through injury, Mullarkey stepped effortlessly into the breech recording a 7.57 average. The two youngsters, Fiala and Garrad, showed remarkable promise, both scoring at plus 6.5, and although Ashley Pullen had been around the second halves for a couple of years without too much success, he too rose to the occasion and became a more-than-useful reserve. The combination of a bit of experience, a lot of youthful enthusiasm and not a little skill boded well for the 1977 campaign and great things were expected of the team.

## 1976 National League

| Date | H/A | Opponent | W/L | Score |
| --- | --- | --- | --- | --- |
| 11 April | H | Ellesmere Port | L | 36-39 |
| 18 April | A | Eastbourne | L | 33-45 |
| 19 April | H | Eastbourne | W | 44-33 |
| 22 April | A | Stoke | L | 36-42 |

Ted Hubbard averaged over eight points per match for Rye House every year from 1976 to 1979.

| 24 April | A | Paisley | L | 35-43 |
|---|---|---|---|---|
| 9 May | H | Peterborough | W | 53-25 |
| 11 May | A | Ellesmere Port | L | 22-56 |
| 23 May | H | Scunthorpe | W | 53-25 |
| 6 June | H | Oxford | W | 46-32 |
| 10 June | A | Oxford | D | 39-39 |
| 13 June | H | Workington | W | 55-23 |
| 20 June | H | Berwick | W | 59-19 |
| 21 June | A | Newcastle | L | 21-57 |
| 4 July | H | Stoke | W | 42-35 |
| 10 July | A | Canterbury | L | 34-44 |
| 11 July | H | Teesside | W | 50-28 |
| 25 July | H | Crayford | W | 40-38 |
| 27 July | A | Crayford | L | 38-40 |
| 1 August | H | Paisley | W | 59-19 |
| 1 August | H | Coatbridge | W | 53-23 |
| 5 August | A | Teesside | W | 45-32 |
| 6 August | A | Coatbridge | L | 35-42 |
| 7 August | A | Berwick | L | 34-44 |
| 8 August | H | Weymouth | W | 54.5-23.5 |
| 15 August | H | Mildenhall | W | 49-29 |
| 18 August | H | Mildenhall | L | 30-48 |
| 22 August | H | Canterbury | L | 38-40 |
| 29 August | A | Boston | L | 38-40 |
| 30 August | H | Boston | W | 48-30 |
| 7 September | A | Weymouth | W | 43-34 |
| 12 September | H | Newcastle | D | 39-39 |
| 17 September | A | Peterborough | L | 30-47 |

P34 W17 D2 L15

For 1,357.5 Against 1,205.5

Position: fifth (out of eighteen)

## Knock Out Cup

First Round
Bye
Second Round

| Date | H/A | Opponent | W/L | Score |
|------|-----|----------|-----|-------|
| 1 May | A | Canterbury | L | 34-44 |
| 2 May | H | Canterbury | W | 45-32 |

Won 79-76 on aggregate
Third Round

| Date | H/A | Opponent | W/L | Score |
|------|-----|----------|-----|-------|
| 18 July | H | Ellesmere Port | L | 38-39 |
| 20 July | A | Ellesmere Port | L | 28-50 |

Lost 66-89 on aggregate

## *1976 National League and Knock-Out Cup*

| Name | M | R | Pts | BP | Total | CMA |
|------|---|---|-----|----|----|-----|
| Ted Hubbard | 35 | 154 | 340 | 13 | 353 | 9.17 |
| Kelvin Mullarkey | 37 | 160 | 263 | 39 | 302 | 7.55 |
| Hugh Saunders | 37 | 144 | 229 | 40 | 269 | 7.47 |
| Brian Foote | 17 | 66 | 105 | 11 | 116 | 7.03 |
| Karl Fiala | 32 | 132 | 198 | 24 | 222 | 6.73 |
| Bob Garrad | 36 | 135 | 186 | 21 | 207 | 6.13 |
| Bob Cooper | 16 | 54 | 61 | 8 | 69 | 5.11 |
| Ashley Pullen | 30 | 94 | 100.5 | 15 | 115.5 | 4.92 |
| John Waldrab | 6 | 16 | 8 | 3 | 11 | 2.75 |

# 1977

Fortunately for Rye House, the team that had finished the season stayed together and the new season started with Hubbard, Saunders, Mullarkey, Fiala, Garrad, Cooper and Pullen all present and correct for the opening two league fixtures, both against Eastbourne. Sadly, all the optimism with which the Rockets went into the season took a bit of a battering as Eastbourne completed the double over their old rivals, 51-27 at Arlington and 47-31 back at Hoddesdon.

There was some excuse for the home loss as Hubbard was injured in his first ride, forcing him to withdraw from the rest of the meeting with concussion, ankle, hip and shoulder injuries. The following week, still without Hubbard, the Rockets travelled to 1976 champions Newcastle and came away with two points thanks to a 12-point maximum from Fiala, paid ten from Mullarkey, nine points from Saunders and paid nine from Garrad, giving them a 42-36 win.

This was the first of a run of four consecutive away matches, from which the Rockets returned to Hoddesdon with five points. Even more remarkable was the fact that Hubbard missed all of them and Karl Fiala broke his leg in a car accident on his way back from the third of the matches at Weymouth, causing him to miss the fourth away fixture at Edinburgh. Even without Hubbard and Fiala, the Rockets still managed to pull off a fine 40-38 victory. It was also the start of four consecutive paid double-figure scores from Mullarkey, who followed up his paid 10 with two more 10s and a paid 15-point maximum at Edinburgh. Back at home for two meetings, he continued his high scoring with paid 13 against Teesside and paid 14 against Stoke. Even better for Rye House's future was the fact that, in the two latter matches, Garrad turned in scores of 14 and 15. And still, without Hubbard and Fiala, Rye House won both matches, 50-28 and 49-29 respectively.

Karl Fiala (left) joined Rye House as a teenager in 1975. By 1979, he had become the Rockets' leading rider. He is pictured here with Crayford's Les Rumsey.

With Hubbard back for the next match away at Boston, the Rockets put on another impressive display to claim both points with a 40-38 win. There then followed a run of ten matches, home and away, which saw Rye House undefeated except narrowly at Oxford, 38-37, in one of the most thrilling matches of the season. And even that might have resulted in a win for the Rockets had Saunders not been injured a week previously in Rye House's 44-34 win over Coatbridge, forcing him to miss the Oxford match. Undoubtedly, the best day during this run of ten matches came on 3 July when the Rockets raced a double-header, beating Berwick 63-14 and then Scunthorpe 51-27. In the victory over Berwick, only Pullen was defeated by an opponent as Hubbard, Mullarkey, Garrad, Saunders, Cooper and Peter Tarrant all scored paid maximum points. In the second match, Mullarkey, Garrad and Saunders were once again unbeaten by any opponent.

Peter Tarrant had been brought in to replace Fiala and was just coming good when he had to make way for Fiala's return in the next match against Ellesmere Port. The team was now back to full strength and remained that way for the next sixteen matches. Mullarkey was improving with every meeting, while Hubbard and Garrad continued to give excellent support. Unfortunately, though, Saunders' form dipped after his injury. As the season progressed, he did begin to improve again and, with Fiala and Pullen also improving, the Rockets became almost invincible by the end of the season. In the run-in, they won seven of their last eight matches. In the last seven matches, Mullarkey recorded an incredible cma of 11.31. In fact, he was unbeaten by any opponent in the last five matches. Hubbard's cma over those last seven matches was 10.71. It was little wonder that the Rockets finished on such a high. Unfortunately for them, Eastbourne were having what was probably their best season ever, losing just seven matches. Rye House only lost nine matches out of 36, but it was just enough for them to fall behind Eastbourne and finish runners-up. It was all a world away from those first two seasons and if they could keep their septet of Hubbard, Saunders, Cooper, Mullarkey, Garrad, Fiala and Pullen together, and if the latter four continued to improve at the rate they were doing, there was every hope that they would be sitting at the top of the National League come the end of the following season.

With Mullarkey now the team's undoubted number one, it was he who represented the Rockets in the National League Riders' Championship final, gaining the highest position so far attained by a Rye House rider when he came fourth with 12 points.

Not only was it Rye House's most successful year on the track, but off the track they also pulled off a major coup when they became the first team to find a commercial sponsor to back all their activities. In a £20,000 sponsorship deal, a local heating appliance manufacturer, Infradex, agreed to provide full support, including equipment and transport, for every member of the team.

The 1977 National League runners-up. From left to right, back row: Ashley Pullen, Bob Cooper, Bob Garrad, Karl Fiala, Ted Hubbard, Kelvin Mullarkey. Front row: Garry Monk, Hugh Saunders (on bike), Kevin Bowen.

In return, Rye House agreed to wear the Infradex logo on their race jackets and leathers. In many ways, the fact that it was Rye House and not one of the glamour clubs of the sport that had managed to pull off the first major sponsorship deal was a tribute to the business acumen of Colin Pratt and there were few now who doubted that Rye House was in good hands. Only three years previously, there were many who felt that the former training and Sunday fun day afternoon track, Rye House, would never be able to support a full league team. But now, with the sponsorship deal, Rye House was free of money worries, crowds were on the increase, the team itself was proving to be one of the best in the country and there was no talk of Rye House closing. What was even better was that the training school was still actively turning out possible stars of the future such as Bobby Garrad and Karl Fiala. All in all, everything looked rosy for the Rye House Rockets as they moved into British speedway's Golden Jubilee year, 1978.

*1977 National League*

| Date | H/A | Opponent | W/L | Score |
| --- | --- | --- | --- | --- |
| 10 April | A | Eastbourne | L | 27–51 |
| 11 April | H | Eastbourne | L | 31–47 |
| 25 April | A | Newcastle | W | 42–36 |
| 26 April | A | Ellesmere Port | L | 28–50 |
| 10 May | A | Weymouth | D | 39–39 |
| 13 May | A | Edinburgh | W | 40–38 |
| 22 May | H | Teesside | W | 50–28 |
| 12 June | H | Stoke | W | 49–29 |
| 19 June | A | Boston | W | 40–38 |
| 26 June | H | Glasgow | W | 44–34 |

| 30 June | A | Oxford | L | 37-38 |
| 3 July | H | Berwick | W | 63-14 |
| 3 July | H | Scunthorpe | W | 51-27 |
| 10 July | H | Ellesmere Port | W | 39-38 |
| 12 July | A | Crayford | W | 38-37 |
| 17 July | H | Crayford | W | 45-33 |
| 21 July | A | Teesside | D | 39-39 |
| 22 July | A | Glasgow | W | 40-38 |
| 23 July | A | Berwick | W | 43-35 |
| 29 July | A | Peterborough | L | 44-34 |
| 31 July | H | Canterbury | W | 43-35 |
| 5 August | A | Workington | W | 43-35 |
| 6 August | A | Stoke | W | 40-38 |
| 10 August | A | Mildenhall | L | 36-42 |
| 21 August | H | Boston | L | 38-40 |
| 22 August | A | Scunthorpe | D | 39-39 |
| 29 August | H | Edinburgh | W | 56-22 |
| 3 September | A | Canterbury | L | 26-52 |
| 9 September | A | Newport | L | 36-42 |
| 4 September | H | Workington | W | 56-22 |
| 11 September | H | Newcastle | W | 44-34 |
| 18 September | H | Newport | W | 59-19 |
| 18 September | H | Weymouth | W | 49-29 |
| 2 October | H | Oxford | W | 45-30 |
| 16 October | H | Mildenhall | W | 46-32 |

P36 W24 D3 L9
For 1,524 Against 1,273
Position: second (out of nineteen)

## Knock-Out Cup

First Round

| Date | H/A | Opponent | W/L | Score |
| --- | --- | --- | --- | --- |
| 14 April | A | Oxford | L | 34-44 |
| 17 April | H | Oxford | W | 44-34 |

Drew 78-78 on aggregate

First Round Replay

| Date | H/A | Opponent | W/L | Score |
| --- | --- | --- | --- | --- |
| 29 May | H | Oxford | W | 42-36 |
| 2 June | A | Oxford | L | 32-45 |

Lost 74-81 on aggregate

## 1977 National League and Knock-Out Cup

| Name | M | R | Pts | BP | Total | CMA |
| --- | --- | --- | --- | --- | --- | --- |
| Kelvin Mullarkey | 40 | 176 | 373 | 29 | 402 | 9.14 |
| Ted Hubbard | 30 | 121 | 245 | 28 | 273 | 9.03 |
| Bob Garrad | 40 | 165 | 301 | 32 | 333 | 8.07 |
| Hugh Saunders | 39 | 158 | 249 | 40 | 289 | 7.32 |
| Karl Fiala | 30 | 110 | 151 | 20 | 171 | 6.22 |
| Ashley Pullen | 40 | 144 | 194 | 26 | 220 | 6.11 |
| Peter Tarrant | 6 | 18 | 22 | 5 | 27 | 6.00 |
| Bob Cooper | 39 | 132 | 135 | 23 | 158 | 4.79 |

Bob Garrad rode for Rye House from 1976 to 1986 and was their leading scorer in 1980, 1981, 1982 and 1984.

## 1978

For the second year running, Rye House started the season with exactly the same seven riders. The opening match against Teesside on 2 April saw them win by the magnificent score of 58-20. Even more encouraging for the Rockets was the fact that Fiala and Pullen both scored paid maximums. Hubbard contributed a paid maximum while Mullarkey dropped just one point to an opponent. With Eastbourne's top scorer from 1977, Colin Richardson, moving on, and their decision not to replace him with another top-class rider, it now seemed very possible that Rye House could at last bring the National League title back to Hoddesdon. The very next meeting threw a big spanner in the works, however, as they lost away at Ellesmere Port, 45-32. Hubbard scored 12 and Mullarkey paid 12, but the young duo of Fiala and Pullen did not have quite such a good time of it. As it happened, these two matches were in some ways to set the pattern for the rest of the season, with good wins at home, but an inability to replicate that form away.

Another good home win against Stoke, 52-26, followed, with Fiala once again unbeaten by an opponent at home, scoring a paid maximum, and Mullarkey scoring a full maximum. For the home match against Barrow on 11 June, Peter Tarrant was brought into the team at the expense of Bob Cooper and helped the Rockets to a 59-19 victory. No less than five of the Rye House team scored full or paid maximums: Fiala, Garrad, Mullarkey, Saunders and Pullen. The same day saw the Rockets also defeat Glasgow 52-26 in the second round of the Knock-Out Cup in a double-header. This time it was Hubbard's turn to record a paid maximum, while Pullen weighed in with 14 points.

In the next match, away at Berwick, another youngster was blooded in the team, the seventeen-year-old Kevin Smith. Smith had been riding for the Rockets' junior side in the Trackstar Anglia League and was so impressive that he was given his chance with the big boys. His first match was not a great success as he only scored one point from three rides, but it wouldn't be long before he would join Garrad, Fiala and Pullen as a major prospect for the future. Rye House lost the match at Berwick by a narrow 40-38 margin.

One of the strangest races ever to take place at Rye House occurred on 2 July in the match against Weymouth. Weymouth's Malcolm Shakespeare led Mullarkey as they came out of the last bend on the first lap of heat seven. As they did so, Shakespeare locked up and Mullarkey ran into him, shooting over the top of his handlebars. Pullen, who was following closely behind, avoided the pair by riding onto the centre green. Shakespeare and his partner, Danny Kennedy, continued to race but the referee put on the red lights. For what seemed like an eternity, but was in reality only about two minutes, the crowd waited for a decision from the referee, Reg Trott. Finally, he decided to rerun the race with the exclusion of Mullarkey. Both Pratt and Mullarkey protested vigorously, arguing that the stoppage was Shakespeare's fault. Eventually, Trott agreed to reinstate

Mullarkey and this time it was the turn of Weymouth to protest. Trott again excluded Mullarkey. As the riders were called to the line, Mullarkey rode his bike out along with the others. When the Weymouth pair protested to the starting marshall, he told them that the referee had informed him that he had allowed Mullarkey back in after all. The race was eventually won by the Weymouth pair, who scored a 5-1. In spite of this setback, Rye House finally won the match, 45-33. Perhaps the biggest irony in all this was that Len Silver was also the Weymouth promoter.

During July, the Rockets managed to put together some away victories, beating Newcastle 41-37 and Barrow 41-36 on consecutive nights. Both matches proved to be real team efforts as the highest score for Rye House in both was eight – Fiala at Newcastle and Garrad and Saunders at Berwick. This, combined with some further big victories at home, 59-19 over Milton Keynes and 54-24 over Berwick, saw the Rockets within sight of taking their first championship. But these hopes were dealt a blow on 3 August in the meeting at Teesside when Saunders crashed and badly injured his back, putting him out of action for just over a month. Although the Rockets continued to reel off victory after victory at home, they suffered a couple of bad defeats during the month as, firstly, they went down to Canterbury, 59-19, and then 54-24 to Eastbourne. To make up for this, the team put on a stunning display to rout Boston 60-18 on 28 August, with Fiala scoring a full maximum and Hubbard, Mullarkey and Garrad contributing paid maximums. Smith also recorded his first maximum with nine points from three rides. However, back on the road again after this, the Rockets went down again, 43-35 at Oxford and 42-36 at Weymouth.

Saunders returned for the next away match at Milton Keynes and helped them to an away victory, 41-37, scoring paid seven from three rides. There were two more big home wins, 58-20 against Glasgow and 57-21 against Workington, but the last three away matches all resulted in defeats.

In the end, it was the relative lack of success away from home that did for the Rockets' hopes of walking off with their first league title. Although they were unbeaten at home, they only managed eight wins away, while both Canterbury, the league champions, and Newcastle, the runners-up, managed 12 each. Nevertheless, third place was still a good effort and with the younger members of the team still improving all the time, it could surely be only a matter of time before Rye House swept all before them, especially if that team could be kept together. All six team members, excluding the reserves, Cooper, Tarrant and Smith, contributed at least three maximums during the year, with Hubbard scoring no less than 12 and Mullarkey and Fiala seven each.

The year 1978 also saw Rye House's best cup run so far as they reached the final to meet the acknowledged Knock-Out Cup kings of the Second Division, Eastbourne. The first leg was held at Arlington on 22 October and was won by the home side, 46-32, leaving the Rockets a 14-point

Two of the regular team members who made Rye House such a potent force between 1977 and 1980: Kelvin Mullarkey and Ashley Pullen.

deficit to make up at Hoddesdon the following week. Garrad was the Rye House hero of the afternoon as he scored 11 points. It was a large crowd that turned out on a sunny day to see if the Rockets could pull back the deficit and win their first trophy since becoming a senior league club five years previously. Fiala and Hubbard started well for Rye House, gaining a 5-1 in the first heat. In the second heat, Smith and Pullen were also heading for a 5-1 when Pullen suffered mechanical trouble and was overtaken by the Eastbourne pair. Once again, in the third heat it was Garrad and Saunders who gated first. Behind them, Eastbourne's Eric Dugard, who had reared at the start and was left well behind, chased after them and, in an electrifying ride, caught the Rye House pair and passed them. Heat seven saw Dugard once again come from behind as he and Mullarkey passed and re-passed before the former just came home by half a wheel. In spite of Dugard's heroics, Rye House had, by heat eight, cut the deficit to eight points, but because they were six points in front on the day, Eastbourne were able to use a tactical substitute. Naturally, it was Dugard who came in. Riding with Mike Sampson, he helped pull back a 5-1. After that, it was more or less all over for the Rockets. Although they won the leg, 41-37, it was not good enough to wrest the cup away from Eastbourne and they had to be content with the runner-up slot. Another highlight that year was the staging of the first Test match in the Great Britain *v.* Denmark series the day after Ole Olsen's World Championship win at Wembley. The Danes won 67-41, with a young Hans Nielsen scoring an 18-point maximum.

Hubbard returned to the top of the Rye House averages and was the team's representative at the National League Riders' Championship, going one better than Mullarkey the previous year by finishing in third place after a run-off against Peterborough's Dave Gooderham.

*1978 National League*

| Date | H/A | Opponent | W/L | Score |
|------|-----|----------|-----|-------|
| 2 April | H | Teesside | W | 58-20 |
| 7 April | A | Ellesmere Port | L | 35-43 |
| 9 April | H | Stoke | W | 52-26 |
| 23 April | H | Ellesmere Port | W | 40-38 |
| 25 April | A | Crayford | W | 44-32 |
| 21 May | H | Peterborough | W | 46-32 |
| 11 June | H | Barrow | W | 59-19 |
| 17 June | A | Berwick | L | 38-40 |
| 21 June | A | Mildenhall | L | 33-45 |
| 25 June | H | Scunthorpe | W | 50-28 |
| 2 July | H | Weymouth | W | 45-33 |
| 3 July | A | Newcastle | W | 41-37 |
| 4 July | A | Barrow | W | 41.5-36.5 |
| 7 July | A | Peterborough | L | 37-41 |
| 23 July | H | Milton Keynes | W | 59-19 |
| 23 July | H | Berwick | W | 54-24 |
| 3 August | A | Teesside | W | 42-36 |
| 4 August | A | Edinburgh | W | 42-36 |
| 6 August | H | Mildenhall | W | 40-38 |
| 13 August | H | Canterbury | W | 42-36 |
| 14 August | A | Scunthorpe | W | 42-36 |
| 19 August | A | Canterbury | L | 17-59 |
| 20 August | H | Edinburgh | W | 54-24 |
| 26 August | A | Boston | W | 41-37 |
| 27 August | A | Eastbourne | L | 24-54 |
| 28 August | H | Eastbourne | W | 42-36 |
| 28 August | H | Boston | W | 60-18 |
| 5 September | A | Weymouth | L | 36-42 |

| 12 September | A | Milton Keynes | W | 41-37 |
| 15 September | A | Workington | L | 38-40 |
| 16 September | A | Stoke | L | 31-47 |
| 17 September | H | Glasgow | W | 58-20 |
| 17 September | H | Workington | W | 57-21 |
| 29 September | A | Glasgow | L | 37-41 |
| 1 October | H | Newcastle | W | 45-33 |
| 8 October | H | Oxford | W | 46-31 |
| 15 October | H | Crayford | W | 48-30 |

P38 W27 D0 L11
For 1,650.5 Against 1,308.5
Position: third (out of twenty)

## Knock-Out Cup

First Round

| Date | H/A | Opponent | W/L | Score |
|---|---|---|---|---|
| 21 May | H | Milton Keynes | W | 58-20 |
| 23 May | A | Milton Keynes | W | 52-26 |

Won 110-46 on aggregate

Second Round

| Date | H/A | Opponent | W/L | Score |
|---|---|---|---|---|
| 11 June | H | Glasgow | W | 52-26 |
| 16 June | A | Glasgow | D | 39-39 |

Won 91-65 on aggregate

Third Round

| Date | H/A | Opponent | W/L | Score |
|---|---|---|---|---|
| 9 July | H | Crayford | W | 44-34 |
| 18 July | A | Crayford | D | 39-39 |

Won 83-73 on aggregate

Semi-Final

| Date | H/A | Opponent | W/L | Score |
|---|---|---|---|---|
| 24 September | H | Canterbury | W | 57-20 |
| 30 September | A | Canterbury | L | 37-41 |

Won 94-61 on aggregate

Final

| Date | H/A | Opponent | W/L | Score |
|---|---|---|---|---|
| 22 October | A | Eastbourne | L | 32-46 |
| 29 October | H | Eastbourne | W | 41-37 |

Lost 73-83 on aggregate

## 1978 National League and Knock-Out Cup

| Name | M | R | Pts | BP | Total | CMA |
|---|---|---|---|---|---|---|
| Ted Hubbard | 46 | 190 | 409.5 | 33 | 442.5 | 9.32 |
| Kelvin Mullarkey | 48 | 201 | 413 | 45 | 458 | 9.11 |
| Karl Fiala | 48 | 187 | 326 | 39 | 365 | 7.81 |
| Hugh Saunders | 36 | 137 | 215 | 50 | 265 | 7.74 |
| Bob Garrad | 46 | 177 | 294 | 39 | 333 | 7.53 |
| Ashley Pullen | 48 | 168 | 256 | 32 | 288 | 6.86 |
| Peter Tarrant | 34 | 103 | 100 | 25 | 125 | 4.85 |
| Bob Cooper | 7 | 19 | 17 | 6 | 23 | 4.84 |
| Kevin Smith | 22 | 68 | 71 | 11 | 82 | 4.82 |

# 1979

Once again, Rye House was able to start the season with the same team that had finished the previous one. The first eight matches saw Hubbard, Mullarkey, Saunders, Garrad, Fiala, Pullen and Smith donning the Rockets' colours, though this year without the Infradex logo as the company had decided to pull out of the sponsorship deal. Of those eight matches, five were away from home and Rye House won three of them while scoring convincing victories in the three home matches. In these early matches, Saunders' form was not what it had been but, to make up for him, Smith had improved out of all recognition from the previous year and on 8 July, when still only seventeen, he scored his first 15-point maximum against Nottingham. This match against Nottingham was the sixth in a run of nineteen consecutive wins that had started on 10 June, when the team beat Peterborough 45-33, and finally came to an end on 1 September, when the Rockets lost away at Stoke, 47-31. This was in spite of the fact that Hubbard missed twelve of the matches through injury. His loss was more than covered by the improved form of all four of the Rye House discoveries, Fiala, Garrad, Pullen and particularly Smith, who in one season had gone from reserve to heat-leader standard. During the run of nineteen victories, he scored three 15-point maximums, but the contribution of the others should not be overlooked either. Fiala became the team's top scorer, while Garrad recorded eight double-figure scores in nine consecutive matches between 22 July and 20 August. Not only were the four youngsters heat-leader standard, but Mullarkey was also racking up a series of big scores so that, when Hubbard returned on 31 August, there were no less than six riders of heat-leader standard in the Rye House team. Even the seventh, Hugh Saunders, was scoring at something like 6.5 per match.

By the time the nineteen-match winning run came to an end, there were only two teams left in the title race: Rye House and Mildenhall. Just at this point, Rye House faltered slightly, losing three matches in the first two weeks of September: at Stoke on the first, 41-37 at Peterborough on the seventh and 45-32 at Glasgow on the fourteenth. At home, the scores were as big as ever and on one memorable day, 2 September, the Rockets won two matches in a double-header, both by the magnificent score of 60-18. Garrad scored two three-ride maximums while Hubbard, Smith, Mullarkey and Fiala all contributed one four-ride maximum each.

Another member of the team of all talents, Kevin Smith rode for Rye House from 1978 to 1980.

The position as the season came to an end in the last two weeks of October was that Rye House had two matches left, while Mildenhall had three. Incredibly, both of Rye House's matches were against their rivals for league honours, while Mildenhall had one further match away at Scunthorpe. If Rye House won both of their matches against Mildenhall, they would win the league title. This was by no means an impossibility as, earlier in the season, they had done just that in the semi-final of the Knock-Out Cup. The first match took place on 21 October at Hoddesdon. Saunders was out of the tie through injury, his place being taken by Peter Tarrant.

A large crowd saw the Rockets get off to a dream start as Smith and Mullarkey began with a 5-1 in heat one, to be followed by another 5-1 from Pullen and Tarrant in heat two and yet another in heat three courtesy of Hubbard and Garrad. So, after three heats, the score was Rye House 15 Mildenhall 3. The Rockets continued to pile up the points and by heat eight they had a 16-point advantage. Mildenhall struck back belatedly in heat ten with a 5-1 of their own, but by then it was far too late and Rye House ran out winners, 46-32. Part one had been accomplished, but in the second half, disaster struck as Smith cracked his collarbone and looked doubtful for the return at Mildenhall a week later.

Sure enough, as the teams took to the track on 28 October, Rye House were without Smith and Saunders. A crowd of 10,000 people, many from Rye House, turned up to see this crucial battle. Once again, it was the Rockets who got off to a good start as Fiala and Hubbard managed a 4-2 in the opening heat. Mildenhall pulled back a 5-1 in the next heat and from then on the scores stayed close with Mildenhall just keeping the edge. At the end of heat twelve, with one heat to go, the score was Mildenhall 38 Rye House 34. A 5-1 for Rye House would give them a draw, leaving them in an unassailable lead in the league on 61 points with Mildenhall on 57 with only one match to ride.

It was a vital heat. The tension around the stadium was almost unbearable as the four riders came up to the tapes. As the riders flew into the first bend, Fiala, Garrad and Mildenhall's Mel Taylor crashed. The referee, Ken Hill, announced a rerun with the exclusion of Fiala as the primary cause of the stoppage. Pratt was on the phone to the referee immediately claiming that it was a first-bend incident and all four riders should be put back, and that in any case if it was anyone's fault it was Taylor's as he had fallen and Fiala had laid his bike down to avoid him, but Hill stuck by his decision. Pratt was so incensed that he withdrew Garrad from the rerun and the Mildenhall pair cruised round to a sensational 5-0 win and a 43-34 match victory. This left Mildenhall just one point behind Rye House in the league.

With their season over, Pratt and Silver took the team off to Spain for a short holiday as a reward for all their fine work during the year. Back at home, sadly for them, Mildenhall were beating Scunthorpe 41-37 to take the league title, leaving Rye House as runners-up for the second time in three years.

But it wasn't all disappointment for Rye House. Following their win over Mildenhall in the Knock-Out Cup semi-final, Rye House met Berwick in the final. The first leg was held at Rye House on 14 October. The Rockets were in sensational form with Fiala scoring a paid maximum and Mullarkey, Garrad and Pullen paid 11 each. The final score was Rye House 54 Berwick 24, giving the Rockets a 30-point cushion to take to Sheffield Park.

The return on 27 October saw Rye House take the lead in the first heat with a 4-2 from Fiala and Hubbard and from then on there was never the remotest chance that Berwick could make up the deficit. A 4-2 to Berwick in the final heat saw them just take the match 40-38 but the final aggregate score was Rye House 92 Berwick 64, giving the Rockets their first major trophy. Once again, Fiala top scored for the Rockets with 11 points, his only loss coming in that last heat.

1979 was certainly Fiala's year as far as Rye House was concerned. It was the year he finally fulfilled his promise for the team, becoming its top scorer with an average of 9.20. Behind him, Garrad on 9.11, Mullarkey, 8.71, Smith, 8.20, Hubbard, 8.16 and Pullen on 7.34 were all of National League heat-leader standard. They were now a major force to be reckoned with in the National League. In the last three years, they had finished second, third and second, and in the Knock-Out Cup they had been runners-up in 1978 and were now champions in 1979. No other team in the National League could point to this sort of record over the last three seasons and if they could once again keep their side together for 1980, it seemed inevitable that they would walk off with their first league title.

## 1979 National League

| Date | H/A | Opponent | W/L | Score |
|------|-----|----------|-----|-------|
| 24 May | A | Oxford | W | 41-37 |
| 27 May | A | Boston | L | 38-39 |
| 5 June | A | Milton Keynes | L | 36-41 |
| 10 June | H | Peterborough | W | 45-33 |
| 24 June | H | Stoke | W | 58-20 |
| 28 June | A | Middlesbrough | W | 44-34 |
| 1 July | H | Milton Keynes | | 40-38 |
| 3 July | A | Crayford | W | 47-31 |
| 8 July | H | Nottingham | W | 47-31 |
| 11 July | A | Nottingham | W | 42-36 |
| 14 July | A | Canterbury | W | 43-35 |
| 22 July | H | Berwick | W | 49-27 |
| 22 July | H | Scunthorpe | W | 59-18 |
| 30 July | H | Boston | W | 60-18 |
| 5 August | H | Newcastle | W | 51-27 |
| 10 August | A | Ellesmere Port | W | 40-38 |
| 12 August | H | Oxford | W | 45-33 |
| 12 August | H | Middlesbrough | W | 57-21 |
| 19 August | H | Edinburgh | W | 55-22 |
| 20 August | A | Scunthorpe | W | 53-25 |
| 24 August | A | Workington | W | 41-37 |
| 31 August | A | Edinburgh | W | 45-33 |
| 1 September | A | Stoke | L | 31-47 |
| 2 September | H | Weymouth | W | 60-18 |
| 2 September | H | Crayford | W | 60-18 |
| 7 September | A | Peterborough | L | 37-41 |
| 9 September | H | Canterbury | W | 53-25 |
| 11 September | A | Weymouth | W | 52-26 |
| 14 September | A | Glasgow | L | 32-45 |
| 15 September | A | Berwick | D | 39-39 |
| 17 September | A | Newcastle | W | 42-36 |
| 30 September | H | Glasgow | W | 54-24 |
| 30 September | H | Workington | W | 47-31 |
| 7 October | H | Ellesmere Port | W | 61-17 |
| 21 October | H | Mildenhall | W | 46-32 |
| 28 October | A | Mildenhall | L | 34-43 |

P36 W29 D1 L6

For 1,684 Against 1,116

Position: second (out of nineteen)

## Knock-Out Cup

First Round

| Date | H/A | Opponent | W/L | Score |
|------|-----|----------|-----|-------|
| 29 April | H | Weymouth | W | 56-22 |
| 22 May | A | Weymouth | W | 44-34 |

Won 100-56 on aggregate

Second Round

| Date | H/A | Opponent | W/L | Score |
|------|-----|----------|-----|-------|
| 3 June | H | Glasgow | W | 54-24 |
| 8 June | A | Glasgow | L | 31-47 |

Won 85-71 on aggregate

Third Round

| Date | H/A | Opponent | W/L | Score |
|------|-----|----------|-----|-------|
| 29 June | A | Workington | L | 29-49 |
| 15 July | H | Workington | W | 59-19 |

Won 88-68 on aggregate

Semi-Final

| Date | H/A | Opponent | W/L | Score |
|------|-----|----------|-----|-------|
| 26 August | A | Mildenhall | W | 40-38 |
| 27 August | H | Mildenhall | W | 44-34 |

Won 84-72 on aggregate

Final

| Date | H/A | Opponent | W/L | Score |
|------|-----|----------|-----|-------|
| 14 October | H | Berwick | W | 54-24 |
| 27 October | A | Berwick | L | 38-40 |

Won 92-64 on aggregate

Rye House Knock-Out Cup champions

## 1979 National League and Knock-Out Cup

| Name | M | R | Pts | BP | Total | CMA |
|------|---|---|-----|----|-------|-----|
| Karl Fiala | 46 | 187 | 387 | 43 | 430 | 9.20 |
| Bob Garrad | 46 | 188 | 404 | 24 | 428 | 9.11 |
| Kelvin Mullarkey | 46 | 191 | 332 | 84 | 416 | 8.71 |
| Kevin Smith | 42 | 164 | 311 | 25 | 336 | 8.20 |
| Ted Hubbard | 31 | 126 | 236 | 21 | 257 | 8.16 |
| Ashley Pullen | 44 | 152 | 239 | 40 | 279 | 7.34 |
| Hugh Saunders | 39 | 129 | 171 | 41 | 212 | 6.57 |
| Peter Tarrant | 18 | 52 | 49 | 19 | 68 | 5.23 |

# The 1980s

## 1980

Towards the end of 1979, due to other business commitments, Colin Pratt decided to part company with Rye House as he felt he no longer had the time to devote to the club. Len Silver bought his shares and once again became the sole director of Rye House Speedway.

Silver knew that the supporters had high hopes for the team in 1980 and he was determined to give them what they wanted. One of the good things about Rye House was that it still, to some extent, retained that Sunday afternoon out feeling with management, riders and supporters all mucking in together. The riders and supporters often travelled to away fixtures together while the riders made a point of attending as many supporters' functions as they could. The big difference from the open era and the Southern Area League days, however, was the sheer professionalism that Silver and Pratt had injected into the club. There was still this closeness between management, riders and fans, but they knew they were now ready to take that final step towards becoming champions.

Before the season started, Hubbard announced he would be unable to ride for the Rockets in 1980 and Saunders retired to be appointed the new team manager in Pratt's place. This left Silver with the relatively young quintet of Garrad, Fiala, Mullarkey, Smith and Pullen. Instead of adding more experienced riders, Silver turned to more young discoveries to make up the other two places. Peter Tarrant was promoted to team duties proper and Simon Aindow, Andy Fines, Barry King and Carl Squirrell were given the reserve spots.

Peter Tarrant, a reserve from 1977 to 1981.

The opening match was against Oxford on 30 March and the Rockets began the season as they intended to continue with a convincing 50-27 victory.

Eleven days later, Rye House had their first away fixture, also against Oxford. After two heats, they were five points down, having suffered a 5-0 in heat two. By heat eight, they were seven points up and went on to win the match 43-34. With the 'famous five' all scoring solidly in both matches, the rest of the league knew that Rye House were the team to beat. A reverse at Ellesmere Port, 42-36, on 25 April was followed by a run of nineteen consecutive victories. At home, the Rockets were totally invincible, knocking up scores of 53-25 against Scunthorpe, 52-26 against Milton Keynes, 56-22 against Canterbury, 57-21 against Milton Keynes, 59-19 against Glasgow, 50-28 against Berwick and 56-22 against Stoke. In these early season encounters, Fiala, Mullarkey, Garrad and Smith were all racking up double-figure scores match after match. By the time of the next defeat on 16 August, at the hands of Berwick, Mullarkey had scored eight full or paid maximums, Fiala seven, Garrad six and Smith four. Pullen had also scored one in the match against Glasgow which saw all five score a maximum.

By the middle of August, the league was becoming more or less a two-horse race between Rye House and Newcastle, who were also having a tremendous run, dropping just five points compared to the Rockets' four. While the top five were continuing to fire on all cylinders, Peter Tarrant was also giving good support from the number six berth. At reserve, Simon Aindow had been injured after the first match. Andy Fines took his place, but after three pointless outings he was replaced by Barry King, the son of former Rye House rider Gerry King. After four matches, Fines returned with Carl Squirrell, taking his place after two more matches. From then until the end of the season, Fines, King and Squirrell swapped about in the reserve berth, though by the end of the season it was Fines who established himself as the best of the three.

Following the defeat at Berwick, the Rockets suffered another setback in the next match away at Boston, and with two further defeats in September at their great rivals Newcastle and Edinburgh, it looked as though they might just miss out on the honours again. Fortunately for Rye House, Newcastle suffered a shock home defeat at the hands of near neighbours Middlesbrough on 15 September and the destiny of the league championship was up in the air again.

It was then that the Rockets really piled on the pressure. Between 21 September and 9 October they raced to four home victories with scores of 52-26 against Nottingham, 63-13 against Workington, 54-24 against Weymouth and 56-22 against Peterborough. During this four-match period, the big five scored nine full or paid maximums between them.

The match against Workington on 28 September was, of course, the highlight of the run. With two 5-0s, nine 5-1s and two 4-2s, the Rockets slaughtered their opponents and showed they were in a completely different class. Fiala, Smith, Garrad and Mullarkey all scored full or paid 12-point maximums, while Tarrant also scored a maximum paid nine points from three rides. Pullen contributed paid ten and Fines paid seven from three rides.

Rye House now had two away matches left, against Middlesbrough, who were unbeaten at home, and Glasgow. They had 60 points, while Newcastle, who also had two matches left, one home and one away, had 57. Rye House's race points were superior to Newcastle, so they just needed one draw from their last two fixtures to take the title.

The best hope seemed to lie in the final match against Glasgow but, nevertheless, hopes were high as the team travelled to Middlesbrough on 9 October.

Hopes of taking the title at the first attempt started well as Fiala and Smith began with a 4-2 in the first heat, but two 5-1s from Middlesbrough in the next two heats showed why they were unbeaten at home and the many supporters who had travelled up with the Rockets team began to feel that perhaps they would have to wait for the Glasgow match after all. After heat nine, the scores were Middlesbrough 30 Rye House 24. Being six points down enabled Saunders to bring in double tactical substitutes in heat ten as Garrad and Fiala came together to produce a 5-1 to put the Rockets back in with a chance. Another 5-1 in heat eleven and suddenly, with just two heats to go, Rye House were two points in front. A 4-2 from Middlesbrough in heat twelve meant that, with just one heat to go, the scores were now level. A 3-3 in the final heat would be enough for the Rockets to take the league title. The line-up was Fiala and Mullarkey for Rye House and Mike Spink and Mark Courtney for Middlesbrough. In the end, it proved all to easy for the Rockets as Courtney fell and the race was rerun, leaving Fiala to punch the air in victory as he came over the line in first place. With Mullarkey coming in third, not only did Rye House get the point they needed, but they actually won the match, 40-38.

As it happened, it was just as well that they managed to pull off a last-gasp win as the final 'easier' match against Glasgow resulted in a whopping 57-21 defeat, though perhaps the Rockets felt entitled to take it easy after the previous night's exertions at Middlesbrough.

Although Rye House won the league and were the cup holders from 1979, their Knock-Out Cup campaign did not go as planned as they were knocked out in the first round by Mildenhall, 79-77. However, this took nothing away from the fact that the Rockets had now won Rye House's first major league championship in their history and were, by any standard, the most successful team over the last four years in the National League. Their record was second, third, second, first, with one Knock-Out Cup victory and one runners-up place.

One of the main reasons for Rye House's success was their stability as a team. Not only had Fiala, Garrad, Mullarkey, Smith and Pullen been the mainstay of the team for the last three years, but in 1980 they all rode in every single match. It was this stability and sheer team effort from these five youngsters that made Rye House the great team they had become. One example of this was the fact that Mullarkey recorded no less than 69 bonus points during the season. The top three, Garrad, Fiala and Mullarkey, all finished the year with 9-plus averages; Smith had an average of 8.43 and Pullen 6.8. With yet another youngster, Andy Fines, coming good towards the end of the season, it looked as though Rye House would become a dominant force for years to come, if only they could stay together.

*1980 National League*

| Date | H/A | Opponent | W/L | Score |
| --- | --- | --- | --- | --- |
| 30 March | H | Oxford | W | 50-27 |
| 10 April | A | Oxford | W | 43-34 |
| 20 April | H | Ellesmere Port | W | 48-30 |
| 25 April | A | Ellesmere Port | L | 36-42 |
| 11 May | H | Scunthorpe | W | 53-25 |
| 12 May | A | Scunthorpe | W | 44-34 |
| 18 May | H | Middlesbrough | W | 43-35 |
| 20 May | A | Milton Keynes | W | 52-26 |
| 6 June | A | Workington | W | 46-31 |
| 15 June | H | Canterbury | W | 56-22 |
| 22 June | H | Crayford | W | 40-38 |
| 30 June | A | Exeter | W | 42-36 |
| 1 July | A | Weymouth | W | 41-36 |
| 5 July | A | Canterbury | W | 42-36 |
| 6 July | H | Milton Keynes | W | 57-21 |
| 13 July | H | Berwick | W | 50-28 |
| 13 July | H | Glasgow | W | 59-19 |
| 25 July | A | Peterborough | W | 41-37 |
| 28 July | H | Boston | W | 47-29 |
| 3 August | H | Stoke | W | 56-22 |
| 4 August | A | Stoke | W | 51-27 |
| 5 August | A | Crayford | W | 43-35 |
| 10 August | H | Edinburgh | W | 52-26 |
| 16 August | A | Berwick | L | 30-47 |

| | | | | |
|---|---|---|---|---|
| 24 August | A | Boston | L | 37-41 |
| 25 August | H | Mildenhall | W | 47-31 |
| 27 August | A | Mildenhall | W | 40-38 |
| 30 August | A | Nottingham | L | 38-40 |
| 31 August | H | Newcastle | W | 45-32 |
| 7 September | H | Exeter | W | 58-20 |
| 8 September | A | Newcastle | L | 29-49 |
| 12 September | A | Edinburgh | L | 33-45 |
| 21 September | H | Nottingham | W | 52-26 |
| 28 September | H | Workington | W | 63-13 |
| 28 September | H | Weymouth | W | 54-24 |
| 5 October | H | Peterborough | W | 56-22 |
| 9 October | A | Middlesbrough | W | 40-38 |
| 10 October | A | Glasgow | L | 21-57 |

P38 W31 D0 L7
For 1,735 Against 1,219
Position: first (out of twenty)

## Knock-Out Cup

First Round

| Date | H/A | Opponent | W/L | Score |
|---|---|---|---|---|
| 25 May | A | Mildenhall | L | 33-45 |
| 26 May | H | Mildenhall | W | 44-34 |

Lost 77-79 on aggregate

## 1980 National League and Knock-Out Cup

| Name | M | R | Pts | BP | Total | CMA |
|---|---|---|---|---|---|---|
| Bob Garrad | 40 | 169 | 410 | 6 | 416 | 9.85 |
| Karl Fiala | 40 | 163 | 360 | 25 | 385 | 9.49 |
| Kelvin Mullarkey | 40 | 161 | 305 | 69 | 374 | 9.29 |
| Kein Smith | 40 | 157 | 292 | 39 | 331 | 8.43 |
| Ashley Pullen | 40 | 152 | 225 | 35 | 260 | 6.84 |
| Peter Tarrant | 35 | 117 | 131 | 38 | 169 | 5.78 |
| Andy Fines | 21 | 61 | 50 | 12 | 62 | 4.07 |
| Carl Squirrell | 12 | 33 | 22 | 3 | 25 | 3.03 |
| Barry King | 11 | 25 | 14 | 1 | 15 | 2.40 |

# 1981

Unfortunately, it was a forlorn hope that the team could stay together for yet another season. Garrad and Smith both felt the time had now come for them to take their chances in the First Division, the British League. Garrad moved on to Len Silver's Hackney, while Smith went to Poole on a reported £10,000 transfer. Pullen too was recalled to his parent club, Reading, also in the British League. Although Silver realised he would have to look for replacements, he still wanted to encourage the youngsters at Rye House. He signed up the comparatively experienced Steve Naylor from Crayford, but to fill the other two places he looked to the likes of Tarrant, Fines, Squirrell and King. He knew the team would be weaker than the all-conquering 1980 Rockets, but, in some ways, he wasn't too dismayed as the home matches had all been runaway victories and Silver felt that some closer meetings would be good for the crowds.

Steve Naylor, heat leader from 1981 to 1985.

With a heat-leader trio of Fiala, Mullarkey and Naylor, backed up by another generation of up-and-coming youngsters, Rye House felt that the season could still be a reasonably good one. But, just as the season was about to start, they suffered a real blow as Fiala decided he'd had enough of speedway and announced his retirement. Kevin Bowen was quickly signed up, but he had only been second string the previous year at Oxford and was certainly not a proper replacement for Fiala. So Rye House entered the 1981 season with just two recognised heat leaders in Mullarkey and Naylor.

The first two matches were home and away against Scunthorpe on 5 and 13 April. Both ended in victories for the Rockets and things did not look so bad after all thanks to Tarrant, who scored a paid maximum at home and paid 11 away, and Fines, who scored paid 10 and a paid maximum. Not only did Rye House win both matches but they were by convincing scores too, 55-22 at home and 49-28 away. From this early season showing, it seemed as though the Rockets were back up to four heat-leader-class riders in Mullarkey, Naylor, Tarrant and Fines. Six days later, however, disaster struck as both Tarrant and Fines, riding in a three-cornered fixture against Peterborough and Mildenhall at Mildenhall, crashed in the same heat and were both taken to hospital. Fines had broken his leg and was out for the rest of the season. Tarrant only received bad bruising but his form over the next few matches suffered as a result and, in just one race, Rye House had lost both their potential league winners. They were now down to two heat leaders. Fines was replaced by the seventeen-year-old Marvyn Cox.

The next match was at home to Glasgow. It was to be Rye House's first loss at home since 1977. Fortress Hoddesdon had been breached and it was not to be the last time that season. The score on 17 May was Rye House 31 Glasgow 46. Of their 31 points, Naylor scored ten and Mullarkey nine. Barry King was the only other rider to put up any sort of show, gaining six points from five rides.

From then on, the season became one of damage limitation rather than of trying to retain the league title. After the home loss to Glasgow, eight successive league defeats plus two in the Knock-Out Cup followed, including five at home. The only bright spot in all this was the return of Bobby Garrad, who had had an unhappy time at Hackney with a long run of mechanical problems. Garrad slotted back in immediately with a run of double-figure scores. Unfortunately, just as it appeared that Rye House were almost back up to strength, Naylor suffered from an inexplicable loss of form, scoring just 13 points in four matches during early July.

*Above:* An action shot from 1981, showing, from left to right: Kevin Bowen, Steve Naylor, Kevin Teager (Scunthorpe). Teager later rode for Rye House.

*Left:* Marvyn Cox came to Rye House as a seventeen-year-old in 1981. By 1983, he was the Rockets' leading rider.

The rot finally stopped on 26 July when the Rockets beat Boston at home, 42-35. This match also coincided with the start of a good run of scores from Kevin Bowen. In contrast to the previous few years, when Rye House had used very few riders, this year a number of riders came and went as Silver tried to find a winning combination. Barry King, Carl Squirrell, Phil Vance, Tony Garrad, Simon Aindow and Colin Tarrant all came and went, but by the beginning of August, the Rockets had found the side that was to see them through the rest of the season. This consisted of Mullarkey, Garrad, Naylor, Bowen, Cox, and youngsters Garry Monk and Wimbledon loanee Peter Johns.

After that initial away win at Scunthorpe, the Rockets were not to taste victory on their travels any more that season, while their home record was also less than impressive with ten wins and eight losses. However, towards the end of the season there was a glimmer of hope as Rye House romped home in the last three home matches by scores of 63-15 over Workington, 59-19 over Peterborough and 51-27 over Milton Keynes. The match against Workington saw Cox score his first maximum in the National League; something he followed up with a paid maximum against Peterborough. By the end of the season, Cox had proved himself to be in the same mould as other Rye House juniors such as Garrad, Fiala and Smith. He crowned his first full season by winning the Anglia Junior League Riders' Championship.

Although slightly down on previous seasons, it was Mullarkey and Garrad who once again proved to be the best of the Rockets with averages of 8.85 and 8.27 respectively, while Naylor turned in 7.67. Fourth man was Bowen with 5.05. It was a far cry from the previous two years when the Rockets had five heat-leader-class riders and it led to them dropping to sixteenth place in the table. Once again, however, there was some optimism for 1982. If the heat leader trio could stay and Cox could improve in the traditional Rye House style, and if Fines could find the form he had exhibited before his broken leg put him out for the season, then...

The 1981 season had also seen more building work at the track as 800 new seats were added, making the seating capacity at the stadium 2,000, larger than a number of British League tracks.

As normal, during the winter, the training school continued, but it was all very different from the time when George Barclay had turned up in 1968, waited for anything up to four hours and then been given a few laps and told to return to the pits immediately. The cost for a three-day training session was now £50 for a rider with his own bike and £90 for one without. On the first day, there was practical instruction in starting techniques and some practice on the track. On the second day, there was practically a whole day of classroom work looking at machine maintenance, with a short time for more on-track practice, and on the third day there was more practice with special instruction on the art of broadsiding. All aspiring trainees had to provide their own helmets, gloves, boots and steel shoe.

## 1981 National League

| Date | H/A | Opponent | W/L | Score |
|---|---|---|---|---|
| 5 April | H | Scunthorpe | W | 55–22 |
| 13 April | A | Scunthorpe | W | 28–49 |
| 17 May | H | Glasgow | L | 31–46 |
| 21 May | A | Wolverhampton | L | 23–55 |
| 22 May | A | Workington | L | 29–49 |
| 24 May | H | Wolverhampton | L | 37–41 |
| 9 June | A | Crayford | L | 23–55 |
| 14 June | H | Exeter | L | 34–44 |
| 21 June | H | Oxford | L | 37–41 |
| 28 June | H | Edinburgh | L | 33–44 |
| 3 July | A | Ellesmere Port | L | 27–51 |
| 9 July | A | Middlesbrough | L | 34–44 |
| 10 July | A | Edinburgh | L | 27–50 |
| 11 July | A | Stoke | L | 30–48 |
| 16 July | A | Oxford | L | 35–43 |
| 26 July | H | Boston | W | 42–35 |
| 1 August | A | Canterbury | L | 33–45 |
| 2 August | H | Stoke | W | 41–36 |
| 9 August | H | Middlesbrough | L | 37–41 |
| 11 August | A | Milton Keynes | L | 38–40 |
| 16 August | H | Crayford | W | 43–35 |
| 21 August | A | Glasgow | L | 32–46 |
| 30 August | A | Mildenhall | L | 37–41 |
| 30 August | A | Boston | L | 31–47 |
| 31 August | H | Weymouth | L | 34–44 |
| 13 September | H | Canterbury | W | 48–30 |
| 15 September | A | Weymouth | L | 24–54 |
| 20 September | H | Ellesmere Port | W | 45–33 |
| 21 September | A | Newcastle | L | 26–52 |
| 25 September | A | Peterborough | L | 36–42 |
| 27 September | H | Newcastle | W | 45–33 |
| 27 September | H | Workington | W | 63–15 |
| 28 September | A | Exeter | L | 21–57 |
| 4 October | H | Peterborough | W | 59–19 |
| 18 October | H | Mildenhall | L | 38–39 |
| 25 October | H | Milton Keynes | W | 51–27 |

P36 W11 D0 L25
For 1,328 Against 1,472
Position sixteenth (out of nineteen)

## Knock Out Cup

First Round
Bye

Second Round

| Date | H/A | Opponent | W/L | Score |
|---|---|---|---|---|
| 29 May | A | Peterborough | L | 26-70 |
| 7 June | H | Peterborough | L | 32-64 |

Lost 58-134 on aggregate

## *1981 National League and Knock-Out Cup*

| Name | M | R | Pts | BP | Total | CMA |
|---|---|---|---|---|---|---|
| Bob Garrad | 25 | 113 | 232 | 18 | 250 | 8.85 |
| Kelvin Mullarkey | 39 | 179 | 345 | 25 | 370 | 8.27 |
| Steve Naylor | 39 | 168 | 307 | 15 | 322 | 7.67 |
| Kevin Bowen | 34 | 114 | 123 | 21 | 144 | 5.05 |
| Peter Johns | 18 | 51 | 49 | 11 | 60 | 4.71 |
| Peter Tarrant | 14 | 58 | 61 | 6 | 67 | 4.62 |
| Marvyn Cox | 37 | 148 | 136 | 33 | 169 | 4.57 |
| Garry Monk | 20 | 47 | 45 | 8 | 53 | 4.51 |
| Barry King | 15 | 59 | 50 | 12 | 62 | 4.20 |
| Tony Garrad | 15 | 44 | 21 | 3 | 24 | 2.18 |

# 1982

Rye House supporters were able to breathe a sigh of relief when the new season started as the first home match against Oxford on 4 April saw Mullarkey, Garrad, Naylor, Fines, Cox, Bowen and Monk take their places in the Rockets' line-up. It proved to be an exciting match with the result resting on the last race. A new sixteen-heat formula had been introduced for that year and the score after fifteen heats was Rye House 46 Oxford 44. Garrad and Bowen lined up for Rye House against Oxford's Mick Handley and Graham Drury. Garrad charged off from the gate but was overtaken on the first bend by Handley. Behind him, Drury kept snapping away at his rear wheel until he eventually managed to find a way past on the final lap, giving Oxford a 5-1 and victory by 49 points to 47. It was certainly not the start the Rockets' faithful had wanted but, on the plus side, Naylor scored a brilliant 15-point maximum while Cox also came good with paid 11.

Rye House's next meeting was away at Peterborough in the first leg of the three-cornered Easter Triangle. Naylor scored his second successive maximum as he led the Rockets to a fine victory over Mildenhall and the home side. Cox once again put in a good performance, scoring seven points. Disaster struck in the second leg at Mildenhall, however, as Bowen hit the safety fence in heat seven, breaking a bone at the base of his spine which put him out of action for most of the rest of the season. Peter Johns returned to the team to take his place.

Rye House did not have another home league meeting until 9 May, when they took on and beat Ellesmere Port 56-40. It was the start of an unbeaten run at home which lasted until the end of the season. In fact, in spite of the first meeting defeat by Oxford, they finished the year with an unbeaten home record – raced 18 won 18. The first match had been declared void as the contract of Graham Drury, who scored 10 points for Oxford, had not been registered at the BSPA. The match was rerun at the end of the season with Oxford being heavily defeated 64-32.

The match against Ellesmere Port also saw the home league debut of Steve Bryenton, who came in for the injured Peter Johns. Two Rockets, Garrad and Naylor, scored full 15-point maximums, while Cox finished with 10 points. A double-header followed the next week, with Garrad scoring a maximum in each as Rye House overwhelmed their Scottish opposition: 53-33 against Glasgow and 57-38 against Edinburgh. Mullarkey and Cox backed him up with double-figure scores in both. Although Naylor's early season form dipped a little, this was more than compensated for by Garrad, who was having his best season yet in Rockets' colours, and Cox, who had come from nowhere the year before to chase Garrad hard all season for that top rider slot. Cox's rise in 1982 was nothing short of sensational. Still only a teenager, he rode for a representative full National League side against Young England and had many a British League promoter paying a visit to Hoddesdon to watch this boy wonder. Garrad's best season saw his average go up by a whole point from the previous season to 9.85 and culminated in third place in the National League Riders' Championship.

While Garrad and Cox were reaching the heights, Mullarkey was continuing to prove what a great team man he was. By the end of the season, he had amassed another 37 bonus points and, even more incredibly, had now raced seven full seasons without missing a single match for the Rockets.

Although Rye House continued to sweep all before them at home, it was their away form which prevented them from mounting a serious challenge on the league title. They only managed to win four times away from Hoddesdon and three of those wins were by the narrowest of margins, 49-47.

One reason for the lack of success away was the Rockets' long tail. Fines never really lived up to the promise he had started to show before his injury the previous year, while Johns and Bryenton, who kept his place in the side when Johns returned because Monk decided to retire, were still learning their trade. Nevertheless, Johns and Bryenton showed flashes of real brilliance at times, Bryenton in particular as he scored paid 15 against Stoke, paid 13 against Middlesbrough and paid 11 against Glasgow. Towards the end of the season, another youngster, former Rye House rider George Barclay's son John, came into the team and showed real promise.

This was a year of consolidation for the Rockets and a real improvement over their dismal showing in 1981. As a result, they shot up the table from sixteenth place to sixth and reached the semi-final of the Knock-Out Cup, having accounted for Crayford and Mildenhall on the way.

Once again, as the season came to an end, there was much reason for hope the following year. If Garrad, Mullarkey, Cox and Naylor stayed and at least one or two of the youngsters, Fines, Johns, Bryenton and Barclay, could show a Cox-like improvement, there was every cause for optimism that the Rockets could once again be battling it out for honours.

## 1982 National League

| Date | H/A | Opponent | W/L | Score |
|---|---|---|---|---|
| 18 April | H | Milton Keynes | W | 54-41 |
| 20 April | A | Crayford | W | 49-47 |
| 28 April | A | Long Eaton | W | 49-47 |
| 29 April | A | Middlesbrough | L | 39-57 |
| 2 May | A | Boston | L | 46-50 |
| 3 May | H | Boston | W | 59-37 |
| 9 May | H | Ellesmere Port | W | 56-40 |
| 16 May | H | Glasgow | W | 63-33 |
| 16 May | H | Edinburgh | W | 57-38 |
| 31 May | H | Weymouth | W | 54-41 |
| 4 June | A | Ellesmere Port | L | 37-59 |
| 12 June | A | Stoke | L | 42-53 |
| 13 June | H | Berwick | W | 64-32 |
| 17 June | A | Oxford | W | 49-47 |
| 27 June | H | Canterbury | W | 55-40 |
| 6 July | A | Weymouth | L | 37-59 |
| 18 July | H | Exeter | W | 61-34 |
| 23 July | A | Edinburgh | W | 51-44 |
| 24 July | A | Berwick | L | 31-64 |
| 1 August | H | Stoke | W | 73-23 |
| 8 August | H | Newcastle | W | 49-47 |
| 15 August | H | Middlesbrough | W | 53-41 |
| 17 August | A | Milton Keynes | L | 43-52 |

| 22 August | H | Scunthorpe | W | 58-38 |
| 23 August | A | Scunthorpe | L | 45-51 |
| 30 August | H | Mildenhall | W | 49-47 |
| 4 September | A | Canterbury | L | 43-53 |
| 5 September | H | Crayford | W | 64-31 |
| 10 September | A | Peterborough | L | 42-54 |
| 12 September | H | Long Eaton | W | 52-43 |
| 13 September | A | Newcastle | L | 28-67 |
| 17 September | A | Glasgow | L | 41-54 |
| 19 September | H | Peterborough | W | 52-44 |
| 26 September | H | Oxford | W | 64-32 |
| 27 September | A | Exeter | L | 19-34* |
| 31 October | A | Mildenhall | L | 35-61 |

* Abandoned after nine heats. Match unable to be rearranged. Score allowed to stand.
P36 W22 D0 L14
For 1,763 Against 1,635
Position: sixth (out of nineteen)

## Knock-Out Cup

First Round
Bye
Second Round

| Date | H/A | Opponent | W/L | Score |
| --- | --- | --- | --- | --- |
| 23 May | H | Crayford | W | 35-25* |
| 25 May | A | Crayford | W | 62-33 |

* Tie abandoned after ten heats. Match rearranged for 31 May but Crayford conceded, leaving Rye House to win 97-58 on aggregate

Third Round

| Date | H/A | Opponent | W/L | Score |
| --- | --- | --- | --- | --- |
| 10 July | A | Mildenhall | L | 39-56 |
| 11 July | H | Mildenhall | W | 60-35 |

Won 99-91 on aggregate
Semi-Final

| Date | H/A | Opponent | W/L | Score |
| --- | --- | --- | --- | --- |
| 20 August | A | Ellesmere Port | L | 25-71 |
| 5 September | H | Ellesmere Port | W | 59-37 |

Lost 84-108 on aggregate

## 1982 National League and Knock-Out Cup

| Name | M | R | Pts | BP | Total | CMA |
| --- | --- | --- | --- | --- | --- | --- |
| Bob Garrad | 42 | 229 | 536 | 28 | 564 | 9.85 |
| Marvyn Cox | 27 | 143 | 287 | 30 | 317 | 8.67 |
| Kelvin Mullarkey | 42 | 220 | 391 | 37 | 428 | 7.78 |
| Steve Naylor | 41 | 212 | 384 | 25 | 409 | 7.72 |
| Peter Johns | 37 | 134 | 130 | 36 | 166 | 4.96 |
| John Barclay | 6 | 19 | 18 | 5 | 23 | 4.84 |
| Andy Fines | 33 | 136 | 134 | 25 | 159 | 4.68 |
| Steve Bryenton | 35 | 144 | 123 | 32 | 155 | 4.31 |
| Garry Monk | 13 | 46 | 31 | 4 | 35 | 3.04 |
| Paul Hilton | 6 | 17 | 6 | 1 | 7 | 1.65 |
| Kevin Bowen | 7 | 17 | 3 | 1 | 4 | 0.94 |

Chris Chaplin rode for Rye House from 1983 to 1986. In the second half and in individual events he always wore his trademark Charlie Chaplin race jacket.

# 1983

There was some very bad news for the Rye House faithful as the 1983 season was about to start. The fans' hero and ever-present, Kelvin Mullarkey, decided he could no longer continue in the sport without a suitable sponsor. Len Silver thought he had found one but Mullarkey had become very disillusioned with the state of the National League. In particular, he was concerned about the pay rates and the new 45-point limit that had been introduced that year. In the end, Mullarkey did return to the saddle, but it was with Canterbury and Rye House were forced to say goodbye to their favourite son – for the time being.

However, they still had three top-class heat leaders in Garrad, Naylor and Cox, and with Peter Johns starting the season with 36 paid points in his first three league matches, it looked as though Rye House could once again be battling it out for top honours. They also had high hopes for another sixteen-year-old discovery, Len Silver's son Andrew, who had shown a lot of promise at the training school over the winter and was given the reserve slot. The other two members of the team were Kevin Bowen and Steve Bryenton.

The first home league match was against Long Eaton and, sure enough, the Rockets scored an emphatic 62-34 win with Johns leading the way with a 13-point haul. Behind him, Naylor and Cox both scored double figures while Garrad had three wins and a fall. Best of all, though, was the paid reserve's maximum from Silver: six points from two races on his league debut.

The next home meeting did not go as planned, however, and with Naylor falling in three of his first four races, they were held to a 48-48 draw by Scunthorpe. With a 53-43 away defeat at Edinburgh following on 22 April, it hadn't been too good a start, but there were still high hopes that once the top four got going, and with Silver to support them, the Rockets would be there or thereabouts at the end of the season. These hopes were dealt a severe blow in the next home match against Crayford, however. Although Rye House scored a narrow 49-46 injury, Johns suffered a broken thumb following a fall in heat six which not only put him out for the rest of that meeting but also for many meetings to come.

Worse was to come when, after scoring paid nine in the next home match against Peterborough, Andrew Silver broke his leg and was ruled out for the rest of the season.

A number of juniors were tried out to fill the positions, including Terry Broadbank (Mike's son), Chris Chaplin and Kerry Gray. John Barclay also returned to the team for a while. The best of the bunch turned out to be Gray, who was given an extended run in the team and finished the season with a 5.73 average.

With Garrad, Cox and Naylor still as the top three, the Rockets were able to hold their own at home, and when Peter Johns returned on 5 June, there was reason to believe that the season would not end in complete disaster, although thoughts of winning the league title again had by now disappeared. After two good scores back in Rockets' colours, Johns was out again following a fall at Peterborough on 17 June in which he injured his back. Worse was to come for Rye House when, on 31 July, Naylor was injured during the Herts Gold Cup individual meeting and he too was out for the rest of the season.

The following meeting saw just three of the riders who had started the season with the Rockets line up for the Knock-Out Cup quarter-final first leg against Exeter. Fortunately, Bryenton was able to step up a gear, scoring 13 points, and with Cox and Garrad still in top form, scoring 17 and 15 respectively, the Rockets gained a 55-41 success. But it was obvious that Rye House now had too long a tail. Away from home, they were losing match after match; their only victory all season had been on 4 May against Long Eaton, when they still had Naylor and Silver going well.

Not only were they losing away from home, but on 10 July the Rockets even lost their unbeaten home record when they went down 49-47 to Middlesbrough. Worse still, they lost again, on 25 September, by an even bigger score, 51-45, to Newcastle.

All in all, 1983 was not a great year for Rye House. A season that had started reasonably well gradually deteriorated as the Rockets were struck hard by the injury jinx. Their final position in the table was eleventh out of eighteen. In the Knock-Out Cup, they defeated Oxford in the first round but were beaten by Exeter in the quarter-finals.

There was some compensation, particularly the form of their two leading riders, Marvyn Cox and Bob Garrad. Still only eighteen, Cox now topped the Rye House score chart with an average of 9.83 just ahead of Garrad's 9.28. Cox represented the team at the National League Riders' Championship, finishing in fourth place with 11 points. He also took the Silver Helmet from Exeter's Keith Millard on 14 August and successfully defended it three times before losing it to Jim McMillan one week later. But there is no doubt that his biggest achievement was his third place in the European Under-21 Junior championship, having scored 11 points following a pointless ride in his first outing.

Garrad also won the Silver Helmet during the season, but only kept it for one day, taking it from Edinburgh's Mark Fiora on 22 April and losing it the following night to Steve McDermott at Berwick.

## 1983 National League

| Date | H/A | Opponent | W/L | Score |
|---|---|---|---|---|
| 10 April | H | Long Eaton | W | 62-34 |
| 17 April | H | Scunthorpe | D | 48-48 |
| 22 April | A | Edinburgh | L | 43-53 |
| 23 April | A | Berwick | L | 39-57 |
| 24 April | H | Crayford | W | 49-46 |
| 2 May | H | Boston | W | 58-38 |
| 4 May | A | Long Eaton | W | 49-47 |
| 5 May | A | Middlesbrough | L | 40-56 |
| 6 May | A | Glasgow | L | 37-59 |
| 8 May | H | Peterborough | W | 64-32 |
| 14 May | A | Canterbury | L | 37-58 |
| 5 June | H | Canterbury | W | 59-37 |
| 12 June | H | Berwick | W | 52-44 |
| 26 June | H | Stoke | W | 59-34 |
| 3 July | H | Exeter | W | 60-35 |
| 5 July | A | Crayford | L | 44-50 |
| 7 July | A | Oxford | L | 47-49 |
| 10 July | H | Middlesbrough | L | 47-49 |
| 17 July | H | Milton Keynes | W | 59-36 |
| 19 July | A | Milton Keynes | L | 44-51 |
| 25 July | A | Scunthorpe | L | 40-56 |
| 7 August | A | Boston | L | 45-50 |

| 8 August | A | Newcastle | L | 45-50 |
| 20 August | A | Stoke | L | 46-50 |
| 21 August | H | Edinburgh | W | 54-42 |
| 21 August | H | Glasgow | W | 58-36 |
| 28 August | A | Mildenhall | L | 40-55 |
| 29 August | H | Mildenhall | W | 51-45 |
| 4 September | H | Oxford | W | 54-42 |
| 5 September | A | Exeter | L | 41-55 |
| 6 September | A | Weymouth | L | 36-60 |
| 25 September | H | Newcastle | L | 45-51 |
| 30 September | A | Peterborough | L | 36-60 |
| 2 October | H | Weymouth | W | 55-40 |

P34 W15 D1 L18
For 1,643 Against 1,605
Position: eleventh (out of eighteen)

## Knock-Out Cup

First Round
Bye
Second Round

| Date | H/A | Opponent | W/L | Score |
|---|---|---|---|---|
| 22 May | H | Oxford | W | 51-45 |
| 9 June | A | Oxford | W | 51-45 |

Won 102-90 on aggregate
Third Round

| Date | H/A | Opponent | W/L | Score |
|---|---|---|---|---|
| 14 August | H | Exeter | W | 55-41 |
| 15 August | A | Exeter | L | 32-64 |

Lost 87-105 on aggregate

## 1983 National League and Knock-Out Cup

| Name | M | R | Pts | BP | Total | CMA |
|---|---|---|---|---|---|---|
| Marvyn Cox | 37 | 210 | 509 | 7 | 516 | 9.83 |
| Bob Garrad | 38 | 213 | 483 | 11 | 494 | 9.28 |
| Steve Naylor | 22 | 106 | 188 | 24 | 212 | 8.00 |
| Peter Johns | 8 | 37 | 57 | 8 | 65 | 7.03 |
| Kerry Gray | 23 | 120 | 152 | 20 | 172 | 5.73 |
| Steve Bryenton | 38 | 200 | 243 | 42 | 285 | 5.70 |
| Andrew Silver | 9 | 29 | 28 | 6 | 34 | 4.69 |
| Kevin Bowen | 15 | 60 | 59 | 10 | 69 | 4.60 |
| Chris Chaplin | 24 | 90 | 53 | 12 | 65 | 2.89 |
| Terry Broadbank | 11 | 39 | 24 | 4 | 28 | 2.87 |
| John Barclay | 16 | 61 | 15 | 4 | 19 | 1.25 |

# 1984

For the opening fixture of 1984 – a home challenge match against Milton Keynes – six of the regular 1983 squad turned out: Garrad, Naylor, Silver, Johns, Bryenton and Gray, with Chaplin filling the seventh place. There were two names missing: Kevin Bowen, who had retired and, of course, Marvyn Cox, who, to nobody's surprise, had left for the higher sphere of racing on offer in the British League. The Rockets won the match easily enough, 47-31, with Garrad scoring a maximum and Naylor paid 11. The pleasingly unexpected high return of Chris Chaplin with nine points gave the team high hopes that they would be able to weather the loss of Cox and put in a good season.

However, in the second half of the match, Naylor fell and fractured a wrist, putting him out for some time. Reality struck home on 13 April as Rye House travelled to Hackney for the first leg of the Knock-Out Cup first round tie and found themselves on the wrong end of a 53-25 beating. Garrad scored over half his team's points with 13. Next in line was Silver with five. Although Silver rode better in the second leg at home, equalling Garrad's score of ten, the Rockets went down 42-36 to lose the tie 95-61 on aggregate. While Rye House had some promising juniors who could come good at times, it was obvious that there was only one real heat-leader-class rider, Bobby Garrad, and the early optimism dissipated very quickly. Len Silver realised he had to move quickly to shore up the team and he decided that his best option was to recall former faithful Rye House servant Kelvin Mullarkey. Although Mullarkey had quit the Rockets at the end of 1982, he was, in fact, still a Rye House contracted rider and was only on loan to Canterbury. Silver's decision to recall Mullarkey did not go down at all well with the Canterbury management, who slapped an injunction on him in an attempt to prevent him from riding for the Rockets. Their manager, Maurice Morley, complained that he had not been given enough notice by either the Rye House management or the rider himself for him to find a suitable replacement. Mullarkey himself was keen to move back to his old track because he was finding some difficulty in riding for Canterbury on their Saturday match day due to business commitments. It was made clear that Mullarkey was not just a temporary replacement for Naylor but was a permanent signing. In fact, so under-strength were the Rockets that, even when Naylor returned, they would still be under the 45 race-point limit then in force.

Shortly after this, Peter Johns left to join Arena Essex and Steve Bryenton was injured. Nevertheless, with Garrad and Mullarkey now at the top of the order and Silver and Chaplin continuing to improve, the next home match saw a revived Rockets team beat Milton Keynes 44-34. Silver, in particular, was looking as though he could easily take the place of Cox in scoring power before the season was over, but after scoring at an average of 9.5 in his first four league outings, he injured his ankle and shoulder and missed a few matches.

If Rye House could have got their full team together during the season, they might have done reasonably well. With Garrad, Naylor and Mullarkey as the three heat leaders, and the ever-improving Silver and Chaplin backing them up, and with Bryenton and Gray in the numbers six and seven spots, it was a team that could have done well in the league, but there was hardly a time when the Rockets were able to put out their strongest line-up.

Len Silver's son, Andrew, rode for Rye House from 1983 to 1985.

When they did, on 10 June against Glasgow, they were able to score a comfortable 43-35 victory. But, not long after Naylor and Silver returned from injury, it was Mullarkey's turn to be sidelined through injury. Bryenton came back and went out again for domestic reasons. A number of junior riders came in to make up the numbers, including Michael Keepe, Mark Chessell and Gary Rolls, but none of them set the Hoddesdon raceway alight, although, once again, all of them showed promise in the true Rye House junior tradition.

In the end, it was a very average season for the Rockets. Once again, they were virtually unbeatable at home, losing just once to Middlesbrough, who actually finished below them in the league, while away from home they failed to win a single match, stretching their record of defeats to twenty-nine consecutive matches. It meant a middle-of-the-table end for the team as they finished eighth out of sixteen teams. Strangely enough, their average score for the season, home and away, was 39-39.

With Garrad able to steer clear of the injury jinx that seemed to affect the rest of the team, he once again put in a solid performance throughout the year, finishing with an 8.69 average. He also took the Silver Helmet from Milton Keynes' Kevin Smart on 29 April and defended it twice before losing it to Dave Perks at Long Eaton on 9 May.

Naylor and Mullarkey gave good backing, injuries permitting, both finishing with plus-seven averages, but the real talk of the terraces was the promoter's son, Andrew Silver. After his return from injury, he did not quite capture his early season form but, nevertheless, he did well enough to force his way into the second heat-leader position with an average of 7.79. If, as looked likely, he could follow in the footsteps of riders like Garrad, Fiala and Cox, and if Chaplin could also continue his more steady improvement, it looked as though the good times would return to Hoddesdon in 1985.

## 1984 National League

| Date | H/A | Opponent | W/L | Score |
| --- | --- | --- | --- | --- |
| 29 April | H | Milton Keynes | W | 44-33 |
| 1 May | A | Milton Keynes | L | 37-41 |
| 7 May | H | Canterbury | W | 42-36 |
| 9 May | A | Long Eaton | L | 31-47 |
| 10 May | A | Middlesbrough | L | 26-52 |
| 11 May | A | Glasgow | L | 35-43 |
| 12 May | A | Stoke | L | 35-43 |
| 19 May | A | Canterbury | L | 33-45 |
| 1 June | A | Hackney | L | 30-48 |
| 10 June | H | Glasgow | W | 43-35 |
| 21 June | A | Arena Essex | L | 36-41 |
| 24 June | H | Middlesbrough | L | 37-40 |
| 1 July | H | Stoke | W | 43-35 |
| 8 July | H | Hackney | W | 42-36 |
| 13 July | A | Edinburgh | L | 37-41 |
| 15 July | H | Weymouth | W | 47-31 |
| 29 July | H | Long Eaton | W | 44-34 |
| 30 July | A | Scunthorpe | L | 35-42 |
| 5 August | H | Berwick | W | 44-32 |
| 19 August | H | Edinburgh | W | 58-20 |
| 26 August | A | Mildenhall | L | 34-44 |
| 27 August | H | Mildenhall | W | 44-34 |
| 27 August | H | Boston | W | 52-26 |
| 9 September | H | Peterborough | W | 44-22* |
| 11 September | A | Weymouth | L | 28-50 |
| 14 September | A | Peterborough | L | 25-52 |

| 16 September | H | Scunthorpe | W | 45-33 |
| 30 September | H | Arena Essex | W | 43-34 |
| 6 October | A | Berwick | L | 34-43 |

★ Match abandoned after eleven heats. Result stands

P30 W14 D0 L16

For 1,159 Against 1,160

Position: eighth (out of sixteen)

## Knock-Out Cup

First Round

| Date | H/A | Opponent | W/L | Score |
|---|---|---|---|---|
| 13 April | A | Hackney | L | 25-53 |
| 15 April | H | Hackney | L | 36-42 |

Lost 61-95 on aggregate

## 1984 National League and Knock-Out Cup

| Name | M | R | Pts | BP | Total | CMA |
|---|---|---|---|---|---|---|
| Bob Garrad | 32 | 150 | 309 | 17 | 326 | 8.69 |
| Andrew Silver | 27 | 117 | 203 | 25 | 228 | 7.80 |
| Steve Naylor | 19 | 77 | 144 | 4 | 148 | 7.69 |
| Kelvin Mullarkey | 24 | 111 | 173 | 24 | 197 | 7.10 |
| Kerry Gray | 26 | 112 | 141 | 19 | 160 | 5.71 |
| Steve Bryenton | 19 | 74 | 82 | 19 | 101 | 5.46 |
| Chris Chaplin | 30 | 95 | 96 | 21 | 117 | 4.93 |
| Michael Keepe | 10 | 28 | 24 | 3 | 27 | 3.86 |
| Mark Chessell | 8 | 27 | 24 | 1 | 25 | 3.70 |
| Gary Rolls | 11 | 29 | 17 | 7 | 24 | 3.31 |

# 1985

The season started without Gray, who decided to return home to Australia, and Bryenton, who moved to Canterbury. Their places were taken by Alastair Stevens, on loan from Oxford, and Neil Cotton, signed up from Peterborough. The opening home match of the season on 31 March saw the two join Garrad, Naylor, Mullarkey, Silver and Chaplin for what, it was hoped, would be the regular line-up for the year. Although the Rockets were able to put out the team they wanted, it was a disastrous start as they went down to an overwhelming 45-30 defeat to Arena Essex in the Herts/Essex Cup first leg. Only Garrad looked able to live with the Hammers, scoring 12 points from five rides. Stevens had a terrible start for his new club, being excluded in his first race for delaying the start. Things could only get better! Or could they? In the second leg, away at the Thurrock Raceway, the Rockets lost by the even bigger margin of 47-31 and then, in the three team Easter Triangle first leg at Hackney, the Rockets were once again badly beaten coming third with 27 points to Hackney's 51 and Mildenhall's 30. The Rockets even came third in their home leg, scoring just 33 points to Hackney's 40 and Mildenhall's 35.

Just as things were looking bad for the Rockets' prospects in 1985, they opened their National League account on 21 April with an excellent 47-30 win over Long Eaton and a fine all-round performance. Silver scored a 12-point maximum, while Garrad backed him up with eight paid 10 and Chaplin, Naylor and Mullarkey all put in a solid seven each.

Sadly, it was a bit of a false dawn as, in the next home league match, the Rockets were crushed 54-23 by Hackney. By this time, Naylor was once again out through injury with Rye House using rider replacement. Naylor was to remain out for the rest of the season, taking over as team manager during the summer. Of the 23 points, Silver and Garrad scored 17 between them. The first round, first leg of the National League fours followed at Wimbledon; the scores were Wimbledon 43, Arena Essex 25, Mildenhall 21 and Rye House a woeful 7. Worse than that for Rye House, with Naylor already sidelined, Mullarkey crashed in heat three and broke his collarbone. From an already poor start to the season with all their riders, the Rockets had now lost Naylor and Mullarkey, while Chaplin had become disillusioned with the state of British speedway after spending a winter in California and decided to retire. To try and overcome the difficulties, two new riders appeared for Rye House on 19 May against Canterbury: Rob Woffinden and former British Junior champion Keith Millard. Woffinden, in particular, had a good debut, scoring eight points and helping Rye House to win the match 42-36. Michael Keepe was also brought back into the side. Canterbury, however, immediately slapped in a protest, saying that the Rockets had used the three riders without proper permission. Three months later, the Control Board ruled in Canterbury's favour and the ten points contributed by the three were deducted from the Rye House score, leaving Canterbury the winners, 36-32.

Two defeats in a season at Fortress Hoddesdon was almost unheard of, but worse was to come as, in a five-match home sequence, starting on 18 August with a 41-36 defeat to Middlesbrough, the Rockets lost three of them. Although the sequence ended with an impressive 57-21 win over Edinburgh with no less than four riders, Garrad, Mullarkey, Silver and Stevens, scoring maximums, by the end of the season, Rye House had lost five home matches, something hitherto unthinkable. Strangely, although this was Rye House's worst home record since 1981, they managed to win two away matches during the year, 44-33 at Long Eaton and 40-38 at Eastbourne, their best away record since 1982.

Both Garrad and Mullarkey's form seemed to have deserted them to some extent, with Garrad's average over the year dropping to 6.34 and Mullarkey's to 5.91. Mullarkey was, however, still the team man he had always been and, in spite of dropping points, managed to turn in 36 bonus points, more than any other Rye House rider. Apart from his year at Canterbury, Mullarkey had now been with the club ten years since 1975 and he was rewarded with a Testimonial, which took place on 27 October, having been postponed from August due to bad weather. After the meeting, Mullarkey announced his retirement.

Ali Stevens, a heat leader for the Rockets in 1985 and 1986.

With their drop in form and the virtual non-appearances of Naylor and Chaplin, it was just as well that Silver continued his rise to the top, becoming the Rockets' number one with an average of 8.61, with Stevens not far behind him on 7.37. Once again, it was a case of hoping that Rye House could keep hold of the two for the following season. Both were still teenagers – Silver was eighteen, while Stevens was just sixteen – with extremely bright-looking futures ahead of them. Stevens' astonishing rise from junior to top-class National League heat-leader in one season culminated in his scoring double figures in every one of his final nine league home matches. Silver did even better by scoring paid double figures in his last nine matches home and away. Over the whole season, his lowest home score was eight. He also won the Silver Helmet on 14 July from Steve Wilcox of Middlesbrough and defended it three times before losing it to Middlesbrough's Martin Dixon on 18 August. Fortunately, he was an ever-present in the side, while Stevens missed just one match. If not for these two, the season would have been an unmitigated disaster, although Woffinden too was just coming good when he broke his collarbone twice and missed ten matches. Injuries played havoc with Rye House and during the season they used no less than eighteen riders. As it was, the Rockets dropped to thirteenth place in the league and, although they managed to get through to the third round of the Knock-Out Cup, this was only by virtue of the fact that they received byes in both the first and second rounds.

Just before the end of the season, Silver brought Julian Parr into the team from Birmingham. He only rode in three matches but posted an average of 9.23. It was to be Silver's last act as Rye House promoter as he handed over control of Rye House to Ronnie Russell. Russell had had plenty of experience of speedway supporting his brother, Terry, at Crayford and Hackney. Silver's departure marked the end of an era at Rye House, but was not, of course, the last Rye House would see of 'Leaping Len'.

Before the end of the year, Russell stated that it was his intention to keep Garrad, Silver, Stevens and Parr in the team, though he was concerned that Oxford would want to recall Stevens, following his amazingly successful debut year.

Russell also had plans for the track as he proposed building a new two-metre high safety fence and improving the track lighting. Norman Kingsbury was brought in as team manager.

## 1985 National League

| Date | H/A | Opponent | W/L | Score |
|---|---|---|---|---|
| 21 April | H | Long Eaton | W | 47-30 |
| 30 April | A | Milton Keynes | L | 36-42 |
| 10 May | A | Peterborough | L | 24-54 |
| 12 May | H | Hackney | L | 23-54 |
| 19 May | H | Canterbury | L | 32-36* |
| 24 May | A | Birmingham | L | 33-44 |
| 31 May | A | Hackney | L | 29-49 |
| 8 June | A | Canterbury | L | 27-51 |
| 9 June | H | Milton Keynes | W | 51-26 |
| 10 June | A | Exeter | L | 30-48 |
| 11 June | A | Poole | L | 23-55 |
| 16 June | H | Eastbourne | W | 39-37 |
| 23 June | H | Arena Essex | W | 43-35 |
| 27 June | A | Arena Essex | L | 34-44 |
| 30 June | H | Ellesmere Port | W | 43-35 |
| 12 July | A | Edinburgh | L | 34-44 |
| 13 July | A | Berwick | L | 21-57 |
| 11 August | H | Berwick | W | 42-36 |
| 14 August | A | Long Eaton | W | 44-33 |
| 15 August | A | Middlesbrough | L | 29-49 |

| 18 August | H | Middlesbrough | L | 36-41 |
| 25 August | A | Mildenhall | L | 31-47 |
| 26 August | H | Mildenhall | L | 38-40 |
| 26 August | H | Glasgow | W | 54-24 |
| 28 August | A | Wimbledon | L | 31-47 |
| 1 September | H | Wimbledon | W | 40-37 |
| 7 September | A | Eastbourne | W | 40-38 |
| 8 September | H | Poole | L | 38-40 |
| 8 September | H | Edinburgh | W | 57-21 |
| 13 September | A | Ellesmere Port | L | 22-56 |
| 22 September | H | Stoke | W | 51-25 |
| 27 September | A | Glasgow | L | 33-45 |
| 28 September | A | Stoke | L | 33-45 |
| 29 September | H | Peterborough | W | 41-36 |
| 6 October | H | Exeter | W | 57-21 |
| 13 October | H | Birmingham | W | 49-29 |

* Score amended after appeal to Control Board. Original score 42-36
P36 W15 D0 L21
For 1,330 Against 1,454
Position thirteenth (out of nineteen)

## Knock-Out Cup

First Round
Bye
Second Round
Bye
Third round

| Date | H/A | Opponent | W/L | Score |
|------|-----|----------|-----|-------|
| 2 June | H | Middlesbrough | L | 37-41 |
| 14 July | A | Middlesbrough | L | 33-45 |

Lost 70-86 on aggregate

## 1985 National League and Knock-Out Cup

| Name | M | R | Pts | BP | Total | CMA |
|------|---|---|-----|----|----|-----|
| Andrew Silver | 38 | 191 | 385 | 26 | 411 | 8.61 |
| Alastair Stevens | 37 | 166 | 274 | 32 | 306 | 7.37 |
| Rob Woffinden | 22 | 100 | 155 | 16 | 171 | 6.84 |
| Bob Garrad | 34 | 154 | 216 | 28 | 244 | 6.34 |
| Kelvin Mullarkey | 34 | 149 | 184 | 36 | 220 | 5.91 |
| Kevin Brice | 23 | 69 | 70 | 6 | 76 | 4.41 |
| Neil Cotton | 10 | 24 | 20 | 6 | 26 | 4.33 |
| Keith Millard | 13 | 36 | 25 | 3 | 28 | 3.11 |
| Gary Rolls | 10 | 27 | 17 | 4 | 21 | 3.11 |
| Nigel Leaver | 8 | 19 | 8 | 2 | 10 | 2.11 |

# 1986

In what turned out to be a bit of an omen for the new promotion, the first three meetings of the new season were rained off, and Rye House were unable to start until 20 April. When the season did get underway at Hoddesdon, it was to prove perhaps even more of an omen as the Rockets went down 49-29 to Hackney in the second leg of the Easter Trophy. There was a third omen of what was in store when, before the season even started, Stevens fractured his skull, broke both his wrists, broke two bones in his neck and fractured two vertebrae in a non-speedway-related accident. Fortunately, he recovered before Rye House's first match of the year.

Although Russell had been able to hold on to Stevens, he had been unable to persuade Silver to stay, as he moved instead to Arena Essex. In his place, he brought in ex-England international Paul Woods for a reported fee of £12,000, along with former Hackney heat leader Paul Bosley, to take Mullarkey's place, and Linden Warner. With a line-up consisting of Garrad, Stevens, Parr, Woods, Bosley, Warner and Kevin Brice, there were high hopes that the Rockets could get back to their winning ways. The poor form shown against Hackney dented these hopes but there followed a strange sequence of matches as the team tried to settle down. After the Hackney defeat, they managed a Knock-Out Cup double over Exeter, but then lost home and away to Eastbourne. This was followed by three consecutive wins, 42-36 at home to Edinburgh, 40-37 away at Long Eaton – in which both Stevens and Woods scored full maximums – and 40-38 at home to Newcastle. But the roller-coaster season continued as they then lost their next three matches. Already showing major inconsistency, the Rockets then suffered from their usual injury problem as first Parr broke his collarbone and then Warner broke his. Bosley followed, aggravating an old back injury, and then it was the turn of junior Colin Lambkin, who had been brought in to cover for the injuries. He broke his leg. Parr returned only to break his other collarbone. Fortunately, Woods, Stevens and Garrad kept going all season and between them missed just one match, home against Canterbury on 7 September, after Woods suffered concussion at Peterborough two days previously.

The worst moment for Rye House came on 1 July when they were humiliated by a rampant Poole team to the tune of 60-17. Worse still, the second half was a National Junior League match which saw the juniors beaten 19-4.

Two successive home defeats followed: on 20 July, 41-37 to Arena Essex and on 27 July, 40-38 to Middlesbrough. Russell tried to counter the injury crisis by signing up Alan Mogridge from Canterbury. At first, Mogridge's introduction to the side seemed to turn the tide as he helped the Rockets to away wins at Canterbury, 41-36, and Glasgow, 42-36. Unfortunately, Mogridge was then recalled by his parent club, Hackney, and Rye House failed to win another away match all season.

Paul Woods, Rye House's leading rider in 1986 and 1987, seen here leading teammate Julian Parr and Mark Courtney.

At least, after the 27 July loss to Middlesbrough, the Rockets managed to remain unbeaten at home and by the end of the year just managed to maintain their middle of the table position, finishing eleventh out of twenty teams.

Following their victory over Exeter in the first round of the Knock-Out Cup, the Rockets lost out to Hackney in the second round by an aggregate score of 83-72. The Junior team fared even worse than the main team, finishing last out of eight in the National Junior League Southern Section with just three home wins to their credit out of six and seven straight away losses. Lambkin was top junior with an average of 7.41.

Paul Woods became the new Rockets' number one with an average of 8.97. For the time he was with them, Mogridge slotted in at number two, while Ali Stevens was the third heat leader with 7.47. It was a steady year of consolidation without the progress that might have been expected of him after his first sensational year, although he was chosen to race for Young England against the Wallabies in the three-match Test series.

Bosley managed to score at just over six per match, while Brice and Garrad managed a shade short of 5.50 each. At the reserve end, Parr and Linden scored at just over and just under five a match respectively. It was a good solid middle and lower order, but what was really lacking was a second top-class heat leader to join Woods.

As well as the start of the season being affected by the weather, three further meetings were rained off during the year. What with that and the less than consistent performance from the team, support began to dwindle and Russell began to get a little concerned about the future of Rye House, though he was sure that if only he could get together a winning team the crowds would return.

1986 was also Bob Garrad's Testimonial year. He had now ridden for Rye House for eleven years, since his first appearance as a sixteen-year-old back in 1976. During that time, he had been the Rockets' number one on four occasions, including 1980, the year of the League Championship. Altogether, he had ridden in 421 matches for the Rockets; more than any other rider. There is no doubt that he had been a great and loyal servant to Rye House and the fans turned out in their thousands to salute him on 5 October. Russell was also determined to do Garrad justice and he got together a meeting which included the World Champion, Hans Nielsen, as well as many old Rockets' favourites, including Kevin Smith, Marvyn Cox and Andrew Silver. Following the meeting, at the grand old age of twenty-six, Garrad hung up his leathers.

## 1986 National League

| Date | H/A | Opponent | W/L | Score |
|---|---|---|---|---|
| 11 April | A | Birmingham | L | 36-42 |
| 4 May | A | Eastbourne | L | 37-41 |
| 5 May | H | Eastbourne | L | 36-42 |
| 11 May | H | Edinburgh | W | 42-36 |
| 14 May | A | Long Eaton | W | 40-37 |
| 18 May | H | Newcastle | W | 40-38 |
| 24 May | A | Boston | L | 31-47 |
| 1 June | H | Wimbledon | W | 40-38 |
| 15 June | H | Poole | W | 42-35 |
| 16 June | A | Newcastle | L | 30-48 |
| 18 June | A | Mildenhall | L | 24-51 |
| 1 July | A | Poole | L | 17-60 |
| 6 July | H | Long Eaton | W | 45-31 |
| 6 July | H | Stoke | W | 42-36 |
| 10 July | A | Middlesbrough | L | 28-50 |
| 11 July | A | Edinburgh | L | 29-48 |
| 20 July | H | Arena Essex | L | 37-41 |

| 24 July | A | Arena Essex | L | 33-44 |
| 27 July | H | Middlesbrough | L | 38-40 |
| 2 August | A | Canterbury | W | 41-36 |
| 4 August | A | Exeter | L | 28-50 |
| 8 August | A | Hackney | L | 35-43 |
| 9 August | A | Stoke | L | 26-51 |
| 15 August | A | Glasgow | W | 42-36 |
| 16 August | A | Berwick | L | 27-51 |
| 17 August | H | Milton Keynes | W | 45-33 |
| 20 August | A | Wimbledon | L | 32-44 |
| 31 August | H | Hackney | W | 41-37 |
| 5 September | A | Peterborough | L | 36-41 |
| 7 September | H | Canterbury | W | 40-38 |
| 14 September | H | Berwick | W | 42-36 |
| 21 September | H | Mildenhall | L | 34-44 |
| 21 September | H | Birmingham | W | 44-31 |
| 23 September | A | Milton Keynes | L | 36-42 |
| 28 September | H | Peterborough | W | 46-32 |
| 28 September | H | Boston | W | 45-33 |
| 12 October | H | Glasgow | W | 42-36 |
| 26 October | H | Exeter | W | 37-24 |

P38 W18 D0 L20

For 1,386 Against 1,543

Position: eleventh (out of twenty)

## Knock-Out Cup

First Round

| Date | H/A | Opponent | W/L | Score |
|---|---|---|---|---|
| 21 April | A | Exeter | W | 41-37 |
| 27 April | H | Exeter | W | 55-23 |

Won 96-60 on aggregate

Second Round

| Date | H/A | Opponent | W/L | Score |
|---|---|---|---|---|
| 27 June | A | Hackney | L | 30-48 |
| 29 June | H | Hackney | W | 42-35 |

Lost 72-83 on aggregate

## 1986 National League and Knock-Out Cup

| Name | M | R | Pts | BP | Total | CMA |
|---|---|---|---|---|---|---|
| Paul Woods | 41 | 177 | 391 | 6 | 397 | 8.97 |
| Alan Mogridge | 18 | 77 | 123 | 22 | 145 | 7.53 |
| Alastair Stevens | 42 | 173 | 301 | 22 | 323 | 7.47 |
| Paul Bosley | 32 | 125 | 176 | 12 | 188 | 6.02 |
| Kevin Brice | 39 | 150 | 173 | 32 | 205 | 5.47 |
| Bob Garrad | 42 | 155 | 180 | 30 | 210 | 5.42 |
| Julian Parr | 30 | 94 | 101 | 17 | 118 | 5.02 |
| Linden Warner | 35 | 99 | 96 | 18 | 114 | 4.61 |
| Colin Lambkin | 9 | 19 | 2 | 1 | 3 | 0.63 |

Barry Thomas first rode at Rye House in 1970 and
returned as a member of the 1987 team.

## 1987

If 1986 didn't go quite as well as hoped for, 1987 was to turn out to be an unmitigated disaster.
Following Garrad's retirement, Bosley also announced his retirement and Stevens, as expected,
was recalled to Oxford. Their places were filled with Gary Rolls and Barry Thomas, by then in
the veteran stage of his career, and Kevin Teager who was talked out of retirement. Theoretically,
the team seemed to be on a par with the 1986 team and, although maybe a challenge for top
honours was a bit too much to hope for, there was reason to expect a year of consolidation and
a base for a future assault on the league title.

Rye House opened the league season with a 43-34 home win over Milton Keynes. The top
two scorers were Teager with ten and Thomas with nine. With the other newcomer, Rolls, also
doing well, winning heat eight and scoring a total of four from the reserve spot, it looked at this
very early stage as though Russell may have made some very shrewd signings. As this was the
first match of the season in the whole of the National League, it meant that Rye House were
top of the table. Unfortunately, that was the only time they were to see that end of the table all
season, as there then followed a run of four defeats, two at home and two away, with both the
away defeats being by large margins: 56-22 at Wimbledon and 55-23 at Eastbourne. There was
a brief respite on 13 May as Rye House managed to score an away win at Long Eaton, 41-37,
thanks to two 5-1s in the last two heats and 11 points each from Woods and Thomas, but, in
truth, this was just a one-off anomaly in an otherwise very disappointing run. Parr, who had a
very disappointing start to the season, announced his retirement at the end of May following
a spectacular crash in the match against Newcastle on 31 May in which he went through the
fence and had to be stretchered off. His place was taken by former Rocket Steve Bryenton.
Shortly afterwards, Warner, who was also having a bad time of it, retired as well. Russell moved
quickly to bring in a rider who he thought was capable of kick-starting the Rockets' season.
Jamie Luckhurst had been a top heat leader with Wimbledon in 1985 and 1986 and had moved
up to the British League, joining Ipswich at the start of 1987, but he couldn't get to grips with
the higher grade of racing and Russell was able to sign him up for Rye House. His debut
match was pencilled in for 5 July, the home fixture against Long Eaton, but he failed to arrive
after experiencing mechanical problems on the way. The following week, however, it seemed
that the wait had been worth it as he scored 11 points against Edinburgh in the Rockets' 41-36
victory.

The next match, on 2 August, was a home tie against Berwick. Luckhurst managed one point and the Rockets went down 49-29. Of those 29 points, 22 were scored by Woods and Thomas. It is true that the track conditions were difficult following heavy rain, but, of course, it was the same for both sides. Even the most hardened Rye House supporters had to admit that Berwick showed greater willingness to overcome the conditions than the home side, with the exception of Woods and Thomas. Stung somewhat by the criticism of their performance, the Rockets next visited Arena Essex and put up a much better show, managing to take a point away from Thurrock with a 39-39 draw that could so easily have been a win for Rye House, as going in to the last heat the score was 37-35 in their favour. Out for the Rockets were Teager and Woods. Teager touched the tapes and was excluded, his place being taken by Gary Rolls. As the tapes went up, Woods and Rolls shot out the gate in the lead, but the referee, Frank Ebdon, called them back, ruling an unsatisfactory start. At the third attempt, the Hammers' Martin Goodwin went clear of Woods, with Rolls and Ian Humphreys locked in a titanic battle for the vital third place. For four laps there was little in it, but it was Humphreys who just crossed the line inches in front of Rolls to rob Rye House of the full two points. Nevertheless, it was a much better performance from the Rockets with Thomas scoring 11, Woods 10 and Luckhurst a paid eight.

After that, however, the season just collapsed completely as Rye House lost their next six matches, including four at home, and slumped to the foot of the table. Thomas, Teager and Luckhurst tried, but they were never really above second string standard, likewise Kevin Brice. Only Paul Woods was able to mix it with the stars of the opposing teams. He was the only real heat leader the Rockets had and, as Rye House discovered, you can't get very far with just one heat leader. As the season wore on, the Rockets suffered more retirements from disillusioned riders. Luckhurst only rode in seven matches before deciding it wasn't working out for him, then Bryenton quit, as did Gary Rolls, after a fall while riding against Middlesbrough. Rye House used rider replacement to cover for Luckhurst, while the places of the other two were taken by Rob Parish and Rob Fortune, but neither of them was able to breathe new life into the Rockets.

Rye House ended their dismal run of defeats on 13 September with a home win against Middlesbrough on a quagmire of a track that produced times eight or nine seconds slower than normal. But that was to be the last win they had in a season which fizzled out with four further defeats, the last two away at Peterborough and Berwick when, as if to epitomise the season as a whole, they went down 59-19 and 60-18 respectively.

The season ended with Rye House stone cold bottom of the league for the first time in their Second Division history. There was no relief in the Knock-Out Cup either as they were bundled out in the first round by Mildenhall, who won both legs: 66-30 at Mildenhall and 48-47 at Hoddesdon.

Paul Woods finished with a respectable average of 8.11, with Barry Thomas second on 6.93. Apart from Luckhurst's seven matches, which netted him an average of 6.40, the third heat-leader spot went to Kevin Brice on 5.10. This was about equal to the average of top-of-the-table Eastbourne's number six man. This lack of top riders saw Rye House slump to eight home defeats, the most they'd suffered since they had entered the league back in 1974. When they finally did obtain another heat leader, Kevin Jolly, on loan from Wimbledon for the end-of-season Kent/Herts Cup match against Canterbury, they were able to put together a winning score and beat the Crusaders, 42-36.

The only bright spot of the season was Paul Woods' success in winning the Silver Helmet on 13 May from Long Eaton's Gerald Short, but even that was because Short suffered an engine failure. Woods lost it the following night to Steve Wilcox of Middlesbrough.

It was a season Ronnie Russell, the team and supporters were only too happy to see the back of. The poor showing of the team had led to more supporters staying away, and the club was in some financial difficulty. Russell launched an appeal fund to help finance the club. He had in mind a target of £20,000 which he hoped to raise by getting 200 fans to put in £100 each. He also looked for sponsorship from local companies and had some success in this area.

But he knew that what he really needed was to strengthen the team for the 1988 campaign as this would be the only way to lay down a sound foundation for future success and therefore increase numbers through the gate.

As the season finished, however, there were two more pieces of bad news that threatened the whole future of the club. Firstly, the bank announced that they were giving Russell fourteen days to come up with a sound business plan for saving Rye House and, secondly, the Speedway Control Board ruled that Rye House still owed Andrew Silver £1,350 from his £9,000 transfer to Arena Essex two years before. The regulations stated that riders were entitled to 17.5 per cent of a transfer fee if they were sold by the club, but nothing if they requested a move themselves. Andrew Silver's case had been going on so long because there had been a dispute over whether he had requested a transfer or whether it was the club's decision. The Board decided in the end that Silver had not asked for a transfer and was therefore entitled to the 17.5 per cent.

For Russell, these two events were ones he could well have done without, especially as his £20,000 appeal was now gathering pace. Former rider Kelvin Mullarkey, for one, had already pledged his £100. But he was up against time and he had to meet a 1 January 1988 deadline for informing the National League whether Rye House would run in 1988 or not. As a consequence, Russell decided to go nationwide with his appeal and called for help from speedway supporters all over the country.

By the time Russell met the Supporters' Club on 20 December, he was able to announce the good news that he fully expected Rye House to run in 1988. Now he had to turn his attention to building a new team. His first two signings were juniors Martin Cobbin and John Wainwright, who were to alternate at the number seven spot.

*1987 National League*

| Date | H/A | Opponent | W/L | Score |
| --- | --- | --- | --- | --- |
| 6 April | H | Milton Keynes | W | 43-34 |
| 12 April | H | Wimbledon | L | 36-42 |
| 22 April | A | Wimbledon | L | 22-56 |
| 26 April | H | Poole | L | 36-42 |
| 3 May | A | Eastbourne | L | 23-55 |
| 4 May | H | Canterbury | W | 43-35 |
| 13 May | A | Long Eaton | W | 41-37 |
| 14 May | A | Middlesbrough | L | 23-55 |
| 15 May | A | Edinburgh | L | 31-46 |
| 19 May | A | Milton Keynes | L | 21-57 |
| 31 May | H | Newcastle | W | 46-31 |
| 6 June | A | Canterbury | L | 36-42 |
| 7 June | H | Exeter | W | 46-32 |
| 9 June | A | Poole | L | 24-54 |
| 27 June | A | Stoke | L | 22-56 |
| 5 July | H | Long Eaton | W | 43-34 |
| 12 July | H | Edinburgh | W | 41-36 |
| 2 August | H | Berwick | L | 29-49 |
| 13 August | A | Arena Essex | D | 39-39 |
| 16 August | H | Stoke | L | 32-46 |
| 23 August | H | Arena Essex | L | 36-39 |
| 31 August | H | Eastbourne | L | 33-45 |
| 6 September | H | Mildenhall | L | 33-39 |
| 7 September | A | Newcastle | L | 34-43 |
| 9 September | A | Mildenhall | L | 29-49 |
| 13 September | H | Middlesbrough | W | 40-36 |
| 14 September | A | Exeter | L | 29-49 |

| 20 September | H | Peterborough | L | 34-44 |
| 9 October | A | Peterborough | L | 19-59 |
| 24 October | A | Berwick | L | 18-60 |

P30 W8 D1 L21
For 982 Against 1,341
Position: sixteenth (out of sixteen)

## Knock-Out Cup

First Round

| Date | H/A | Opponent | W/L | Score |
|------|-----|----------|-----|-------|
| 24 May | A | Mildenhall | L | 30-66 |
| 25 May | H | Mildenhall | L | 47-48 |

Lost 77-115 on aggregate

## 1987 National League and Knock-Out Cup

| Name | M | R | Pts | BP | Total | CMA |
|------|---|---|-----|----|----|-----|
| Paul Woods | 31 | 146 | 288 | 8 | 296 | 8.11 |
| Barry Thomas | 31 | 142 | 228 | 18 | 246 | 6.93 |
| Jamie Luckhurst | 7 | 30 | 45 | 3 | 48 | 6.40 |
| Kevin Brice | 31 | 124 | 147 | 11 | 158 | 5.10 |
| Linden Warner | 19 | 69 | 147 | 15 | 86 | 4.99 |
| Kevin Teager | 31 | 128 | 123 | 31 | 154 | 4.81 |
| Gary Rolls | 21 | 63 | 56 | 14 | 70 | 4.44 |
| Rob Parish | 8 | 27 | 25 | 3 | 28 | 4.15 |
| Steve Bryenton | 10 | 23 | 19 | 4 | 23 | 4.00 |
| Julian Parr | 13 | 41 | 27 | 9 | 36 | 3.51 |

# 1988

Having battled hard to keep Rye House in business, Russell now found himself locked in a different sort of battle. Just as the 1988 season was about to start, his next two proposed signings created a furore in the National League. As well as an upper limit for team strength, there was also a lower limit that teams had to meet before they were allowed to take part in the league. In 1988, this was 38 points. Of the riders who had represented Rye House in 1987, no fewer than seven had said they would not be back: Thomas, Bryenton, Parr, Warner, Rolls, Luckhurst and Parish. The team average was already very low and Russell needed some top-class riders just to bring the team up to 38, never mind 45. As far as he could see, all the British riders were taken, so he looked abroad and came up with Denmark's Jens Rasmussen and Peter Schroek from Germany. The only problem was that foreign riders, apart from Australians and New Zealanders, were banned from the National League. Most of the other promoters protested but Russell maintained that it was the only way he could get a team together. Just as the season was about to start, a compromise settlement was reached. Rye House were allowed to use Rasmussen because he had been living in Great Britain for five years and had an English wife and child, but it was a definite no for Schroek.

The other riders signed up to start the season were Steve Wilcox, Mark Lyndon and Carl Chalcraft. Along with the survivors from 1987, Woods, Brice and Teager, they formed the basis of the Rockets team for the start of 1988.

The opening three home fixtures of the season gave the Rye House faithful some hope that things were going to be different this year. In particular, the form of Jens Rasmussen was quite astonishing. In the opening match, a challenge against Milton Keynes, he scored 13 points in the Rockets' 49-43 win. In the second, the Easter Triangle against Hackney and Mildenhall, he scored a maximum 12, although the Rockets themselves came second to Hackney – Hackney 46, Rye House 36, Mildenhall 26 – and in the third, the Herts-Essex Cup against Arena Essex, he scored a 15-point maximum in the 49-46 victory. With Paul Woods giving strong backing in each of these matches and the rest of the team beginning to settle into their mostly new surroundings, the previous year's nightmare was already beginning to look like a distant memory.

The opening league fixture of the season was away at Poole and, although the Rockets were heavily defeated, 60-36, it was not altogether too depressing a performance. Rasmussen scored a paid 12 but what was particularly hopeful was the form of Wilcox, who top scored with 14 well-earned points. The first home fixture was against Long Eaton and this time it was Brice's turn to top score with a paid maximum 15 points. Woods also scored a paid 15, but from six rides, and Rasmussen continued his purple patch with paid 11, which included an engine failure.

For some inexplicable reason, it all came crashing down the following week as the Rockets put up a miserable performance, losing at home to Edinburgh, 58-37. Rasmussen put in another great performance with 13 points and Woods supported him with paid nine and an engine failure, but after those two, the support seemed to disappear. Ironically, Edinburgh's top performer, with an unbeaten 18 points, was Jamie Luckhurst.

But it wasn't just the match score that caused problems. Russell had decided to include Schroeck in the team after all and Edinburgh rode the match under protest. The following week, Rye House again lost at home, this time to Berwick, 53-42. Once again, it was Rasmussen and Woods who carried the fight, this time with good support from Chalcraft. These three scored 39 of the 42 points between them and, after the optimistic start to the season, it looked as though they had not laid the ghost of 1987 to rest after all. The Rockets then fell at the first hurdle in the Knock-Out Cup, losing 97-94 to Peterborough.

Eventually, the National League promoters relented and sanctioned the signing of Schroeck, but he did not turn out to be the saviour Russell had hoped for and, after a few more matches, he was dropped from the side anyway.

Jens Rasmussen was the first European to ride in the National League when he signed for the Rockets in 1988.

As the season continued, Rasmussen and Woods continued to lead from the front, but behind them the others were having very inconsistent seasons. One week, Brice, Wilcox or Chalcraft might do well, the next they would score next to nothing. Away from home, the Rockets managed just one win all season, just as in 1987. This was at Long Eaton on 1 June, when, for once, all six team members came good together for a crushing 60-36 victory. At home, the inconsistency took its toll and the team won seven and lost seven, drawing one. Towards the end of the season, Schroeck returned to the team and top scored with 14 away at Middlesbrough on a night when Rasmussen and Woods were both absent.

At least Rye House had the satisfaction at the end of the season of not finishing bottom again: this 'honour' was reserved for Long Eaton. They had, in fact, risen two places to finish fourteenth out of sixteen. But it was far from what they had hoped for at the beginning of the season. Rasmussen was, of course, the undoubted success of the season. He averaged 9.28 over the season – the first Rye House rider to top the nine-point mark since Garrad and Cox five years previously. He also broke the track record, recording a time of 59.0 seconds on 4 September in the match against Poole. Woods gave excellent support, although his average was slightly down to 7.38, mainly due to persistent mechanical problems rather than a lack of determination or skill. Wilcox finished the season as third heat-leader on 6.27.

The final meeting at Rye House in 1988 was a best pairs event which was won by Mark Lyndon and Nigel Leaver. Kelvin Mullarkey made a reappearance and, with some typical daredevil riding that held the crowd spellbound, managed to score six points from his four rides. In many ways, the sight of a full-throttle Mullarkey was a nostalgic but poignant reminder of the team the supporters had once seen sporting the Rockets colours in the late 1970s and early '80s when they were the strongest force in the National League.

As the final-night firework display got underway, Russell came to the mike to make a farewell speech. He told the crowd that he had just promoted his last meeting at Rye House. The financial position was such that he felt he could no longer carry on and, although he hoped that someone else would be willing to take over the reigns, he held out little hope that this would in fact happen. Although all the riders said they would like to ride for the Rockets again in 1989, it seemed that there would be no team for them to ride for. As the supporters went home that night, many felt they had seen their last ever meeting at Rye House.

It later emerged that the main reason for Russell's decision to leave Rye House was a dispute over the stadium rental for 1989. The stadium wished to increase the rent from £10,000 per year to £30,000. With Russell deciding to pull out, the stadium owners contacted the National League promoters and said they were willing to compromise rather than see speedway disappear altogether. Following this communication, Russell arranged a meeting with Eddie Leslie, the stadium manager, and reported to the Supporters' Club that, in spite of the stadium's original stance that the terms for next year's lease were non-negotiable, it now seemed they were negotiable after all and he was hopeful that a settlement could be reached in time to enter a team into the league for 1989.

Following the meeting, a new rent was agreed as well as a number of other outstanding issues, such as use of the stadium pump. There was also hope that a long-term solution to the question of rent could be agreed to save the yearly uncertainty. However, there was one problem still remaining. In September, the small stand on the home straight had been demolished, but there was still a dispute over who should pay for this, the stadium or Rye House Speedway. The cost was £10,500 and neither side were willing to foot the bill. Russell reported to the next Supporters' Club meeting that he was now fifty per cent hopeful that the Rockets would run in 1989 with himself still in charge.

Towards the end of the year, Russell announced that he hoped to find a co-promoter to help out at Rye House and ease some of his financial burden as well as some of the workload, but he was unable to interest anyone because of the ongoing dispute over payment for the stand demolition.

## 1988 National League

| Date | H/A | Opponent | W/L | Score |
|---|---|---|---|---|
| 12 April | A | Poole | L | 36–60 |
| 17 April | H | Long Eaton | W | 55–41 |
| 24 April | H | Edinburgh | L | 37–58 |
| 27 April | A | Wimbledon | L | 32–64 |
| 1 May | H | Berwick | L | 42–53 |
| 22 May | H | Wimbledon | W | 51–45 |
| 23 May | A | Exeter | L | 44–52 |
| 29 May | A | Mildenhall | L | 40–56 |
| 1 June | A | Long Eaton | W | 60–36 |
| 12 June | H | Glasgow | L | 44–52 |
| 23 June | A | Arena Essex | L | 45–51 |
| 26 June | H | Peterborough | W | 51–44 |
| 10 July | H | Hackney | L | 33–61 |
| 15 July | A | Hackney | L | 34–62 |
| 17 July | H | Arena Essex | W | 50–46 |
| 29 July | A | Peterborough | L | 29–67 |
| 31 July | H | Exeter | W | 61–34 |
| 5 August | A | Glasgow | L | 38–58 |
| 6 August | A | Berwick | L | 28–68 |
| 21 August | H | Mildenhall | W | 49–47 |
| 28 August | A | Eastbourne | L | 34–60 |
| 29 August | H | Eastbourne | L | 47–48 |
| 4 September | H | Poole | L | 47–49 |
| 11 September | H | Middlesbrough | D | 48–48 |
| 17 September | A | Stoke | L | 33–63 |
| 18 September | H | Stoke | W | 50–45 |
| 25 September | H | Milton Keynes | L | 39–55 |
| 6 October | A | Middlesbrough | L | 46–50 |
| 7 October | A | Edinburgh | L | 41–55 |
| 18 October | A | Milton Keynes | L | 36–60 |

P30 W8 D1 L21
For 1,280 Against 1,588
Position: fourteenth (out of sixteen)

## Knock Out Cup

First Round

| Date | H/A | Opponent | W/L | Score |
|---|---|---|---|---|
| 13 May | A | Peterborough | L | 38–58 |
| 14 May | H | Peterborough | W | 56–39 |

Lost 94–97 on aggregate

## 1988 National League and Knock-Out Cup

| Name | M | R | Pts | BP | Total | CMA |
|---|---|---|---|---|---|---|
| Jens Rasmussen | 30 | 162 | 367 | 9 | 376 | 9.28 |
| Paul Woods | 24 | 133 | 254 | 16 | 270 | 8.12 |
| Steve Wilcox | 32 | 173 | 235 | 36 | 271 | 6.27 |
| Mark Lyndon | 27 | 136 | 171 | 19 | 190 | 5.59 |
| Kevin Brice | 28 | 127 | 126 | 18 | 144 | 4.54 |

| | | | | | |
|---|---|---|---|---|---|
| Carl Chalcraft | 28 | 119 | 110 | 24 | 134 | 4.50 |
| Peter Schroeck | 19 | 82 | 62 | 9 | 71 | 3.46 |
| John Wainwright | 18 | 45 | 27 | 3 | 30 | 2.67 |
| Kevin Teager | 12 | 42 | 20 | 5 | 25 | 2.38 |

# 1989

As the New Year started, Russell at last found his co-promoter in Barry Klatt, the former Mildenhall co-promoter, who, it was hoped, would be able to bring a lot of expertise with him and help Russell turn things around at Rye House. They announced that season ticket prices for the 1989 season would be £90 for adults and £40 for children and senior citizens.

As far as the riders went, they promised an incentive of £1,000 a point for their average at the end of the season if the Rockets won the league. They also proposed having an eight-man squad. Rasmussen, Woods, Brice, Chalcraft and Schroeck were retained from the 1988 team. The other three riders were new signings: Mel Taylor, an established star with Mildenhall, who had averaged over 10 points a match for the last two seasons, and Australians Glen Baxter and Jamie Fagg, who had finished third in the Australian Championship. Once again, it looked as though Rye House could at last shake off the last few seasons and put in a serious challenge for the league title. With Rasmussen, Taylor and Woods they now had three top-class heat leaders and, with some good class riders in support, things were at last looking up for the Rockets.

The season at Hoddesdon began on 27 March with the Easter Triangle second leg. It was a triumph for the Rockets as they won the tie with 43 points to Ipswich's 41 and Mildenhall's 24. Taylor top scored with a paid maximum of 12, Rasmussen and Chalcraft grabbed a paid 10 each and Schroeck, riding at reserve, scored six points from his two rides.

The Rockets began their official fixtures on 9 April with a Knock-Out Cup first round, first leg tie against Exeter. Once again, the Rockets were in the ascendant as they trounced the Falcons, 57-39. Rasmussen scored a 15-point maximum, Schroeck added a paid 14, Woods a paid 13 and Taylor 11 from four completed rides. The following night's return at Exeter, however, did not go according to plan and the Rockets found themselves on the end of an even bigger beating as Exeter thrashed them 62-34. Woods had a poor night, contributing just two points. Taylor, Rasmussen and Baxter were top scorers, all with paid tens. Sadly, it meant an early exit from the Cup by an aggregate score of 101-91.

Mel Taylor rode for Rye House from 1989 to 1991.

There was worse to come as Rye House lost their opening home league fixture to Hackney on 16 April, 50-45. It was a very unfortunate end to the meeting that finally did for the Rockets. Going into the last heat, heat sixteen, the scores were level at 45 each. With Rasmussen and Woods out for them, the Rockets were reasonably confident of at least a draw. Hackney's two riders were Andy Galvin and Paul Whittaker. As the tapes went up, the Rye House pair got a good start and, coming round in to the back straight, Rasmussen was in the lead with Woods in third place. Unfortunately, Woods and Whittaker collided and fell and the race had to be rerun. The referee, Frank Ebdon, immediately put on Woods' light as the main cause of the stoppage. In the rerun, Rasmussen once again got the start he needed and was leading as Galvin caught up to him. Once again, there was a collision, this time between Rasmussen and Galvin; both fell. There was a rerun and, again, it was the Rye House rider who was excluded, leaving just the two Hackney riders to potter round for a 5-0 and a 50-45 victory.

Although they had lost, there was an element of bad luck attached and, with Woods, Taylor and Rasmussen all going well, there was no reason to panic yet.

A run of three away matches followed, all of which Rye House lost, but by reasonably close margins. The one bright spot was Baxter scoring a 15-point maximum in the 52-44 away loss at Peterborough. Woods, however, did not seem to be his usual self in these away matches and it was suggested that maybe the fall he had against Hackney had affected him more than at first thought. He had received conflicting reports from the hospital: as first he was told that he'd chipped a bone in his hand, then that he'd broken his scaphoid and then that he'd not broken anything. Sadly, a visit to a specialist confirmed that he had, in fact, fractured his wrist, an injury that was to put him out for the rest of the season and revive memories of the injury jinx that had dogged Rye House for the last four or five years.

Fortunately, Baxter was now hitting top form and was only too ready to take over Woods' place as heat leader. In the next home match on 30 April, he scored 11 points in the Rockets' comprehensive 61-34 despatch of Middlesbrough. Rasmussen came up with yet another paid maximum. A good away win at Milton Keynes followed on 9 May as a paid maximum from Baxter plus scores of 13 from Taylor and 11 from Rasmussen helped the Rockets to a 52-43 victory. From then on, the pattern of home wins and away losses established itself until the Rockets lost at home by the narrowest margin possible, 48-47, to Stoke on 16 July. Another home loss followed on 6 August to Berwick while Taylor was missing through injury. The loss of Taylor for a couple of matches highlighted the problem with the Rockets team that had followed the loss of Woods early in the season. Yes, they had Rasmussen, Taylor and Baxter all performing well, but there was very little in the way of back-up. Brice would sometimes post a good score, but not always, and apart from him there was nothing. The Rockets lost at home again on 6 August, 57-38 to Berwick, in a match that Taylor missed. The following week, Rye House, still without Taylor, again lost at home, this time 49-46 to Arena Essex in the Herts/Essex Cup first leg.

Taylor returned for the next home match against Poole on 20 August, much against medical advice. But he wasn't the only returnee, as Rye House stunned the speedway world by announcing that former Rocket and darling of the crowd, thirty-eight-year-old Kelvin Mullarkey, was to make a comeback after a four-year absence. His appearance brought some welcome relief to a dispirited Rye House audience as he battled his way from the back in his typical never-say-die style and looked as though he had never been away. Sadly, although both Taylor and Mullarkey were back, the Rockets suffered their fourth home defeat in five matches. The match was also marred by an incident after heat ten when Taylor and Poole's Craig Boyce came to blows on the centre green after the latter had been excluded for unfair riding.

The run-in to the end of the season saw Rye House lose all their away matches and one more home match, against Ipswich on 3 September, when they went down 50.5-43.5. The season had promised much at the beginning, but the injury to Woods finished off any realistic chance they had of battling it out for honours, and the further loss of Taylor for a few matches during the season consigned them to the bottom end of the table as they finished up in fourteenth place out of eighteen teams.

Once again, the undoubted success of the season was Jens Rasmussen, who averaged 9.29. He was also the most successful Silver Helmet holder in the league as he won the title on 16 April from Hackney's Steve Schofield and successfully defended it seven times before losing it to David Norris of Eastbourne on 29 May. Behind him, Baxter and Taylor both turned in seven-plus averages. Next highest was Mullarkey, who averaged 5.63 in his 11 matches. Brice, Fagg, Schroeck and Chalcraft all hovered around the four-point mark and it was this long tail that really crippled the Rockets.

At the end of the season, Mullarkey retired again, saying he had only returned to help his old club out over a difficult patch. Brice and Taylor also banged in transfer requests.

After the season finished, the stadium owners announced a £2 million project of stadium improvements which included building a new grandstand on the home straight and a new pits area on the first bend. Along with the new building work, hardcore was put down on the car park to prevent the puddles which had always been a feature of the area.

## 1989 National League

| Date | H/A | Opponent | W/L | Score |
| --- | --- | --- | --- | --- |
| 16 April | H | Hackney | L | 45–50 |
| 10 April | A | Arena Essex | L | 45–51 |
| 26 April | A | Wimbledon | L | 45–51 |
| 28 April | A | Peterborough | L | 44–52 |
| 30 April | H | Middlesbrough | W | 61–34 |
| 7 May | H | Peterborough | W | 52–44 |
| 9 May | A | Milton Keynes | W | 52–43 |
| 14 May | H | Arena Essex | W | 53–42 |
| 29 May | H | Eastbourne | W | 51–45 |
| 2 June | A | Glasgow | L | 46–50 |
| 3 June | A | Berwick | L | 23–72 |
| 4 June | H | Long Eaton | W | 60–35 |
| 17 June | A | Stoke | L | 40–56 |
| 25 June | H | Exeter | W | 53–42 |
| 2 July | H | Wimbledon | W | 51–44 |
| 9 July | H | Edinburgh | W | 49–46 |
| 16 July | H | Stoke | L | 47–48 |
| 17 July | A | Newcastle | L | 46–50 |
| 28 July | A | Hackney | L | 35–61 |
| 30 July | H | Milton Keynes | W | 61–34 |
| 2 August | A | Long Eaton | L | 37–59 |
| 6 August | H | Berwick | L | 38–57 |
| 20 August | H | Poole | L | 44–51 |
| 21 August | A | Exeter | L | 37–59 |
| 23 August | A | Mildenhall | L | 46–50 |
| 27 August | A | Eastbourne | L | 37–59 |
| 28 August | H | Mildenhall | W | 55–41 |
| 31 August | A | Ipswich | L | 41–55 |
| 3 September | H | Ipswich | L | 43.5–50.5 |
| 7 September | A | Middlesbrough | L | 44–51 |
| 8 September | A | Edinburgh | L | 41–55 |
| 10 September | H | Glasgow | W | 52–44 |
| 12 September | A | Poole | L | 41–55 |
| 17 September | H | Newcastle | W | 49–46 |

P34 W13 D0 L21
For 1,564.5 Against 1,682.5
Position: fourteenth (out of eighteen)

## Knock-Out Cup

First Round

| Date | H/A | Opponent | W/L | Score |
|------|-----|----------|-----|-------|
| 9 April | H | Exeter | W | 57-39 |
| 10 April | A | Exeter | L | 34-62 |

Lost 91–101 on aggregate

## 1989 National League and Knock-Out Cup

| Name | M | R | Pts | BP | Total | CMA |
|------|---|---|-----|----|-------|-----|
| Jens Rasmussen | 36 | 192 | 416 | 30 | 446 | 9.29 |
| Glen Baxter | 35 | 192 | 363 | 20 | 383 | 7.98 |
| Mel Taylor | 33 | 171 | 326 | 6 | 332 | 7.77 |
| Paul Woods | 6 | 28 | 34 | 10 | 44 | 6.29 |
| Kelvin Mullarkey | 11 | 54 | 58 | 18 | 76 | 5.63 |
| Kevin Brice | 31 | 145 | 145 | 22 | 167 | 4.61 |
| Jamie Fagg | 25 | 103 | 91 | 16 | 107 | 4.16 |
| Peter Schroeck | 22 | 93 | 76 | 18 | 94 | 4.04 |
| Carl Chalcraft | 32 | 109 | 86 | 22 | 108 | 3.96 |
| Trevor O'Brien | 13 | 53 | 41.5 | 6 | 47.5 | 3.59 |

# The 1990s

## 1990

Rye House were able to hold on to their three heat leaders for the 1990 campaign after Taylor withdrew his transfer request as well as Jamie Fagg, but there was a new look about the rest of the team. Woods left for Eastbourne, Brice, after five years with the team, moved to Arena Essex, Schroeck transferred to Wimbledon, while Chalcraft joined Mullarkey in retirement. In their places, Russell and Klatt signed up Roger Johns from Wimbledon and Nigel Sparshott from Long Eaton. Once again, there was optimism as the season started that these five would form the basis of a team capable of taking on the best. Indeed, it seemed this optimism was well founded as Rye House opened the season on 25 March with a 57-37 defeat of Poole in a Challenge match, with Taylor, Rasmussen and Baxter all scoring well and Johns, Fagg and reserve Trevor O'Brien all scoring eight points. In fact, O'Brien scored a paid nine from three rides.

But the optimism was to crumble by the time the opening match of the season was over. Firstly, Taylor was injured before the league season even started. In the last heat of a Challenge match against Ipswich on 1 April, while attempting an outside overtake of Alan Mogridge on the third bend, Taylor crashed through the fence and broke his arm. He was not to return to racing until August.

As if that wasn't bad enough, on 8 April, in the Rockets' opening league fixture of the season against Peterborough, Baxter was involved in a three-man pile-up in heat twelve and broke his hand, while in the very next heat, Rasmussen also crashed and was taken to hospital

Trevor O'Brien rode for the Rockets during the difficult late 1980s and early '90s.

with suspected breaks in both legs. That Rye House lost the match 49-47 was the least of their worries given that they had now lost all three of their heat leaders.

The next day, Rye House were due to meet Exeter in a National League match. As it happened, during the winter the National League had decided to do away with guest riders under any circumstances, so the Rockets were facing the prospect of an away match at the County Ground knowing they were going to get hammered. However, a degree of common sense prevailed and it was agreed to turn the match into a Challenge match to allow Rye House the use of guests. So, with Andy Galvin and Frank Andersen in the team, they made the long trek to the South West but still lost 59-37.

Fortunately for Rye House, the news wasn't quite as bad as first feared and Rasmussen was declared fit for their next home match, the Easter Triangle first leg against Hackney and Arena Essex, as it was found he had not broken any bones after all. With Taylor and Baxter out and operating rider replacement, Rye House won the match with 39 points to Hackney's 38 and Arena Essex's 31. Although Rasmussen rode well for his ten points, the two heroes for the Rockets were O'Brien, who scored paid 11, and Johns who recorded paid 16. With the additional good news that Baxter wasn't as badly hurt as had first been feared, the Rockets' fans allowed a bit of optimism to creep back in to their thinking. Before he could return, Rye House lost two league matches, one away at Ipswich, 67-28, and one at home to Stoke, 49-45. Even when he did return, at home to Wimbledon on 29 April, the Rockets' were on the losing end of a narrow 49-47 scoreline.

However, the team came good for the next home match on 6 May against Exeter with Fagg and O'Brien both picking up 11 points. The next home match also resulted in a victory over Middlesbrough, 59-37. But that was about as good as it got for the Rockets for a while as they suffered more injuries, with Fagg breaking his leg and Johns missing the rest of the season with a broken scaphoid. There then followed a run of 10 matches without a single victory, including four at home. During this period, practically all of Rye House's points came from Rasmussen and Baxter, with O'Brien now and again putting in a good score.

Towards the end of this sequence, further disaster struck as Baxter fell in the match away at Glasgow on 6 July and broke his wrist, keeping him out for the next four matches.

With the team in dire straights and now anchored to the bottom of the league, they once again called on Kelvin Mullarkey to help them out in their hour of need. Sure enough, Mullarkey was only too willing to come to the aid of his old team and answered the call. His first reappearance came on 15 July in a home match against Milton Keynes. Although Mullarkey himself only scored one point, his very appearance seemed to inspire the team as they won their first match since 20 May, 51-45. Rasmussen scored a 21-point maximum while O'Brien weighed in with 13. Linden Warner, who had returned earlier in the season, added a further nine.

Taylor returned on 4 August in an away fixture at Eastbourne and the Rockets were more or less at full strength with a team consisting of Rasmussen, Taylor, Baxter, O'Brien, Mullarkey, Kevin Teager, who had also returned earlier in the season, and Scott Humphries, making his debut at reserve. It was not a happy ending, though, as Rye House went down 61-34, Taylor only managing to score 6 points.

The following week, Taylor was back to something approaching his best form and the Rockets managed to string together a run of three consecutive wins, including an away win at Wimbledon, 49-47. Unfortunately, the season finished with a run of four more defeats and Rye House finished in fifteenth place out of seventeen, having lost nine home matches.

They did not fare any better in the Knock-Out Cup, being knocked out in the second round by Milton Keynes, 101-90, after a bye in the first round.

Once again, a season that had promised much was wrecked by injury and all Rye House could do was struggle through to finish the season. Rasmussen was once again far and away Rye House's top rider, finishing with an average of 9.36. Behind him was Mel Taylor, whose 11 matches at the end of the season netted him 8.86 and showed what might have been had he not broken his arm.

On 16 September, in the home match against Glasgow, Mullarkey fell and never again returned to the track. It was a sad end for the Rockets' most loyal servant. Nevertheless, his fifteen-year career as a Rye House rider had been a wonderful example to other riders. His

The most popular rider to wear the Rockets' colours, Kelvin Mullarkey rode for Rye House on and off for fifteen years. Between 1975 and 1983 he was ever-present, riding in 295 consecutive matches. His all-action style and devotion to the team endeared him to the fans.

exuberant never-say-die attitude had been an outstanding feature of the team for ten years. He had been a heat leader for seven years, captain of the team that won the cup in 1979 and the league in 1980 and was responsible for holding the team together in the potentially disastrous 1981 season. His commitment to the team was second to none as his massive tally of bonus points in 1979 and 1980, in particular, showed. From September 1975 until he left for Canterbury on loan at the start of the 1983 season, he did not miss a single match for Rye House, racking up a total of 295 consecutive league appearances. In 1989, at the age of thirty-eight, he made himself available to answer the call of the club when they were in desperate trouble and did the same again in 1990. There is no doubt that Mullarkey had written himself into the Rye House record books as the most popular rider ever to wear the Rockets' colours

## 1990 National League

| Date | H/A | Opponent | W/L | Score |
| --- | --- | --- | --- | --- |
| 8 April | H | Peterborough | L | 47-49 |
| 19 April | A | Ipswich | L | 28-67 |
| 22 April | H | Stoke | L | 45-49 |
| 29 April | H | Wimbledon | L | 47-49 |
| 3 May | A | Middlesbrough | L | 37-58 |
| 4 May | A | Edinburgh | L | 45-51 |
| 6 May | H | Exeter | W | 55-40 |
| 20 May | H | Middlesbrough | W | 59-37 |
| 27 May | H | Ipswich | L | 44-52 |
| 18 June | A | Newcastle | L | 44-51 |
| 22 June | A | Peterborough | L | 39-57 |
| 24 June | H | Poole | L | 36-60 |
| 29 June | A | Hackney | L | 28-68 |
| 30 June | A | Arena Essex | L | 45-51 |
| 1 July | H | Edinburgh | L | 43-52 |
| 6 July | A | Glasgow | L | 36-60 |
| 7 July | A | Berwick | L | 28-68 |
| 8 July | H | Newcastle | L | 39-57 |
| 15 July | H | Milton Keynes | W | 51-45 |
| 17 July | A | Poole | L | 23-73 |

| 22 July | H | Arena Essex | L | 46-49 |
| 4 August | A | Eastbourne | L | 34-61 |
| 12 August | H | Long Eaton | W | 56-39 |
| 15 August | A | Wimbledon | W | 49-47 |
| 26 August | H | Berwick | W | 52-43 |
| 28 August | A | Milton Keynes | L | 47-48 |
| 2 September | H | Hackney | W | 50-46 |
| 9 September | H | Eastbourne | W | 62-33 |
| 10 September | A | Exeter | L | 32-64 |
| 12 September | A | Long Eaton | L | 47-49 |
| 16 September | H | Glasgow | L | 46-49 |
| 20 October | A | Stoke | L | 46-50 |

P32 W8 D0 L24
For 1,386 Against 1,672
Position: fifteenth (out of seventeen)

## *Knock-Out Cup*

First Round
Bye
Second Round

| Date | H/A | Opponent | W/L | Score |
| --- | --- | --- | --- | --- |
| 5 June | A | Milton Keynes | L | 39-56 |
| 10 June | H | Milton Keynes | W | 51-45 |

Lost 90-101 on aggregate

## *1990 National League and Knock-Out Cup*

| Name | M | R | Pts | BP | Total | CMA |
| --- | --- | --- | --- | --- | --- | --- |
| Jens Rasmussen | 33 | 191 | 441 | 6 | 447 | 9.36 |
| Mel Taylor | 11 | 56 | 119 | 5 | 124 | 8.86 |
| Glen Baxter | 28 | 160 | 293 | 15 | 308 | 7.70 |
| Roger Johns | 13 | 75 | 103 | 11 | 114 | 6.08 |
| Jamie Fagg | 9 | 42 | 49 | 11 | 60 | 5.71 |
| Trevor O'Brien | 34 | 187 | 218 | 34 | 252 | 5.39 |
| Scott Humphries | 11 | 58 | 57 | 11 | 68 | 4.69 |
| Wayne Baxter | 24 | 91 | 72 | 9 | 81 | 3.56 |
| Nigel Sparshott | 14 | 56 | 34 | 10 | 44 | 3.14 |
| Kevin Teager | 6 | 27 | 16 | 3 | 19 | 2.82 |
| Kelvin Mullarkey | 13 | 47 | 25 | 8 | 33 | 2.81 |
| Linden Warner | 14 | 69 | 32 | 7 | 39 | 2.26 |

# 1991

Ever since Ronnie Russell had taken over at the end of 1985, and even before that, there had been an optimistic start to each season. Then, the fates seemed to conspire against the Rockets, mostly in the form of injuries, to scupper their chances of any success in the league or cup. Sadly, 1991 was to prove to be no different.

There was a big reorganisation of the leagues in 1991. At the end of the 1990 season, there were seventeen teams in the National League and only nine in the Sunbrite British League. Both leagues agreed to amalgamate and to form more even First and Second Divisions of the British League, with automatic promotion and relegation between the two. To facilitate this plan, four teams, Poole, Ipswich, Berwick and Wimbledon were promoted to the British League Division One, while the rest of the old National League became the British League Division Two.

Rasmussen and Taylor stayed on to spearhead the Rockets, while new signing, Martin Goodwin, on loan from Arena Essex in place of Glen Baxter, on an 8.5 average, gave the top order a very solid-looking aspect. With Trevor O'Brien, Roger Johns and Glen Baxter's brother, Wayne, staying on along with John Wainwright, there was also some good-looking support.

It was too much to expect, however, that the three heat leaders would stay together throughout the whole season and, sure enough, Rasmussen managed to break his collarbone in a fall in the Rockets' very first home meeting. He missed several matches and, even when he returned, he was not the rider he had been in the previous three seasons. Towards the end of the season, he also contrived to break his leg and therefore missed the last few matches. Taylor broke his wrist and suffered concussion following a bad crash in a home match against Glasgow which the Rockets lost by the mammoth score of 60-29.

Fortunately, Goodwin managed to avoid injury, but, nevertheless, was still hit by the Rye House jinx. He started the season in tremendous form, scoring 17 in his first two home matches against Exeter and Hackney. These were followed by 14 against Peterborough and paid 13 against Ipswich. In July, however, he was suspended for the rest of the season following an incident at Hackney in May when he smashed the window of the referee's box at Hackney with his crash helmet. In between the time of the incident and the tribunal's ruling, he continued to post high scores, helping the Rockets to a first round Knock-Out Cup victory over Stoke, when his winning ride in the last race of a very exciting second leg gave Rye House a 90-89 aggregate score. His loss was a bitter blow to the team. Without the three heat leaders that had started the season, the team struggled through to the end of the season, finishing in ninth place out of twelve (Hackney had withdrawn during the season). In the Knock-Out Cup, the Rockets only got as far as the second round, where they went out to Long Eaton, 93-86 on aggregate.

## 1991 British League Division Two

| Date | H/A | Opponent | W/L | Score |
|------|-----|----------|-----|-------|
| 17 May | A | Edinburgh | L | 35-54 |
| 18 May | A | Stoke | W | 46-44 |
| 7 June | A | Peterborough | L | 41-49 |
| 16 June | H | Middlesbrough | W | 57-33 |
| 6 July | A | Arena Essex | L | 33-57 |
| 7 July | H | Stoke | W | 47-41 |
| 22 July | A | Newcastle | L | 34-49★ |
| 24 July | A | Long Eaton | L | 40-50 |
| 28 July | H | Edinburgh | L | 43-47 |
| 4 August | H | Newcastle | L | 43-47 |
| 11 August | H | Sheffield | W | 54-36 |
| 18 August | H | Long Eaton | W | 50-38 |
| 22 August | A | Sheffield | L | 27-57★ |
| 26 August | H | Arena Essex | L | 31-59 |
| 1 September | H | Milton Keynes | W | 52-37 |
| 8 September | H | Peterborough | W | 50-40 |
| 15 September | H | Glasgow | L | 29-60 |
| 22 September | H | Exeter | W | 45-44 |
| 23 September | A | Exeter | L | 29-61 |
| 1 October | A | Milton Keynes | L | 37-53 |

★ Abandoned after 14 heats. Score stands

P20 W8 D0 L12

For 857 Against 956

Position: ninth (out of twelve)

## Knock-Out Cup

First Round

| Date | H/A | Opponent | W/L | Score |
|------|-----|----------|-----|-------|
| 1 June | A | Stoke | W | 46-44 |
| 2 June | H | Stoke | W | 54-35 |

Won 100-79 on aggregate

Second Round

| Date | H/A | Opponent | W/L | Score |
|------|-----|----------|-----|-------|
| 30 June | H | Long Eaton | W | 46-43 |
| 3 July | A | Long Eaton | L | 40-50 |

Lost 86-93 on aggregate

## Gold Cup (Southern Section)

| Date | H/A | Opponent | W/L | Score |
|------|-----|----------|-----|-------|
| 7 April | H | Exeter | W | 50-40 |
| 8 April | A | Exeter | L | 32-58 |
| 12 April | A | Peterborough | L | 24-66 |
| 14 April | H | Hackney | W | 46-44 |
| 21 April | H | Peterborough | L | 44-46 |
| 3 May | A | Hackney | L | 37-52 |
| 5 May | A | Milton Keynes | L | 44-46 |
| 6 May | H | Milton Keynes | W | 51-39 |
| 25 May | A | Arena Essex | L | 37-53 |
| 27 May | H | Arena Essex | L | 44-46 |

P10 W3 D0 L7
For 409 Against 490
Position: fifth (out of six)

## 1991 British League Division Two and Knock-Out Cup

| Name | M | R | Pts | BP | Total | CMA |
|------|---|---|-----|-----|-------|-----|
| Martin Goodwin | 10 | 55 | 112 | 5 | 117 | 8.51 |
| Jens Rasmussen | 18 | 90 | 165 | 11 | 176 | 7.82 |
| Trevor O'Brien | 26 | 144 | 249 | 24 | 273 | 7.58 |
| Mel Taylor | 23 | 112 | 198 | 10 | 208 | 7.43 |
| Roger Johns | 19 | 86 | 106 | 11 | 117 | 5.44 |
| Rob Tilbury | 15 | 58 | 56 | 8 | 64 | 5.44 |
| Wayne Baxter | 24 | 90 | 68 | 16 | 84 | 3.73 |
| John Wainwright | 20 | 78 | 51 | 17 | 68 | 3.49 |

# 1992

Once again, Ronnie Russell put together a potential championship team ready for the 1992 season. Rasmussen and Goodwin were joined by Jan Pedersen from Arena Essex, while Mark and Sean Courtney were signed from Berwick and Glasgow. To make way for them, Taylor and Johns moved on. Although Rasmussen missed the opening Gold Cup competition as a result of his 1991 injury, there was still a solid feel about the team and, sure enough, the opening fixture on 5 April at home to Exeter resulted in a 51-39 win for the Rockets. The whole team rode well, with Goodwin top scoring on his comeback. There then followed a run of fairly predictable results with home wins and away losses, but what really shocked the team was a massive home loss to Mildenhall as they went down 53-35. The riders themselves felt they had let Russell and the supporters down. In some ways it was a wake-up call for them and from then on till the end of the season they did not lose another home league or Knock-Out Cup match.

Before the league season started, the Rockets took on and beat Sheffield in the first round of the Knock-Out Cup. The first leg marked the return of Rasmussen to the team and saw him score eight points in four rides as the Rockets went down 50-40. Ten points down from the first leg, Rye House laid into the Tigers the following night and trounced them 63-26, Goodwin scoring a 15-point maximum, supported by the Courtney brothers, who both recorded paid 11, and Rasmussen and O'Brien with paid tens. The Knock-Out Cup also marked the debut of Chris Young, a youngster with great potential who had performed extremely well in the Reserves' League. With Rasmussen returning and Young coming in to the team, Wainwright and Baxter were dropped.

With Rasmussen back and no injuries to any of the team, it looked as though, for the first time in many years, the Rockets would be able to fulfil their potential and challenge for honours.

Although they had now found the winning pattern at home, the Rockets were still finding those away points very elusive and their first win away from home did not come until 16 July when they travelled to Middlesbrough and came away with a 53-37 victory.

Three days before this, however, Rye House suffered their first injury as O'Brien, riding in the Westernapolis at Exeter on 13 July, crashed in heat six and was taken to a hospital with a broken leg. He was not to return to the saddle for the rest of the season. His place was taken by the Swedish Mikael Teurnberg, who scored 11 points on his debut at Middlesbrough.

Although Rye House were having a much better season on the track than they had been used to in recent years, behind the scenes all was not well. The year 1992 was not a particularly good one for speedway. Mildenhall and Milton Keynes had been forced to close through lack of support and it was rumoured that even clubs like King's Lynn and Sheffield were going through financial difficulties. On 12 July, after a good home win, 59-31 against Sheffield, Russell told

In 1993, Martin Goodwin became the first Rye House rider in history to reach the World Championship British final.

the crowd that Rye House was in danger of closing unless attendances improved. He revealed that the club had already been given a subsidy by his brother Terry and Ivan Henry of Arena Essex to keep them afloat. He explained that he had hoped that, with a better year on the track, attendances would pick up, but he had been disappointed. In spite of the fact that the team were doing much better in the league and had got through to the Knock-Out Cup quarter-finals, attendances had not picked up. He urged people to try and spread the word to get others along, otherwise this could be the last season at Hoddesdon.

Back on the track, Rye House managed another away win at Edinburgh on 4 September, but they were not winning enough away from home to be able to mount a serious challenge for the league title, although their 100 per cent home record meant that they were a world away from where they had been in the previous few seasons. In the end, they finished in fifth place.

Having disposed of Sheffield in the first round of the Knock-Out Cup, Rye House were lucky enough to obtain a bye in the quarter-finals following the closure of Milton Keynes. The first leg of the semi-final saw them hammer Berwick, 60-28. Pedersen top scored with paid 13 and paid 11 each from Teurnberg and new junior Robert Ledwith, who had been promoted from the ranks of the junior team. Although the Rockets lost the second leg, 53-37 at Berwick, they had a big enough lead to see them through to the final for the first time since they won it back in 1979.

The first leg of the final was due to take place on 23 October against league champions Peterborough. Before that, however, the Rockets had a league match against the same team. When they thrashed the new champions out of sight, 62-28, the speedway world sat up and took notice: Rye House were in with a real chance of lifting the cup.

Sadly, it was not to be. Peterborough won the first leg on their own track 60-30, with only Rasmussen and Goodwin putting up any real fight. The return was due to take place on 25 October but was rained off. Peterborough refused to ride out of season on the following Sunday, which was 1 November, as two of their riders were returning to Australia that day, so Rye House's home tie had to be switched to Arena Essex. Although the Rockets put up a much better display, they could only win 51-39 and so lost the final on aggregate, 99-81.

Altogether, though, it had been a much better season for the Rockets. With just the one injury to Trevor O'Brien, they had been able to put up a much better performance during the year, which shows what might have been all the other years if only they'd managed to steer clear of injury. Goodwin was a star performer, averaging 9.67 over the year, while behind him both O'Brien and Rasmussen scored more than seven and Teurnberg and Sean Courtney over six.

There was also cause for optimism with the juniors as they finished second in the Reserves League. They had three outstanding riders in Young, average 10.40, Ledwith, average 9.14, and Martin Cobbin, average 8.24.

Good things could be expected for 1993 if only the financial position could improve and the team would actually run. Fortunately, with the late run of success for the team, the crowds had picked up just enough for Russell to contemplate running again the following year. In December, he revealed that he had had successful negotiations with two businessmen, Peter Redfern and Roger Shout, and that they would now come in with him as co-promoters, thus easing his own financial burden. He also erected new floodlights with the intention of being able to run evening meetings at Rye House, hoping that this would increase the attendance figures. Season ticket prices had been set at £120 for adults and £60 for children and senior citizens. All of which meant that Rye House were definite starters for 1993.

## 1992 British League Division Two

| Date | H/A | Opponent | W/L | Score |
| --- | --- | --- | --- | --- |
| 14 June | H | Berwick | W | 46-44 |
| 19 June | A | Peterborough | L | 40-50 |
| 22 June | A | Exeter | L | 33-56 |

| 12 July | H | Sheffield | W | 59-31 |
|---|---|---|---|---|
| 16 July | A | Middlesbrough | W | 53-37 |
| 19 July | H | Glasgow | W | 47-43 |
| 2 August | H | Middlesbrough | W | 52-35 |
| 5 August | A | Long Eaton | L | 27-63 |
| 9 August | H | Stoke | W | 51-39 |
| 10 August | A | Newcastle | L | 33-57 |
| 20 August | A | Sheffield | L | 32-58 |
| 31 August | H | Newcastle | W | 48-41 |
| 4 September | A | Edinburgh | W | 46-43 |
| 5 September | A | Berwick | L | 38-52 |
| 20 September | H | Long Eaton | W | 50-39 |
| 4 October | H | Edinburgh | W | 53-37 |
| 11 October | H | Peterborough | W | 62-28 |
| 18 October | H | Exeter | W | 55-35 |
| 21 October | A | Glasgow★ | | |
| 31 October | A | Stoke | L | 33-57 |

★ Match postponed till 28 October when it was postponed again. The match was never raced. Both sides were awarded one point.

P19 W12 D0 L7

For 858 Against 845

Position: fifth (out of eleven)

## Knock-Out Cup

First Round

| Date | H/A | Opponent | W/L | Score |
|---|---|---|---|---|
| 24 May | A | Sheffield | L | 40-50 |
| 25 May | H | Sheffield | W | 63-26 |

Won 103-76 on aggregate

Second Round

Through on default after Milton Keynes' closure

Semi-Final

| Date | H/A | Opponent | W/L | Score |
|---|---|---|---|---|
| 27 September | H | Berwick | W | 60-28 |
| 10 October | A | Berwick | L | 53-37 |

Won 97-81 on aggregate

Final

| Date | H/A | Opponent | W/L | Score |
|---|---|---|---|---|
| 23 October | A | Peterborough | L | 30-60 |
| 30 October | H★ | Peterborough | W | 51-39 |

★ Raced at Arena Essex

Lost 81-99 on aggregate

## Gold Cup (Southern Section)

| Date | H/A | Opponent | W/L | Score |
|---|---|---|---|---|
| 5 April | H | Exeter | W | 51-39 |
| 6 April | A | Exeter | L | 37-53 |
| 7 April | A | Milton Keynes★ | | |
| 12 April | H | Peterborough | W | 49-41 |
| 17 April | A | Peterborough | L | 31-59 |
| 19 April | A | Mildenhall | L | 41-49 |

| 20 April | H | Mildenhall | L | 35-53 |
| 26 April | H | Milton Keynes | W | 53-35 |
| 29 April | A | Long Eaton | L | 42-48 |
| 2 May | A | Stoke | L | 42-48 |
| 10 May | H | Long Eaton | W | 46-44 |
| 31 May | H | Stoke | W | 46-42 |

* Match abandoned after four heats and never restaged

P11 W5 D0 L6

For 473 Against 511

Position: sixth (out of seven)

### 1992 National League and Knock-Out Cup

| Name | M | R | Pts | BP | Total | CMA |
|---|---|---|---|---|---|---|
| Martin Goodwin | 17 | 79 | 185 | 12 | 197 | 9.98 |
| Jens Rasmussen | 19 | 83 | 145 | 6 | 151 | 7.37 |
| Jan Pedersen | 19 | 91 | 147 | 18 | 165 | 7.25 |
| Mikael Teurnberg | 15 | 67 | 92 | 11 | 103 | 6.15 |
| Mark Courtney | 16 | 65 | 87 | 12 | 99 | 6.09 |
| Sean Courtney | 18 | 83 | 101 | 21 | 122 | 5.88 |
| Robert Ledwith | 12 | 48 | 47 | 9 | 56 | 4.67 |
| Chris Young | 12 | 39 | 29 | 5 | 34 | 3.49 |

# 1993

Rye House lost the Courtney brothers for the 1993 campaign but held on to Rasmussen, Goodwin, Pedersen, Teurnberg, O'Brien and Young. Into the team came Paul Whittaker from Middlesbrough and junior discovery Martin Cobbin. Once again, it looked like a team ready and able to do business, although the old injury jinx struck again as Pedersen broke his collarbone in a practice session at Arena Essex before the season started. Fortunately, he recovered sufficiently to be able to take his place in the Rockets' line-up for the opening Division Two fixture on 28 March at home to Exeter. Not only was he fit, but he scored paid 14 from five rides. Goodwin and Teurnberg both scored paid maximums in a great start to the season as Rye House opened the proceedings with a 69-39 win. This was followed by a narrow 55-53 victory a week later over Swindon and then a defeat away at Exeter, 61-46. For the first eight matches of the season, the scores followed the normal pattern of home wins and away losses. Goodwin was riding exceptionally well with strong backing from Pedersen. Rasmussen was a bit down on his best, but nevertheless there was not too much cause for concern.

On 23 May, the Rockets lost their first home match as they went down 61-46 to Long Eaton. Part of the reason for this was, ironically, that Goodwin was having such a brilliant start to the season: he had won the World Championship British quarter-final at Swindon and scored eight points in the semi-final at Ipswich. This was enough to take him through to the British final at Coventry, the first Rye House rider ever to reach this stage of the competition. Undeterred by the First Division opposition, Goodwin went even further and qualified for the Commonwealth final at King's Lynn. Unfortunately, this event took place on 23 May, the same day as the Rockets' home match against King's Lynn. Rye House were forced to use rider replacement but, as Goodwin was by some distance the Rockets' best rider at the time, none of the replacement rides could make up for his absence.

Martin Cobbin left the team due to a broken ankle and Darren Spicer was brought in on loan from King's Lynn to replace him. Soon afterwards, Lawrence Hare was brought in from Ipswich as a replacement for Young, who was finding life a bit difficult.

Jan Pedersen signed from
Arena Essex in 1992 and stayed
until Rye House's closure the
following season.

Rye House suffered their second home defeat on 6 June as they went down 56-52 to Edinburgh, strangely enough just two days after their first away win at, of all places, Edinburgh.

It was obvious by mid-season that attendances at Rye House were not picking up as hoped. Russell had previously introduced a six o'clock start time for midsummer matches but he now reverted to the traditional four o'clock start in the hope this would encourage more supporters through the gate. He also introduced other attractions, such as a 'Fun Day' built round the meeting on 8 August against Sheffield.

Martin Goodwin recalls that that last season was a real struggle financially for Ronnie Russell:

> He called all the riders into the office one day and asked us if we would mind not getting paid for a couple of weeks. He said he would understand if any rider was unable to agree with this but it would help the club out over a very difficult period. All the riders agreed to his proposal because we held Ronnie in such high regard. He was a true gentleman and a man of his word. We knew that we would get our money eventually as indeed we all did. He was the best promoter I ever rode for. A gentle giant and maybe, in some ways, too kind for his own good.

In spite of the two home setbacks against Long Eaton and Edinburgh, and then a third against Glasgow on 18 July, the Rockets were still going well and towards the end of the season they began to put up much better displays away from home than they had done in previous seasons. They were just missing out on bringing home the points as they ran into a number of narrow defeats during September and October: 56-52 at Long Eaton, 56-52 at Middlesbrough and 55-53 at Edinburgh. In all three matches, the whole team contributed useful scores but they were never quite enough. After the home defeat on 18 July, Rye House went to the end of the season without losing another match at home, but the lack of success away meant that the Rockets could only finish the season in eighth place out of eleven teams.

There was no success in the Knock-Out Cup either, as the Rockets went out in the second round, 115-100 to Peterborough, having been given a bye in the first round.

Overall, Goodwin ended up as top scorer for the club with an average of 8.23, although Rasmussen had a much better home record, scoring at over one point per match better than Goodwin, 9.46 to 8.41. But his away form let him down as he returned just 6.63. Pedersen, the third heat leader, recorded 7.33. Behind him, the two mid-season signings did well, with Hare on 7.11 and Spicer on 6.93. Teurnberg also had a good average for a number six with 6.30, while O'Brien and Whittaker both averaged over five points per match. It was a good, solid all-round performance from the team but they were not quite able to take those vital away matches. Although racing at the Hoddesdon Raceway was, as always, very exciting, the lack of success was doing nothing to bring back the crowds and once again there were serious doubts expressed about the future of Rye House.

Redfern and Shute decided they could no longer continue in partnership with Russell, who immediately began looking round for other prospective co-promoters to come in with him in a consortium. The deadline for declarations of intent to run in 1994 was 31 December, but the BSPA agreed to allow Rye House an extension to see if Russell could come up with the necessary support he needed to be able to continue. Sadly, he was unable to and on 21 January 1994 he contacted the BSPA to tell them that the Rockets would not be racing that season. He asked for the licence to be put on ice and the riders to be loaned out so that he could spend time trying to get together a workable package for 1995.

It was a very sad day for the promoter, riders and supporters. Although Rye House had now been a major league team for twenty years and the facilities had been improved out of all recognition from the non-league days, there was still nothing in speedway to equal the family day out atmosphere of an afternoon by the River Lea watching your favourite sport. There was still a lot of socialising between the supporters and the riders, with a real bond between them that wasn't so apparent at many other clubs. But now it was gone. Russell's hopes of re-opening in 1995 did not materialise and it was to be another five years before attempts were made to revive the Rockets and Rye House speedway.

## 1993 British League Division Two

| Date | H/A | Opponent | W/L | Score |
|---|---|---|---|---|
| 28 March | H | Exeter | W | 69–39 |
| 4 April | H | Swindon | W | 55–53 |
| 5 April | A | Exeter | L | 46–61 |
| 12 April | H | Newcastle | W | 57–51 |
| 14 April | A | Glasgow | L | 42–66 |
| 16 April | A | Peterborough | L | 35–73 |
| 18 April | H | Peterborough | W | 62–46 |
| 1 May | A | Swindon | L | 40–67 |
| 3 May | H | Oxford | W | 64–44 |
| 23 May | H | Long Eaton | L | 46–61 |
| 30 May | A | Newcastle | L | 29–78 |
| 31 May | H | Glasgow | W | 59–49 |
| 3 June | A | Middlesbrough | L | 49–59 |
| 4 June | A | Edinburgh | W | 55–53 |
| 6 June | H | Edinburgh | L | 52–56 |
| 11 June | A | Oxford | L | 53–55 |
| 13 June | H | Middlesbrough | W | 59–49 |
| 17 June | A | Sheffield | L | 41–67 |
| 20 June | H | Sheffield | W | 65–42 |
| 27 June | H | Oxford | W | 70–37 |
| 2 July | A | Peterborough | L | 37–71 |
| 7 July | A | Long Eaton | L | 50–58 |
| 11 July | H | Edinburgh | W | 63–45 |
| 16 July | A | Glasgow | L | 35–72 |
| 18 July | H | Glasgow | L | 52–56 |
| 30 July | A | Oxford | W | 57–51 |
| 1 August | H | Middlesbrough | W | 55–53 |
| 8 August | H | Sheffield | W | 70–38 |
| 22 August | H | Long Eaton | W | 57–50 |
| 29 August | A | Newcastle | L | 46–62 |

| 30 August | H | Newcastle | W | 64-44 |
| 1 September | A | Long Eaton | L | 52-56 |
| 5 September | H | Peterborough | W | 66-41 |
| 9 September | A | Middlesbrough | L | 52-56 |
| 3 October | H | Exeter | W | 73-35 |
| 4 October | A | Exeter | L | 46-62 |
| 10 October | H | Swindon | W | 55-52 |
| 15 October | A | Edinburgh | L | 53-55 |
| 21 October | A | Sheffield | W | 55-53 |
| 23 October | A | Swindon | L | 47-61 |

P40 W20 D0 L20
For 2,133 Against 2,177
Position: eighth (out of eleven)

## Knock-Out Cup

First Round

| Date | H/A | Opponent | | W/L | Score |
| --- | --- | --- | --- | --- | --- |
| 13 August | A | Peterborough | L | 36-72 | |
| 15 August | H | Peterborough | W | 64-43 | |

Lost 100-115 on aggregate

## 1993 British League Division Two and Knock-Out Cup

| Name | M | R | Pts | BP | Total | CMA |
| --- | --- | --- | --- | --- | --- | --- |
| Martin Goodwin | 39 | 207 | 401 | 25 | 426 | 8.23 |
| Jens Rasmussen | 42 | 215 | 405 | 27 | 432 | 8.04 |
| Jan Pedersen | 36 | 190 | 312 | 36 | 348 | 7.33 |
| Lawrence Hare | 27 | 108 | 166 | 26 | 192 | 7.11 |
| Darren Spicer | 35 | 131 | 187 | 40 | 227 | 6.93 |
| Mikael Teurnberg | 42 | 217 | 303 | 39 | 342 | 6.30 |
| Trevor O'Brien | 39 | 182 | 206 | 31 | 237 | 5.21 |
| Paul Whittaker | 39 | 187 | 196 | 40 | 236 | 5.05 |
| Martin Cobbin | 7 | 28 | 28 | 3 | 31 | 4.43 |
| Chris Young | 15 | 47 | 29 | 7 | 36 | 3.06 |

# 1999

During the winter of 1998/99, Rye House supporters Steve Ribbons and David Entwistle called a meeting for former Rye House supporters to discuss the possibility of running a Rockets team in the Conference League in the following season. The proposal was greeted enthusiastically and the meeting agreed to ask supporters to put £50 into a kitty so that they could get a team together. Ribbons was elected treasurer of the reformed club and John Stoneman chairman. Unfortunately, in the intervening years since the end of speedway at Hoddesdon, the track had been tarmacked over and was being used as a stock car circuit, so the immediate plan was to get the team to race their home fixtures on another track. As a former promoter, Len Silver was asked if he would like to contribute £50 towards reviving the team. He recalls that he was approached by the Supporters' Club chairman, John Stoneman, to contribute £50, but that he offered to do more than that and agreed to sponsor the team. He also said he would look for possible venues in which the team could race and soon arranged with Dingle Brown for the Rockets to race their home fixtures at Mildenhall. In the meantime, Ribbons had been putting a team together. His first signing was Jamie Barton, followed by Simon Wolstenholme, who was appointed captain.

The big day that Rockets fans had been waiting for for five years finally came on 9 May 1999 when the new team took to the track for their first home fixture, actually at Eastbourne as Mildenhall was unavailable that day. John Sampford, the current team manager, remembers the day particularly well. He had been following the Rockets since their Rayleigh days as a diehard supporter on the terraces. After the announcement that the Rye House team was to return, he was approached and asked if he would like to be the team manager. As he had had no experience of the role he said he would be willing to learn and was told that a former rider would act as team manager for the first few matches while he could understudy and learn the ropes. On arriving at Eastbourne, Sampford went to the pits and asked who the Rockets team manager was. The reply he received was, 'you are'. There was no former rider and Sampford discovered that he had been thrown in at the deep end. As well as Barton and Wolstenholme, the riders who turned out on that historic occasion were Frenchman Patrice Deloubes, Ian Clarke, Dean Chapman and Chris Morgan. One hundred and fifty Rockets fans made their way to Arlington to see their team take on King's Lynn in a Conference League fixture. It proved to be a nail-biting return for Rye House as they fell well behind in the first few heats, only to claw their way back to a last-heat decider, thanks in part to the tactical decisions made by their untried new team manager. And when King's Lynn's Freddie Stephenson, in second place at the time, was excluded on the last lap for crossing the white line, it meant a win for the Rockets by the narrowest possible margin, 44-43. It was an afternoon of celebration for the fans, who had not only seen their team resurrected against all the odds but had seen a magnificent afternoon's racing and, to top it all, had seen their team win at the first attempt. Wolstenholme had played a true captain's part, scoring paid 15, while Morgan, in his first and only outing for the Rockets, backed him up with paid nine. For Sampford, it was the start of a new career as team manager, one that is still going strong today.

For Len Silver too it was a great day. As a former rider and promoter and now sponsor of the club, he had gone down to Eastbourne to see the team to which he had given so much time over the years and found that the speedway bug had bitten again. He decided he wanted to get more involved with the team and as the season progressed he could be seen in the pits on race days giving the riders the benefit of his advice and years of experience.

The Rockets' next match was an away tie against Buxton. With only five fit riders, two Belle Vue juniors were put into the team. Then the referee told Rye House that they could not use rider replacement for the injured Jamie Barton, but as another rider had turned up at Buxton looking for rides the referee put him in at number two for the Rockets. The result of all this was a heavy defeat for Rye House as they went down 52-37. The only good thing to come out of the meeting was the form of Simon Moon, who was making his debut for the Rockets. He scored paid 10.

Rye House made their debut at their adopted Mildenhall home on 20 June with a match against Linlithgow which they won 48-41. Once again, Wolstenholme was top man with a score of 17. Moon added paid 11 and newcomer to the squad Peter Collyer paid 16. A heavy 67-23 defeat at St Austell followed and then defeat in the first round of the Knock-Out Cup, 100-79 to Newport. A massive home defeat came next as they were massacred 62-28 by St Austell. Then, on 15 August came the Rockets' first away win as they travelled to King's Lynn and won 48-40. It was becoming apparent that Rye House were relying on three men to get the bulk of their scores – Wolstenholme, Moon and Collyer – and the committee felt they needed another good rider if they were to have any chance of challenging for the league title.

Before the next league meeting, Rye House undertook a Challenge match against another team from a defunct track, Southampton. They took the opportunity to bring in another rider for this challenge as David Mason was persuaded out of retirement. He showed his real class and, but for an engine failure, would have scored an 18-point maximum. He was then drafted into the team for the next league match, a home fixture against Buxton. This time he did score an 18-point maximum and, with Wolstenholme also scoring a paid maximum, the Rockets won the match 48-42.

The 1999 Rye House team, from left to right, back row: David Mason, Chris Courage, Darren Andrews, Garry Sweet, John Sampford (team manager). Front row: Nathan Morton, Simon Wolstenholm (on bike), Daniel Giffard.

Because of their patchy start to the season, Rye House had by now lost their chance of the championship as Newport and St Austell were well out in the lead, but there was still an outside chance of third place. Unfortunately, the Rockets lost their last two matches, 66-23 away at Newport and 48-41 away at Mildenhall, though in reality this was just as much a home match for the Rockets as it was for Mildenhall.

Nevertheless, fourth place in their first season back under a Supporters' Club committee was a good reward for all the hard work and effort the supporters, led by Ribbons and Stoneman, had put into reviving their dream.

Wolstenholme had played a true captain's part throughout the year, ending the season with an average of 8.43. Though, in the five league matches in which he appeared, David Mason was the undoubted star. He never once dropped below double figures and finished the season with an astonishing average of 10.67.

*1999 Conference League (home matches raced at Mildenhall unless otherwise stated)*

| Date | H/A | Opponent | W/L | Score |
|---|---|---|---|---|
| 9 May | H (Eastbourne) | King's Lynn | W | 44-43 |
| 23 May | A | Buxton | L | 37-52 |
| 20 June | H | Linlithgow | W | 48-41 |
| 22 June | A | St Austell | L | 23-67 |
| 18 July | H | St Austell | L | 28-62 |
| 7 July | A | Linlithgow | L | 38-51 |
| 15 August | A | King's Lynn | W | 48-40 |

| 5 September | H | Buxton | W | 48-42 |
| 19 September | H (King's Lynn) | Mildenhall | W | 50-40 |
| 2 October | H | Newport | W | 56-34 |
| 9 October | A | Newport | L | 23-66 |
| 17 October | A | Mildenhall | L | 41-48 |

P12 W6 D0 L6
For 484 Against 586
Position: fourth (out of six)

## Knock-Out Cup

First Round

| Date | H/A | Opponent | W/L | Score |
|------|-----|----------|-----|-------|
| 25 June | A | Newport | L | 32-57 |
| 3 July | H | Newport | W | 47-43 |

Lost on aggregate 79-100

## 1999 Conference League and Knock-Out Cup

| Name | M | R | Pts | BP | Total | CMA |
|------|---|---|-----|----|----|-----|
| Simon Wolstenholme | 14 | 83 | 168 | 7 | 175 | 8.43 |
| Simon Moon | 12 | 62 | 84 | 12 | 96 | 6.19 |
| Peter Collyer | 10 | 54 | 71 | 12 | 83 | 6.15 |
| Jamie Barton | 7 | 29 | 31 | 2 | 33 | 4.55 |
| Dean Chapman | 12 | 51 | 37 | 12 | 49 | 3.84 |
| Ian Clarke | 13 | 52 | 36 | 10 | 46 | 3.54 |

# The 2000s

## 2000

While Rye House were back racing as a team, the real dream of the supporters was, naturally, to get racing back at the stadium. To this end, Steve Ribbons contacted the stadium owner, Eddie Leslie, to discuss the possibility of a return to Hoddesdon. Leslie was not entirely opposed to the idea, though his first priority was to the greyhounds and the stock car racing. Towards the end of 1999, Len Silver was introduced to Leslie by Ribbons and between the three of them they came to an agreement. Firstly, Silver agreed to take over financial responsibility for the club to relieve the supporters' club of that particular load and, secondly, Leslie agreed that the stadium could stage speedway on the understanding that the club be responsible for laying a shale surface before every match and then lifting it again in time for the stock car meetings. This was a tremendous burden, but Silver, with the Supporters' Club, agreed that this would be done even though it would need a massive force of volunteers twice a week throughout the season to ensure it would happen. The speedway world was stunned by the news and many felt that the venture was doomed to failure.

Indeed, when Silver took his first look at the track, he was appalled by what he saw. The stock car organisers had allowed the stadium to be turned in to a tip, with old tyres and bits of broken cars littering the place. Before it could be considered a home fit for a speedway team, Silver had to spend thousands of pounds and many hours of time in clearing the place up. But on 15 May 2000, the roar of speedway bikes and the cheers of the supporters were heard at Rye House for the first time since the end of the 1993 season. In a Challenge match, the Rockets defeated the Southampton Saints 48-42.

Not surprisingly, the first two names signed up for the 2000 Rockets were Wolstenholme and Mason. Moon was also retained from the 1999 squad and in came Gary Sweet from Mildenhall and Nathan Morton on loan from Arena Essex. The last two places went to Geoff Batt and the sixteen-year-old Steven Eaves.

The first meeting was scheduled for the May Day bank holiday, but rain put paid to that. When racing finally did return to Hoddesdon, one of the biggest crowds seen at Rye House for many years turned out to welcome their team back. One of the problems with the track having been lifted and relaid was that there was no opportunity to practice, which showed in the Rockets' first three matches of the season, all away and all ending in defeat, although Mason showed no signs of rustiness as he reeled off two scores of 13 and one of 14 in those first three matches.

Rye House's first official home fixture came on 22 May when they took on and beat Boston 52-38 in the Conference League Cup. Mason scored another 14, while Wolstenholme added a paid 12, Sweet 10 and Morton 4. The following week saw another big win for the home side, this time in the Conference League itself as they defeated St Austell, 57-32. This time, Mason scored a paid 15-point maximum. Support came from Wolstenholme and Sweet again; the former scoring paid 13, the latter paid 17 from six rides. This match also saw the debut of Phil Ambrose.

After losing to Boston, 59-31, away, the Rockets embarked on a run of five consecutive victories including one away at Somerset in the Knock-Out Cup, ensuring their passage through to the semi-final. David Osborn was brought in at reserve for this match and remained in the team for most of the season.

David Mason made the successful transition from the Conference League to the Premier League side.

The next four matches followed the old familiar pattern of two wins at home and two losses away but then came the Knock-Out Cup semi-final and a trip up to their 1999 surrogate home, Mildenhall. A narrow 48-42 defeat gave the Rockets plenty of hope that they would make the final. The match itself was a bad-tempered affair, but it was all forgotten the next night as the return leg was raced at Hoddesdon. After Mildenhall's top man, Steve Camden, went out with a broken arm in heat one, there was little doubt who the victors were going to be and, sure enough, the Rockets' 55-35 victory saw them through to their first Knock-Out Cup final since 1992. Phil Ambrose had returned for this match, having been out since an injury in June after knocking up a string of double-figure scores. Unfortunately, he was to have just one more match before going out again through another injury. Once again, the real star of the afternoon was David Mason with a 15-point maximum.

The Conference League continued with the same run of home wins and away losses until the Rockets, somewhat unexpectedly, lost at home to Somerset on 2 October, 46-44. It was the first and only match they lost all season. Going into the last heat, the Rockets needed a 5-1 to preserve their unbeaten record. Mason was out the gate clear, with Wolstenholme behind him neck and neck with Somerset's Glen Phillips, but on the third lap Wolstenholme drifted wide on the first and second bends allowing Phillips to get the better of him and denying Rye House their record. In the end, Rye House finished sixth out of ten teams. Not great, but the supporters were just glad to have racing back on their own track.

There was still, however, the little matter of the Knock-Out Cup final against Boston. The first leg was held on 21 October away. In spite of magnificent performances yet again from Mason and Wolstenholme, who scored paid 13 and paid 12 respectively, the Rockets went down 53-37. In the second leg, the Rockets put up a tremendous performance, in spite of the large deficit, and pulled off a tremendous 50-38 victory, Gary Sweet adding paid 14 points to Mason's 16, but it was just not enough and Boston became Knock-Out Cup champions by an aggregate score of 91-87. This was also the last match of Rye House's first season back home at Hoddesdon.

The Rockets had found themselves the undoubted star of the Conference League in David Mason. He went through the whole season of twenty-eight official fixtures in the league, Knock-Out Cup and League Cup, home and away, without his score once dropping below double figures. It was an amazing achievement and only once was that score as low as 10. He scored eight maximums and was top of the Conference League averages with a superlative 10.34 average. In the opening meeting of the season, he took the Bronze Helmet from Buxton's Paul Burnett and held it through eleven successful defences before surrendering it to Newport's Chris Courage on 9 July. He then won it back from Andrew Moore of Sheffield on 21 August and held it until the end of the season.

Wolstenholme continued to give tremendous support, recording an average of 8.50, while Moon, Sweet and Morton all ended the season with plus-six averages. It was unfortunate for the Rockets that Ambrose only managed to fit in nine matches between injuries as his average of 7.24 could have gone a long way to giving them a few extra wins if he had been more available. The other regular member of the team, David Osborn, added a useful 4.52 from the reserve position.

Although the team had had a reasonably successful season on the track, it was what was going on off the track during the season that was really making the headlines. Firstly, with his growing involvement in the club, Len Silver and the Supporters' Club agreed that it would make more sense for Silver to take over the promotion of the club, but it was the announcement in July that once again stunned the speedway world as Silver announced that he had bought Rye House stadium. The weekly laying and lifting of the track, although physically possible, was not the ideal way to go about presenting speedway at the stadium every week. In addition to the sheer hard work, there were always going to be conflicting interests between the users of the stadium – the speedway, the greyhounds, the stock cars, the ministox and the mini motorbikes – and, as Silver said later, all this was a distraction and sometimes caused gross interference with the running of speedway. He came to the conclusion that the only way to solve this problem was to buy the stadium and so, after successful negotiations with Eddie Leslie, Silver became the owner of Rye House stadium on 14 July 2000. He then gave all the other users, apart from the greyhounds, notice to quit. It meant that Silver could stop spending two days of each week sorting out the track and get on with managing the club's affairs. He had always been able to rely on very strong support from the team manager, John Sampford, in this, and still could, but Silver was nevertheless relieved to be able to spend more time on the team itself. Silver also looked forward to the possibility of laying a permanent track as he was always considered to be an expert in this field. His track at Hackney, when he was promoter there, had long been considered one of the best racing strips in speedway, now he proposed doing the same for Rye House. In fact, even as early as that very first year, in September, the track was held in such high regard by the other promoters that it was awarded a Young England versus Young Australia Test match. Mason was chosen for England and justified his inclusion by twice beating Elite League rider Travis McGowan and scoring eight points.

It had been an amazing two years in the life of Rye House. From being just one of many defunct speedway teams, the club was now back in business in its own stadium. For the supporters like Steve Ribbons and John Stoneman, to whom this had been a dream just a short while previously, their foresight, hard work and enthusiasm, together with the single-mindedness, tenacity and expertise of Len Silver, had turned that dream into something far more than they had ever dared hope for. It had long been Silver's ambition to own his own stadium. 'Apart from my sheer love of the sport,' he said, 'owning the stadium gives me the opportunity to make my mark.'

## 2000 *Conference League*

| Date | H/A | Opponent | W/L | Score |
|------|-----|----------|-----|-------|
| 23 April | A | Buxton | L | 42-48 |
| 14 May | A | Peterborough | L | 44-46 |
| 29 May | H | St Austell | W | 57-32 |
| 5 June | H | Ashfield | W | 53-37 |
| 19 June | H | Boston | W | 46-44 |
| 4 July | A | St Austell | L | 37-53 |
| 9 July | A | Newport | L | 29-61 |
| 17 July | H | Newport | W | 50-40 |

| 24 July | H | Buxton | W | 63-27 |
|---|---|---|---|---|
| 6 August | A | Boston | L | 38-52 |
| 14 August | H | Peterborough | W | 64-26 |
| 21 August | H | Sheffield | W | 58-32 |
| 3 September | A | Mildenhall | L | 38-51 |
| 4 September | H | Mildenhall | W | 55-34 |
| 10 September | A | Ashfield | L | 42-48 |
| 29 September | A | Somerset | L | 39-51 |
| 2 October | H | Somerset | L | 44-46 |
| 8 October | A | Sheffield | L | 38-40 |

P18 W8 D0 L10
For 711 Against 721
Position: sixth (out of ten)

## Knock-Out Cup

First Round

| Date | H/A | Opponent | W/L | Score |
|---|---|---|---|---|
| 9 June | A | Somerset | W | 47.5-42.5 |
| 12 June | H | Somerset | W | 58-32 |

Won 105.5-74.5 on aggregate
Semi-Final

| Date | H/A | Opponent | W/L | Score |
|---|---|---|---|---|
| 30 July | A | Mildenhall | L | 42-48 |
| 31 July | H | Mildenhall | W | 55-35 |

Won 97-83 on aggregate
Final

| Date | H/A | Opponent | W/L | Score |
|---|---|---|---|---|
| 21 October | A | Boston | L | 37-53 |
| 23 October | H | Boston | W | 50-38 |

Lost 87-91 on aggregate

## Conference League Cup

| Date | H/A | Opponent | W/L | Score |
|---|---|---|---|---|
| 7 May | A | Mildenhall | L | 37-53 |
| 22 May | H | Boston | W | 52-38 |
| 31 May | A | Boston | L | 31-59 |
| 26 June | H | Mildenhall | W | 47-41 |

Finished in second place

## 2000 Conference League, League Cup and Knock-Out Cup

| Name | M | R | Pts | BP | Total | CMA |
|---|---|---|---|---|---|---|
| David Mason | 28 | 159 | 406 | 5 | 411 | 10.34 |
| Simon Wolstenholme | 28 | 160 | 317 | 23 | 340 | 8.50 |
| Phil Ambrose | 9 | 45 | 72.5 | 9 | 81.5 | 7.24 |
| Simon Moon | 22 | 107 | 142 | 28 | 170 | 6.36 |
| Garry Sweet | 24 | 102 | 135 | 22 | 157 | 6.16 |
| Nathan Morton | 24 | 94 | 124 | 18 | 142 | 6.04 |
| David Osborn | 17 | 69 | 58 | 20 | 78 | 4.52 |
| Geoff Batt | 10 | 35 | 15 | 6 | 21 | 2.40 |
| Steven Eaves | 7 | 23 | 5 | 2 | 7 | 1.22 |

2001

Over the winter, Silver was really able to get to work on the track. The stock car track had now been fully replaced by a speedway track with sweeping bends. A new inside line was installed, hopefully to prevent riders crossing onto the grass, as had been the case on a number of occasions the previous year, and a new chain-link safety fence was erected. New lighting was also put in, taken from Canterbury's former home at Kingsmead. As a result of all this work, the Conference League's top meeting of the season, the Conference League Riders' Championship, was awarded to Rye House.

While Silver was busy supervising alterations to the track, Sampford was looking after team matters. Fortunately, he was able to hang on to all the riders who had finished the 2000 season, with the addition of Darren Andrews, who had performed so well in practice that he was signed up as the number eight.

The season started for the Rockets with a two-leg challenge match against Mildenhall. Although Mason and Wolstenholme naturally performed well in the opening leg away at Mildenhall, it was teenager Daniel Giffard who made the fans sit up and take notice as he reeled off 17 points plus two bonus points from the reserve position and seemed to have no difficulty at all in beating Mildenhall's heat leaders on their own track. His contribution enabled Rye House to start the season with a 47-41 win and boosted confidence for the coming season, although there was one worrying factor in that both Ambrose and Sweet had to be taken to hospital following falls. The second leg and the Rockets' opening fixture on their home track saw Giffard once again turn in an amazing performance as he fought his way to paid 14 points from five rides from the reserve position. In almost every case, he did so the hard way, as he missed the gate and had to come from behind. But, once again, this didn't seem to stop him beating all the Mildenhall heat leaders. As well as Giffard, Andrews, who had come in for the injured Ambrose, put on a brilliant display as he scored paid 13 from the number six spot. Together with Mason's 17 points, the Rockets showed their superiority on the day and pulled off a great 59-31 victory, winning the challenge 106-72 on aggregate.

With Mason, Wolstenholme, Giffard and Andrews all starting the season so strongly, and with the prospect of Ambrose returning in the near future, Rye House looked, on paper, as though they could be the strongest team in the league.

However, there was a quick dose of reality in the next match as the Rockets went down 48-42 away at Boston in the Conference League Trophy. Although Mason and Wolstenholme once again turned in superlative performances, 12 for Mason and 15 for Wolstenholme, Giffard only managed to pick up one point, having been excluded in his first race and suffering engine failure in his second two. Ambrose returned for this match but in heat nine he seemed to lose control of his machine while being strongly challenged on the last corner of the last lap and hurtled into the safety fence. Although he did not seem to be too badly injured, he withdrew from the rest of the meeting. Mason began where he had left off in 2000 by retaining the Bronze Helmet, defeating Luke Clifton.

The Rockets got their revenge the following day, however, as they comprehensively whipped Boston 55-34 at home. Andrews and Giffard were back on form and, with Morton also adding paid nine, thoughts of the league title returned to the minds of the supporters.

A defeat away at Somerset was followed by two more stunning victories: 62-28 at home and 61-28 away against Buxton. Mason scored 15-point maximums in both, while Andrews chimed in with a 12-point maximum at home and 12 points from five rides away. Wolstenholme added 11 from four away and a maximum 12 from four at home. Gary Sweet also returned for these two matches and the Rockets were able to track their strongest side of the season: Wolstenholme, Mason, Morton, Sweet, Ambrose, Andrews and Giffard.

Sadly, Rye House's challenge for honours ground to a halt shortly after these displays of strength as Wolstenholme was badly injured on 2 June in the Ace of Herts Trophy meeting and was unable to ride again until late July. The meeting against Peterborough on 3 June was the first he had missed since being appointed captain in 1999. Worse was to come as Andrews was injured at work and also missed several matches. Chris Courage was signed up as a replacement and settled into the team immediately, scoring paid 12 on his debut at home to Mildenhall on 23 June. However, already without Wolstenholme and Andrews, the title-challenging team took a further knock when, on 30 June, Mason was injured in a home tie against Somerset.

It was a much depleted line-up that took on Boston in the first leg of the Knock-Out Cup first round the following week: no Wolstenholme, no Mason, no Andrews. The remainder of the team, however, rode their hearts out to pull off a 51-39 victory over the reigning cup holders. Giffard and Courage spearheaded the win with paid 16 and 15 respectively. Morton added 11 and Sweet paid 10. Crucially, it was just enough to see the Rockets through to the semi-final as they just held on in the second leg, going down 50-40 at Boston to scrape through on aggregate, 91-89.

The big day came on 21 July when Wolstenholme, Mason and Andrews all returned for the same match, a home league match against Newport. And what a magic day for the Rye House faithful it was, as Wolstenholme and Mason carried on as though they'd never been away, both turning in paid maximums. With Giffard, Morton and Courage adding three more, the match turned in to a 70-19 rout.

Another emphatic win the following week, 63-26 in the first leg of the Knock-Out Cup semi-final, saw them within reach of the final for the second year running. Strangely, no one managed a maximum in this match, but Wolstenholme, Mason, Andrews, Giffard, Sweet and Courage all managed paid double scores. The only rider to miss out was Phil Ambrose, making his return from injury. Once again, Rye House were at full strength and, although they lost the second leg, 49-41, they were through to meet Somerset in the cup final.

Before meeting them in the final, the Rockets had to meet Somerset in the league and, in what was probably the best match of the season, managed to beat them by a single point, 45-44 with Courage top scoring on 12.

The league season ended with a succession of home wins and away losses, apart from a fighting effort at Boston as the Rockets drew 45-45, finally finishing the season in fourth spot, though things might have been different if they had not suffered so badly from injuries early in the season.

There was still, however, the Knock-Out Cup final. The first leg was held at home on 20 October but, against a very strong Somerset side, the Rockets were unable to overcome their opponents and went down 52-38, which made the away leg something of a formality, with the Rebels defeating Rye House 57-33 and 109-71 on aggregate.

It had been a bit of a disappointing year for Rye House after all the hopes at the beginning but, nevertheless, they had held their position in the league and had once again reached the cup final, so, after reflection, the riders, management and supporters were happy enough with the way things had turned out.

Mason was once again the Rockets' top man. His overall average was slightly down at 9.91, but it was still a great average. Wolstenholme was second on 8.54 and Courage third with 8.14. Giffard and Andrews, who had started the season as the numbers six and seven, scored at 6.34 and 5.67 respectively.

In Mason, Rye House also had the Conference League Riders' champion. The meeting to find the champion, held in front a very large crowd at Hoddesdon, saw Mason and Wolstenholme both in contention for the title. In heat nineteen, the two were drawn together and whoever won the race was going to win the title. Mason gated first but Wolstenholme was not far behind and for four laps they rode neck and neck, with Mason just maintaining his lead on the line. Unfortunately, Wolstenholme lost in a run-off for second place, but, nevertheless, first and third for Rye House riders was a great achievement and added further proof that, in David Mason, the Rockets had the best rider in the Conference League and, in Simon Wolstenholme, probably the best captain.

In the space of three years, the Rockets had been resurrected, they had returned to their own track and their promoter was now the owner of the stadium. Could there be any more pleasant surprises for the Rye House faithful? Not one to take things easy, Silver announced towards the end of the season that in 2002 he intended to run two teams, one in the Conference League and another in the Premier League. To show they were ready for it, he challenged Arena Essex to a match on 27 October to finish the season.

Because of the big difference in the leagues, Rye House brought in Brent Werner and Phil Morris from the Premier League. Jamie Smith, who had recorded a 10.53 average for Somerset was regarded as one of the best Conference League riders and he lowered the Rye House track record on 25 August to 58.8. But really everyone was watching the three Rockets' heat leaders, Mason, Wolstenholme and Courage, to see how they would get on at this level. As it turned out, they did not do so well in this higher level, with Mason scoring paid four, and Wolstenholme and Courage two each. The real difference was the speed of gating and the way the Premier boys took the first corner. The final score was Rye House 39 Arena Essex 51. Silver knew that he was going to have to build a new team for the Premier League, nevertheless, he announced soon afterwards that Mason and Courage would both take the step up, while Wolstenholme would stay on as captain of the Conference League team.

Rye House was still one of the major training tracks in the country. Sessions continued throughout the winter with a cost of £35 for anyone wishing to try their hand. As the owner of the stadium, Silver now saw the chance to help those juniors who showed promise by giving them first a chance to race for a team at Conference level and then, if they progressed still further, to move up to the Premier League. He had been involved in speedway for fifty years and he felt this was one way of helping to repay the sport he loved.

## 2001 Conference League

| Date | H/A | Opponent | W/L | Score |
|------|-----|----------|-----|-------|
| 3 June | A | Peterborough | L | 40-49 |
| 29 June | A | Newport | L | 39-51 |
| 14 July | H | Peterborough | W | 47-43 |
| 15 July | A | Buxton | L | 41-47 |
| 21 July | H | Newport | W | 70-19 |
| 17 August | A | Somerset | L | 36-54 |
| 25 August | H | Somerset | W | 45-44 |
| 1 September | H | Mildenhall | W | 63-27 |
| 9 September | A | Mildenhall | L | 44-46 |
| 15 September | H | Buxton | W | 51-39 |
| 17 September | A | Sheffield | L | 31-59 |
| 22 September | H | Sheffield | W | 46-44 |
| 13 October | H | Boston | W | 49-41 |
| 16 October | A | Boston | D | 45-45 |

P14 W7 D1 L6
For 647 Against 608
Position fourth (out of eight)

## Knock-Out Cup

First Round

| Date | H/A | Opponent | W/L | Score |
|------|-----|----------|-----|-------|
| 7 July | H | Boston | W | 51-39 |
| 12 July | A | Boston | L | 40-50 |

Won 91-89 on aggregate
Semi-Final

| Date | H/A | Opponent | W/L | Score |
|------|-----|----------|-----|-------|
| 28 July | H | Sheffield | W | 63-26 |
| 30 July | A | Sheffield | L | 41-49 |

Won 104-75 on aggregate
Final

| Date | H/A | Opponent | W/L | Score |
|------|-----|----------|-----|-------|
| 20 October | H | Somerset | L | 38–52 |
| 26 October | A | Somerset | L | 33–57 |

Lost 71–109 on aggregate

## 2001 Conference League and Knock-Out Cup

| Name | M | R | Pts | BP | Total | CMA |
|------|---|---|-----|-----|-------|-----|
| David Mason | 24 | 132 | 319 | 8 | 327 | 9.91 |
| Simon Wolstenholme | 19 | 89 | 179 | 11 | 190 | 8.54 |
| Chris Courage | 22 | 117 | 227 | 11 | 238 | 8.14 |
| Nathan Morton | 12 | 54 | 72 | 15 | 87 | 6.44 |
| Daniel Giffard | 28 | 123 | 168 | 27 | 195 | 6.34 |
| Darren Andrews | 20 | 79 | 96 | 16 | 112 | 5.67 |
| Garry Sweet | 18 | 70 | 80 | 16 | 96 | 5.49 |
| Phil Ambrose | 26 | 122 | 138 | 29 | 167 | 5.48 |
| James Cockle | 12 | 37 | 23 | 8 | 31 | 3.35 |

## 2002

The first new rider to be signed up for the Premier League team was Elite League rider Nigel Sadler, who had contacted Silver at the end of the 2001 season to ask if he could ride in the Challenge match against Arena Essex as he was considering stepping down from Peterborough to ride in the Premier League. Although he did not find a place in that team, he was the first rider on Silver's list for 2002. With him, from Peterborough, came Scott Swain, while Brent Warner, who had ridden in the Challenge match against Arena Essex, was also signed on. The last two names on the team sheet were Mark Courtney, signed for £1,000 from Trelawney, and Scott Robson.

The new team took to the track for the first time on 29 March at Arena Essex in a two-leg challenge, followed the next day by their first appearance at Hoddesdon in the second leg. Then the serious business began with their first official fixture, a home Premier Trophy tie against Isle of Wight. It was a promising start as John Sampford, team manager at this level for the first time in his life, steered the Rockets through to a 47–42 victory. Werner and Courtney both put in paid 11s. Mason scored just one point and was to take a while to settle down to this level of racing, but Courage put up a good performance, totalling paid seven.

The trophy matches followed a familiar pattern for Rye House supporters over the years, with three home wins and three away losses. The preliminary round of the Knock-Out Cup followed on 20 April with a good 53–37 home win over Somerset, who had also taken the plunge this year and promoted themselves to the Premier League. Unfortunately, just as he was beginning to show real promise, Courage suffered an injury and was sidelined for a number of matches, his place being taken by Adam Pryer. The second leg of the Cup match was an exciting affair, with little between the two teams on the night. In the end, the match finished 45–45, which meant that the Rockets were through on aggregate, 98–82. Swain, who had not shown his true form in the early season matches, really came good in this leg, putting in a magnificent paid 17 from six races.

The following week, the Rockets met Somerset again in a league encounter at Hoddesdon. This match was notable for the fact that it was the only time in the whole season that a Rye House rider recorded a full maximum, when Werner scored 15 points in the Rockets' 52–38 win.

The first few league matches followed the same home wins, away losses pattern until, in the second round cup tie against Swindon, the Rockets once again drew away. It seemed as though Rye House were certainties to go through to the next round, but a spirited performance from Swindon saw them push Rye House all the way, with the Rockets just managing to pull off a narrow 46–44 win, going through on aggregate 91–89.

Brent Werner, mainstay of the Rye House Premier League from 2002 to 2005.

The pattern of away losses in the league was broken at the beginning of June as, thanks to a brilliant ten points from David Mason, the Rockets drew at Workington, 45-45. Unfortunately, just six days later, the pattern of home wins was also broken as Berwick took the two points back with them after defeating the home side 49-41. However, another away draw, this time at Edinburgh, followed on 19 July, making four matches in league and cup that Rye House had now drawn away.

The first leg of the Knock-Out Cup quarter-final took place on 28 July. Sadly, it was to see Rye House's second home defeat of the season as they went down 46-44 to Hull. However, a fighting performance at Hull three days later saw them nearly pull off an amazing cup victory after they had been all but written off. With one heat to go, the Rockets were still in with a chance and, when Werner got away in front, it looked as though they might have done enough to grab a last-heat victory and draw the tie on aggregate. Unfortunately, he hit a big bump in the track, throwing him off line and giving Hull's Gary Stead just enough room to pass him. The final score was 45-45, giving Hull a 91-89 win on aggregate. Amazingly, it was the third time in as many rounds that the Rockets had drawn the away leg 45-45.

Following their exit from the cup, however, things went from bad to worse in the league for Rye House. On 19 August, they embarked on a run of six matches, three at home and three away, without a single victory, going down at home to Swindon, Stoke and Hull, all by very narrow margins, but enough to lose them the points. Part of the reason for this was injuries to three key riders. First, the early season injury to Chris Courage. Although he had returned to the team, he was no longer the promising rider he had seemed at the beginning of the year and, after running up a string of low scores, was dropped from the team. Second was Mark Courtney, whose injury at the end of July put him out for the rest of the season. Third was a knee injury to Scott Swain. Towards the end of the season, their places were taken by Adam Pryer, who returned to the team at the end of August, Troy Pratt, son of former manager Colin, and new young find Edward Kennett. Daniel Giffard was also given a few outings, but failed to make any impression.

The run of six losses was followed by a run of three victories in late September, including a 46-44 victory away at Somerset, thanks to a paid 17 from Werner and a paid 15 from Robson. The last two matches of the year, however, were lost and the season was over. Rye House finished their first season back in second division racing in thirteenth place out of seventeen.

Not great, but it had only ever really been a chance to find their feet again and the team proved that, in general, they were able to mix it at this level.

Werner was the best of the new Rockets make-up, finishing with an average of 8.47, while Sadler gave him strong support, also finishing with an eight-plus average. Sadler was named joint Rider of the Year by the Rye House supporters, not just for his scoring but also for his all-action way of riding, which kept the crowd on their toes throughout the season. The other man to join him as Rider of the Year was, in some ways, the biggest success story of all at Hoddesdon, David Mason. Before the season started, there was much speculation as to how the former Conference star would make out in the Premier League. After a hesitant start, he really came good towards the end of May, turning in three double-figure scores and earning promotion to the team proper from reserve. Over the rest of the season, he recorded four more paid double-figure scores and could mostly be relied upon, with one or two exceptions, to be around the seven or eight mark. By the end of the season, there was no doubt that the former Conference star had made out very well. Meanwhile, back in the Conference League…

With the Rockets moving up to the Premier League, a new name had to be found for the Conference League side. A poll was held amongst supporters to decide the new name. Some called for a return to the Red Devils, but the overwhelming winner was the Rye House Raiders. With Courage and Mason stepping up with the Rockets, it was important to find top-class replacements. Wolstenholme stayed on as captain and Giffard remained with the team. James Cockle was promoted from the junior team as was Edward Kennett. The winter training school had thrown up a couple of good prospects in Luke Bowen, son of Kevin, and Steve Boxall. In the end, only one top-class Conference League rider was brought in as a replacement, that being Barrie Evans. Nevertheless, the team looked very solid and, if able to avoid injuries, a definite contender for Conference League honours. It seemed even more likely after the first official fixture of the season, a home Conference League match against Boston on 1 April, when the Raiders stormed to a 61-30 victory. Wolstenholme and Evans both scored paid maximums, while Kennett added paid 15 from six rides and Cockle paid 11 from four. There then followed a string of four away matches, all of which were fairly close, but the Raiders were just unable to win. Their best was a 45-45 draw at Newcastle. With Evans missing the first three and then scoring paid 16 from six rides in the one match he did ride in, it was very much an 'if only' scenario. There was one more away match in the sequence against Mildenhall, when the Raiders were on the receiving end of a 54-36 thumping, but they were without Wolstenholme as well as Evans for this one. Throughout this period, newcomer Kennett had been going like an express train and moving straight into the third heat-leader spot. Evans returned on 4 June and rode in the next three matches, all of which Rye House won, including one away at King's Lynn which they won by the mammoth score of 61-29. Although Evans had returned, this big win owed itself more to Giffard and newcomer Scott Courtney, Mark's son, who both scored maximums. In the home match against King's Lynn that followed five days later, Giffard scored another maximum, along with Kennett, Wolstenholme and another newcomer to the team, Steve Boxall, to win by the even bigger score of 65-25. An away draw at Boston followed and then three more big home wins – 55-33 against Buxton, 65-25 against Camarthen and 53-35 against Newcastle – and a 48-40 away win against Wimbledon. After this run of victories, Rye House found themselves on top of the Conference League, but the early season losses had effectively scuppered their chances of remaining on top as most of their challengers had matches in hand over them. Although winning the League seemed unlikely, Silver felt very confident about the forthcoming Knock-Out Cup matches. The first leg of the semi-final tie was held on 25 August at Newport, after Rye House had been awarded a walkover against Wimbledon in the first round. Thanks to a good all-round performance, the Raiders won 49-40, but an injury to Wolstenholme in the Conference League Riders' championship put him out for the second leg. At home, however, and using rider replacement, Rye House managed to dispose of Newport, 49-41, winning the semi-final 98-81 on aggregate. This match was notable for the stunning 18-point maximum scored by Kennett, who was now showing amazing form for a sixteen-year-old in his first year of competitive league racing and also for the impressive form

Teenager Edward Kennett (left) topped the Conference League averages in 2003 with an astonishing 11.30. In the same year, he was also Rye House's top rider in the Premier League. On the right is Chris Neath, who played a leading role in Rye House's 2005 successful Premier League team.

of Steve Boxall, who scored a paid 18 from seven rides. For the third year running, Rye House were in the Knock-Out Cup final. Unfortunately, the second leg also saw a nasty accident to Barrie Evans as he was taken into the fence by his teammate Scott Courtney when the latter picked up too much drive coming out of the first bend in heat ten.

The first leg of the final was held on 13 October away at Buxton and, although Wolstenholme and Evans both turned out on the day, it became apparent quite soon that neither of them were back to full fitness. Both men managed three points each, far below what might have been expected if they'd been fully fit. As a result, Buxton took the tie 58-32 to set themselves up for an overall aggregate win. The Raiders' only heat winner of the afternoon was Kennett, who managed a win in heat twelve. Apart from that, a Buxton rider won every single heat.

Wolstenholme was unable to take part in the second leg as the first leg had aggravated the hand injury he had sustained earlier. His place was covered by rider replacement. At home, Rye House put up a better performance, winning the tie 49-41. Once again, it was the two youngsters, Kennett and Boxall, who led the way for the Raiders, scoring paid 14 and paid 16 respectively. But, of course, it was not enough to overcome the first leg deficit and, for the third year running, Rye House had to be content with the Knock-Out Cup runner-up spot.

It had been a season of 'almost, but not quite' for the Raiders. There is no doubt that, but for injuries, they might have done better in both the league and the cup. The early season injury to Evans had lost them matches that could have put them in contention for the League – as it was they finished fourth out of eleven – and the injuries to Evans and Wolstenholme at the end of the season virtually finished off any chance they may have had of winning the Cup. Although he only managed twelve matches during the season, Evans finished up as top scorer for Rye House with an average of 8.80; Wolstenholme finished on 8.24. But the two real finds of the season were Kennett and training school discovery, the fifteen-year-old Steve Boxall. Both finished with eight-point averages as well: Kennett on 8.70, Boxall on 8.00 exactly. Scott Courtney also had an 8.00 average. Five riders with 8-point averages. If only they could all have ridden together for the whole season, things might have been very different.

Kennett also came within an ace of proving himself the best rider in the Conference League as he finished runner-up in the Conference League Riders' Championship to Boston's Jamie Birkinshaw. Considering that a number of the riders in the Championship had been doubling up for Premier League teams throughout the season, and this was the sixteen-year-old Kennett's first season of Conference League racing, it was an astonishing achievement for the youngster.

At the beginning of the season, Silver was concerned that, by running two teams, the supporters would only turn out to support the Premier League side. But the fans were magnificent, showing their support for the Raiders as well as the Rockets, encouraging Silver to continue with the two-team approach for 2003.

At the end of the season, Wolstenholme announced his retirement.

## 2002 Premier League

| Date | H/A | Opponent | W/L | Score |
|------|-----|----------|-----|-------|
| 4 May | H | Newcastle | W | 49-41 |
| 9 May | A | Swindon | L | 35-55 |
| 11 May | H | Somerset | W | 52-38 |
| 12 May | A | Newport | L | 36-54 |
| 18 May | H | Glasgow | W | 49-41 |
| 25 May | H | Exeter | W | 56-34 |
| 3 June | A | Workington | D | 45-45 |
| 4 June | H | Workington | W | 49-41 |
| 9 June | H | Berwick | L | 41-49 |
| 10 June | A | Exeter | L | 28-62 |
| 15 June | H | Trelawny | W | 53-37 |
| 19 June | A | Hull | L | 41-49 |
| 22 June | H | Sheffield | W | 47-43 |
| 27 June | A | Sheffield | L | 32-58 |
| 6 July | H | Edinburgh | W | 51-39 |
| 14 July | H | Reading | W | 47-43 |
| 19 July | A | Edinburgh | D | 45-45 |
| 20 July | A | Berwick | L | 35-55 |
| 27 July | A | Stoke | L | 34-56 |
| 30 July | A | Isle of Wight | L | 34-55 |
| 11 August | H | Isle of Wight | W | 48-42 |
| 19 August | A | Newcastle | L | 33-45 |
| 24 August | H | Swindon | L | 41-51 |
| 26 June | H | Stoke | L | 44-46 |
| 26 August | H | Hull | L | 44-46 |
| 1 September | A | Trelawny | L | 41-49 |
| 13 September | A | Arena Essex | L | 44-46 |
| 14 September | H | Arena Essex | W | 51-39 |
| 20 September | A | Somerset | W | 46-44 |
| 21 September | H | Newport | W | 46-44 |
| 23 September | A | Reading | L | 38-52 |
| 29 September | A | Glasgow | L | 38-52 |

P32 W13 D2 L17
For 1,373 Against 1,496
Position thirteenth (out of seventeen)

## Knock-Out Cup

Preliminary Round

| Date | H/A | Opponent | W/L | Score |
|------|-----|----------|-----|-------|
| 20 April | H | Somerset | W | 53-37 |
| 10 May | A | Somerset | D | 45-45 |

Won 98-82 on aggregate

First Round

| Date | H/A | Opponent | W/L | Score |
|------|-----|----------|-----|-------|
| 30 May | A | Swindon | D | 45-45 |
| 1 June | H | Swindon | W | 46-44 |

Won 91-89 on aggregate

Second Round

| Date | H/A | Opponent | W/L | Score |
|------|-----|----------|-----|-------|
| 28 July | H | Hull | L | 44-46 |
| 31 July | A | Hull | D | 45-45 |

Lost 89-91 on aggregate

## Premier Trophy (Southern Section)

| Date | H/A | Opponent | W/L | Score |
|------|-----|----------|-----|-------|
| 6 April | H | Isle of Wight | W | 47-42 |
| 9 April | A | Isle of Wight | L | 40-50 |
| 13 April | H | Reading | W | 53-36 |
| 15 April | A | Reading | L | 25-65 |
| 19 April | A | Arena Essex | L | 42-48 |
| 27 April | H | Arena Essex | W | 47-43 |

P6 W3 D0 L3
For 254 Against 284
Position third (out of four)

## 2002 Premier League, Premier Trophy and Knock-Out Cup

| Name | M | R | Pts | BP | Total | CMA |
|------|---|---|-----|----|-------|-----|
| Brent Werner | 41 | 212 | 425 | 24 | 449 | 8.47 |
| Nigel Sadler | 44 | 220 | 423 | 23 | 446 | 8.11 |
| Scott Robson | 44 | 206 | 354 | 33 | 387 | 7.51 |
| Mark Courtney | 30 | 117 | 166 | 27 | 193 | 6.60 |
| David Mason | 41 | 175 | 198 | 38 | 236 | 5.39 |
| Scott Swain | 35 | 145 | 158 | 30 | 188 | 5.19 |
| Troy Pratt | 7 | 29 | 30 | 2 | 32 | 4.41 |
| Edward Kennett | 6 | 21 | 16 | 5 | 21 | 4.00 |
| Adam Pryer | 15 | 53 | 34 | 7 | 41 | 3.09 |
| Chris Courage | 22 | 80 | 46 | 10 | 56 | 2.80 |
| Daniel Giffard | 7 | 20 | 5 | 2 | 7 | 1.40 |

## 2002 Conference League

| Date | H/A | Opponent | W/L | Score |
|------|-----|----------|-----|-------|
| 1 April | H | Boston | W | 61-30 |
| 7 April | A | Newcastle | D | 45-45 |
| 21 April | A | Buxton | L | 42-47 |
| 28 April | A | Carmarthen | L | 40-50 |
| 12 May | A | Newport | L | 44-46 |
| 19 May | A | Mildenhall | L | 36-54 |
| 4 June | H | Sheffield | W | 58-32 |
| 12 June | A | King's Lynn | W | 61-29 |
| 17 June | H | King's Lynn | W | 65-25 |
| 23 June | A | Boston | D | 45-45 |
| 29 June | H | Mildenhall | W | 52-38 |
| 15 July | H | Newport | W | 65-25 |
| 21 July | H | Peterborough | W | 52-38 |
| 22 July | A | Sheffield | L | 30-60 |
| 29 July | H | Buxton | W | 55-33 |
| 12 August | H | Carmarthen | W | 65-25 |

| 17 August | H | Newcastle | W | 53-35 |
| 22 August | A | Wimbledon | W | 48-40 |
| 16 September | H | Wimbledon | W | 58-32 |
| 17 September | A | Peterborough | L | 30-60 |

P20 W12 D2 L6
For 1,005 Against 789
Position fourth (out of eleven)

## Knock-Out Cup

First Round
Walkover against Wimbledon
Semi-Final

| Date | H/A | Opponent | W/L | Score |
| --- | --- | --- | --- | --- |
| 25 August | A | Newport | W | 49-40 |
| 2 September | H | Newport | W | 49-41 |

Won 98-81 on aggregate
Final

| Date | H/A | Opponent | W/L | Score |
| --- | --- | --- | --- | --- |
| 13 October | A | Buxton | L | 32-58 |
| 19 October | H | Buxton | W | 49-41 |

Lost 81-99 on aggregate

## *2002 Conference League and Knock-Out Cup*

| Name | M | R | Pts | BP | Total | CMA |
| --- | --- | --- | --- | --- | --- | --- |
| Barrie Evans | 12 | 50 | 101 | 9 | 110 | 8.80 |
| Edward Kennett | 24 | 126 | 258 | 16 | 274 | 8.70 |
| Simon Wolstenholme | 19 | 82 | 146 | 23 | 169 | 8.24 |
| Steve Boxall | 19 | 99 | 173 | 25 | 198 | 8.00 |
| Scott Courtney | 16 | 79 | 143 | 15 | 158 | 8.00 |
| Daniel Giffard | 19 | 83 | 138 | 15 | 153 | 7.37 |
| James Cockle | 19 | 92 | 141 | 18 | 159 | 6.91 |
| Robert McNeil | 6 | 29 | 27 | 7 | 34 | 4.69 |
| Luke Bowen | 6 | 26 | 12 | 3 | 15 | 2.31 |

# 2003

Apart from the addition of Brett Woodifield, brought in for Scott Swain, the Premier League team remained the same as the one that had finished 2002. This meant the permanent promotion of Edward Kennett to the Premier League side after his sensational year in the Conference League. Silver was taking a bit of a chance on Woodifield as he had been out of action for something like eighteen months. However, his six-point average was well below his capabilities and if he could get back to his best form there was no doubt he would be a strong addition to the team.

The Rockets' opening league fixture was at home against Reading on 5 April. Fittingly, it was Kennett who sewed up the match for them. In five rides, from the reserve berth, he scored 9 paid 11, and it was his overtaking of Swindon's Swedish star, Jonas Davidsson, in heat fourteen that secured the match. Woodifield too rode well, scoring paid eight from his four rides, enough to give Silver confidence that he had made the right choice in signing him up. Unfortunately, after scoring paid six in the next match against Ipswich, Woodifield then broke his ankle in the first leg of the Knock-Out Cup match against Arena Essex and was out again for several weeks. Although this happened in his opening ride, the Rockets still managed to go on and win the tie, 46-44. Once again, the hero was Kennett, who finished the evening with a paid 15 haul, twice beating former World Long Track champion Kelvin Tatum on the way. After two disappointing matches, Mark Courtney also came good, scoring paid 13, while captain David Mason contributed eight points from the reserve berth. With a first leg victory behind them and the home leg to come, Rye House looked sure to progress to the second round, but things didn't quite go according to plan. Leigh Lanham for Arena Essex was on brilliant form, and with the other two heat leaders, Tatum and Joonas Kylmakorpi, they were more than a match for the Rockets' trio of Sadler, Robson and Werner. However, with the strong support of Courtney, Kennett and Mason, Rye House had a narrow four-point advantage going into heat thirteen (six points overall), but it was the two 'big' heats, thirteen and fifteen, that spelt disaster for the Rockets as Arena Essex won both of them with 5-1s. Fortunately, Robson and Mason were able to stem the tide with a 4-2 in heat fourteen and the match ended 46-44 in favour of Arena Essex, making the overall score 90-90.

Thanks mainly to Kennett, Mason, Courtney and Robson, Rye House won their next three official home fixtures, but Sadler and Werner were not scoring the points that might be expected of them. It transpired later that Sadler was going through a difficult time personally, but no one was aware of this at the time. Werner was suffering from a long string of mechanical problems.

Although they were just managing to hang on at home, away from home Rye House were suffering some very bad defeats: 62-27 at Exeter, 60.5-29.5 at Trelawny and 57-32 at Stoke. By the time of the rerun Knock-Out Cup first round tie on 23 May, Kennett had amazingly moved from reserve position to become the Rockets' leading rider. Given the string of poor away results, however, the omens did not look good for the Cup tie and, sure enough, in the first leg away at Arena Essex, Rye House went down 55-40, Kennett scoring paid 12 and Werner paid ten from five rides. Before the second leg, the Rockets had a home league match against Stoke, without Kennett, who was taking part in the World Junior Championship qualifying round at Poole, which they lost by the hefty score of 54-35.

Tommy Allen was top scorer for the 2004 Conference League team.

Despite Kennett returning for the Knock-Out Cup replay second leg, the Rockets still went down, 46-44, losing the tie 101-84 on aggregate. Two more losses in the league followed, one home and one away, and any hope Rye House had of finishing in the top half of the table had all but disappeared. Kennett scored his first Premier League maximum on 12 July in a home draw with Newport, but then, just over a week later, he was out for the rest of the season. In an away fixture at Reading on 21 July, in heat five, his footrest touched the fence in the back straight, dragging him into it and sending him flying down the track. The resulting leg injury put him out for the rest of the season. Already losing matches at home and away, without their new young star, Rye House were now in real trouble, although an away win at Peterborough on 22 August gave the Rockets second place in the newly instituted British League Cup Group B and progression through to the quarter-finals.

The first leg of the quarter-final took place on 24 September against Elite League's Belle Vue, who included top riders such as Joe Screen, Steve Johnston and Jason Lyons in their line-up. The Rockets put up a spirited performance against their top class rivals and came away from Kirkmanshulme Lane, just eight points down on the night, 49-41, thanks to a great effort from Robson, who scored 16 points and beat both Screen and Johnston in the last heat. Woodfield also put in one of his best performances of the season to score paid 13 from the reserve berth. For the second leg back at Hoddesdon, Rye House brought in Hull's Paul Thorpe as a guest for Kennett, but this time Belle Vue made no mistakes as their big three, Screen, Johnston and Lyons, had little difficulty with the opposition (with the exception of Thorp, who managed to defeat all three of them). In the end, the Aces ran out victors, 48-42, and winners on aggregate, 97-83. From Rye House's point of view, the best thing about the tie was the size of the crowd that had come to see probably the most famous team in speedway racing for the first time ever at Hoddesdon.

Three more league matches were left at the end of the season, with the Rockets winning the home match against Isle of Wight, 50-40, and losing the two away, 53-37 at Arena Essex and 50-40 at Somerset.

It had not been the season the fans had hoped for and the team did no better than in their first Premier League season, finishing fourteenth out of eighteen teams. Kennett was top of the averages with 7.82, with Robson close on his heels at 7.62. Werner's average dropped to 7.07. Woodifield justified his six-point average by scoring at 6.14, though it might have been more if the early season injury hadn't set him back for a while. The only permanent team member from 2002 to increase his average was David Mason, now in his fifth year at the club. He was let down by his away record as his home average had gone up to 6.82, but overall he was averaging 5.14.

Although Wolstenholme had now retired, the Raiders still had a very strong-looking side. Kennett, Evans, Boxall, Cockle and Scott Courtney were all back, while Luke Bowen and Joel Parsons made up the initial squad. In the first official fixture of the season, a league match against Mildenhall, in just his second ride, Courtney fell and injured himself and was out for the rest of the season. Nevertheless, the Raiders took a comfortable win, beating Mildenhall 51-40, with Kennett leading the way with a scorching 15-point maximum. He also relieved Wayne Broadhurst of the Bronze Helmet. As if that wasn't enough, he set a new Conference League track record of 57.0 seconds.

Even without Courtney, Rye House reeled off five consecutive wins, two of them away. Kennett, who was doubling up with the Rockets of course, rode in three of them and scored maximums in all of them. In the first nine matches he rode in, up until 18 June, he only dropped one point, and that was when he was brought in as a golden double against Mildenhall on 1 June and had a fifteen-yard handicap.

The match against Mildenhall was also the only loss the Raiders suffered in their first thirteen official fixtures. Kennett's unfortunate injury, mentioned above, came after the eleventh of those twelve victories and, for most of the rest of the season, the Raiders were forced to use rider replacement to cover him. Jamie Courtney had been brought into the side in April, but he too was injured at about the same time and his place was taken by Harland Cook, another promising fifteen-year-old discovery. With Kennett out, the rest of the team pulled together magnificently, with Evans, Parsons and Boxall, in particular, all putting together a string of excellent scores.

In the league, the Raiders were absolutely unbeatable at home, while away they were also picking up a significant number of wins and, by the time of the last league match of the season, they were lying in second place with a real chance of taking the title. The last league match was an away fixture at Sheffield. Earlier in the season, Rye House had trounced the Prowlers 58-31 at home. If they could now beat them at Sheffield, the three points gained from the win and the bonus point would make them Conference League champions for the first time.

Sadly, the meeting opened with two 5-1s for Sheffield and, just when they needed all their riders on top form, the Raiders probably put up their worst performance of the season. To make matters worse, their top rider on the night, Parsons, crashed in heat seven and dislocated his knee, putting him out for the rest of the night. Sheffield finished proceedings with four straight 5-1s, consigning the Raiders to their worst defeat of the season, 64-26. They hadn't even won the bonus point, never mind the match, and so had to be content with the runner-up spot in the league.

However, there was still the Knock-Out Cup final to come. For the fourth year running, the Raiders had made the Conference League Knock-Out Cup final, having disposed of Carmarthen, 117-63, and Armadale, 99-71, on the way. They were now up against new league champions and old rivals Mildenhall in the final.

The opening match was at home on 18 October. Edward Kennett defied doctor's orders to return to the line-up for this important match, which saw him line up with Cockle, Evans, Boxall, Parsons, Cook and yet another young teenage discovery, Barry Burchatt. Although the Raiders won the tie, it was only by a narrow three-point margin, 46-43. It could have been more had Burchatt's cut-out not come away when he was leading in the race of his life against Mildenhall's Nick Simmons and Matthew Wright in heat fourteen, turning a 5-1 into a 3-3. Rye House also felt they were hard done by with Mildenhall's inclusion of Daniel King at reserve. It seemed to many that a rider of his standing had no place at reserve when there were riders of a much lower calibre in the team itself. However, his use at reserve was sanctioned and he almost proved a match winner for Mildenhall, scoring paid 17 points. For Rye House, Kennett showed what the team had been missing for most of the season by turning in a brilliant 14-point performance.

Although with not as big a lead as they would have liked, the Raiders, nevertheless, were still in with a good chance of taking the cup. As the second leg progressed, Mildenhall gradually built up a steady lead and, by heat twelve, they were leading by nine points (six overall), but a 5-1 in that heat from Evans and Parsons brought the Raiders right back into contention. After heat fourteen, the scores were 45-38 to Mildenhall, or 88-84 on aggregate. If the Raiders could get a 5-1 in the last heat, it would go to a run-off, and, with the form Kennett was in, he was undoubtedly the favourite to beat any rider Mildenhall might put up to race him.

Lining up for Rye House were Kennett and Boxall, and for Mildenhall, Paul Lee and Matthew Wright. Kennett had already scored 10 points from five rides including an exclusion in his first race. Boxall had scored 13, while Lee had nine plus one exclusion and Wright four. The Raiders were still in with a real chance. It was like 1979 all over again, with an atmosphere that could be cut with a knife descending over the stadium. Former Rocket Steve Naylor, now the Raiders' team manager, won the toss and elected to take positions one and three. Lee's starting had been fairly poor all night but, as the tapes rose, he flew off from the start and increased his lead lap on lap. Kennett and Boxall could only watch his back wheel in despair as the resulting 3-3 gave Mildenhall the tie 48-41 and the Cup, 91-87 on aggregate. It had been an exhilarating match with some first-class speedway but, unfortunately, Rye House found themselves yet again on the wrong end of the score in the Conference League Cup final. Four years running they had reached the final, and four years running they had to be content with the runner-up spot.

It had been a good year for the Raiders, but they were just pipped in both main competitions by arch rivals Mildenhall, although they did manage to win the inaugural Conference League

Fours, beating Mildenhall on their own track as well as Peterborough and Boston in the final. The team for the final, which had to be run as a separate meeting after the original meeting had been abandoned following the semi-finals due to rain, consisted of Evans, Parsons, Boxall and Bowen. Like the Knock-Out Cup final, it was an eventful meeting. After thirteen of the sixteen heats had been run, it was obviously a two-horse race between the Raiders and Mildenhall, with the scores standing at Rye House 24, Mildenhall 26. Heat fourteen proved to be the most exciting race of the night as Boxall shot away from the tapes in front of Mildenhall's Cup hero Paul Lee. Lee hung on, trying to get through on the inside, but as the pair hit the last bend, he switched positions and, in a death-defying move, swept round the outside, his knuckles almost scraping the fence, to grab victory literally on the line. With just two heats to go, Mildenhall were now three points up and had Nick Simmons and Wayne Broadhurst to come, who, between them, had scored 13 points from six rides. It seemed odds on yet another runner-up place for the Raiders. However, it wasn't all over yet as, in heat fifteen, Broadhurst fell, leaving Parsons to take the three points and level the scores. It now came down to a winner-takes-all race between Evans and Simmons, with Peterborough's top man, Daniel King, thrown in for good measure. Simmons gated badly and, in an effort to catch up, overdid it on the second lap, also falling. Evans, who was in third place, decided that was all that was needed and came home for the vital point that gave the Raiders their first ever trophy.

One trophy and two runner-up places, but it might have been three trophies if Kennett had been fit all year. His average of 11.30 was absolutely stunning. Out of sixty-three rides in league and cup matches, he was only beaten by an opponent six times. He was quite clearly the Conference League rider of the year and it was a shame he missed out on the Conference League Riders' Championship because of his injury. However, this did allow another Rye House rider, Barrie Evans, to take the coveted title with 14 points. Parsons was involved in a four-man run-off for third place, but came second to Boston's Trevor Harding to finish in fourth place.

Once again, Rye House had run a successful season with two teams. The level of support for both was such that their future seemed certain as the club entered its seventieth anniversary year.

## *2003 Premier League*

| Date | H/A | Opponent | W/L | Score |
|------|-----|----------|-----|-------|
| 5 April | H | Reading | W | 48–42 |
| 26 April | H | Exeter | W | 55–35 |
| 27 April | A | Newport | L | 39–51 |
| 5 May | H | Workington | W | 50–40 |
| 19 May | A | Exeter | L | 27–62 |
| 20 May | A | Trelawny | L | 29.5–60.5 |
| 24 May | A | Stoke | L | 32–57 |
| 25 May | H | Stoke | L | 35–54 |
| 31 May | H | Swindon | L | 44.5–45.5 |
| 4 June | A | Hull | L | 41–49 |
| 7 June | H | Glasgow | W | 49–39 |
| 15 June | H | Sheffield | L | 44–46 |
| 17 June | A | Isle of Wight | L | 29–61 |
| 21 June | H | Somerset | W | 57–33 |
| 6 July | A | Workington | L | 36–54 |
| 7 July | H | Trelawny | W | 52–38 |
| 12 July | H | Newport | D | 45–45 |
| 17 July | A | Sheffield | L | 34–56 |
| 21 July | A | Reading | L | 42–48 |

| | | | | |
|---|---|---|---|---|
| 2 August | H | Newcastle | W | 49-41 |
| 20 August | A | King's Lynn | L | 42-48 |
| 25 August | H | King's Lynn | W | 49-41 |
| 29 August | A | Edinburgh | L | 34-55 |
| 30 August | A | Berwick | L | 23-67 |
| 1 September | H | Berwick | W | 62-27 |
| 4 September | A | Swindon | L | 41-49 |
| 6 September | H | Hull | W | 47-43 |
| 7 September | A | Newcastle | L | 44-46 |
| 13 September | H | Edinburgh | L | 43-47 |
| 20 September | H | Arena Essex | W | 48-42 |
| 21 September | A | Glasgow | L | 43-47 |
| 4 October | H | Isle of Wight | W | 50-40 |
| 10 October | A | Arena Essex | L | 37-53 |
| 17 October | A | Somerset | L | 40-50 |

P34 W12 D1 L21
For 1,441 Against 1,612
Position: fourteenth (out of eighteen)

## Knock-Out Cup

First Round

| Date | H/A | Opponent | W/L | Score |
|---|---|---|---|---|
| 18 April | A | Arena Essex | W | 46-44 |
| 19 April | H | Arena Essex | L | 44-46 |

Drew 90-90 on aggregate

First Round Replay

| Date | H/A | Opponent | W/L | Score |
|---|---|---|---|---|
| 23 May | A | Arena Essex | L | 40-55 |
| 26 May | H | Arena Essex | L | 44-46 |

Lost 84-101 on aggregate

## British League Cup

First Round Group B (Eastern Group)

| Date | H/A | Opponent | W/L | Score |
|---|---|---|---|---|
| 12 April | H | Ipswich | W | 46-44 |
| 10 May | H | King's Lynn | W | 55-35 |
| 11 June | A | King's Lynn | L | 41-49 |
| 26 July | H | Peterborough | W | 42-36 |
| 7 August | A | Ipswich | L | 44-46 |
| 8 August | A | Arena Essex | L | 41-49 |
| 16 August | H | Arena Essex | W | 53-37 |
| 22 August | A | Peterborough | W | 46-44 |

P8 W5 D0 L3
For 368 Against 340
Position: second (out of five)

Quarter-Final

| Date | H/A | Opponent | W/L | Score |
|---|---|---|---|---|
| 24 September | A | Belle Vue | L | 41-49 |
| 27 September | H | Belle Vue | L | 42-48 |

Lost 83-97 on aggregate

## 2003 Premier League, Knock-Out Cup and British League Cup

| Name | M | R | Pts | BP | Total | CMA |
|------|------|------|------|------|------|------|
| Edward Kennett | 23 | 111 | 193 | 24 | 217 | 7.82 |
| Scott Robson | 48 | 242 | 424 | 37 | 461 | 7.62 |
| Brent Werner | 47 | 234 | 383.5 | 30 | 413.5 | 7.07 |
| Nigel Sadler | 47 | 225 | 327.5 | 28 | 355.5 | 6.32 |
| Brett Woodifield | 44 | 181 | 231 | 47 | 278 | 6.14 |
| David Mason | 44 | 165 | 173 | 39 | 212 | 5.14 |
| Mark Courtney | 47 | 178 | 199 | 27 | 226 | 5.08 |
| Joel Parsons | 6 | 16 | 6 | 1 | 7 | 1.75 |

## 2003 Conference League

| Date | H/A | Opponent | W/L | Score |
|------|------|------|------|------|
| 21 April | H | Mildenhall | W | 51–40 |
| 27 April | A | Newport | W | 44–34★ |
| 3 May | H | Oxford | W | 53–37 |
| 24 May | H | Wolverhampton | W | 57–33 |
| 27 May | A | Wolverhampton | W | 47–38 |
| 1 June | A | Mildenhall | L | 44–48 |
| 8 June | A | Carmarthen | W | 54–36 |
| 15 June | H | Sheffield | W | 58–31 |
| 18 June | A | Wimbledon | W | 47–42 |
| 12 July | H | Newport | W | 57–32 |
| 2 August | H | Newcastle | W | 53–36 |
| 10 August | A | Buxton | L | 44–46 |
| 18 August | H | Carmarthen | W | 58–30 |
| 23 August | H | Boston | W | 64–26 |
| 25 August | H | Peterborough | W | 57–33 |
| 7 September | A | Newcastle | L | 40–50 |
| 8 September | H | Buxton | W | 50–39 |
| 12 September | A | Boston | W | 49–41 |
| 16 September | A | Peterborough | W | 55–32† |
| 26 September | A | Oxford | L | 25–63 |
| 4 October | H | Wimbledon | W | 69–19 |
| 9 October | A | Swindon | L | 29–43‡ |
| 11 October | H | Swindon | W | 47–43 |
| 13 October | A | Sheffield | L | 26–64 |

★ Abandoned after thirteen heats. Result stands
† Raced at King's Lynn
‡ Abandoned after twelve heats. Result stands
P24 W18 D0 L6
For 1,178 Against 936
Position: second (out of thirteen)

## Knock-Out Cup

### First Round

| Date | H/A | Opponent | W/L | Score |
|------|------|------|------|------|
| 8 June | A | Carmarthen | W | 50–40 |
| 9 June | H | Carmarthen | W | 67–23 |

Won 117-63 on aggregate

Semi-Final

| Date | H/A | Opponent | W/L | Score |
|------|-----|----------|-----|-------|
| 15 September | H | Armadale | W | 59-31 |
| 20 September | A | Armadale | W | 50-40 |

Won 109-71 on aggregate

Final

| Date | H/A | Opponent | W/L | Score |
|------|-----|----------|-----|-------|
| 18 October | H | Mildenhall | W | 46-43 |
| 19 October | A | Mildenhall | L | 41-48 |

Lost 87-91 on aggregate

## *2003 Conference League and Knock Out Cup*

| Name | M | R | Pts | BP | Total | CMA |
|------|---|---|-----|----|----|-----|
| Edward Kennett | 12 | 63 | 177 | 1 | 178 | 11.30 |
| Barrie Evans | 25 | 129 | 284 | 29 | 313 | 9.71 |
| Joel Parsons | 29 | 161 | 317 | 33 | 350 | 8.70 |
| Steve Boxall | 27 | 133 | 245 | 24 | 269 | 8.09 |
| Luke Bowen | 26 | 111 | 156 | 33 | 189 | 6.81 |
| Jamie Courtney | 10 | 40 | 50 | 10 | 60 | 6.00 |
| James Cockle | 30 | 130 | 160 | 26 | 186 | 5.72 |
| Harland Cook | 17 | 70 | 74 | 10 | 84 | 4.80 |
| Barry Burchatt | 6 | 24 | 12 | 2 | 14 | 2.33 |
| James Theobald | 7 | 19 | 8 | 1 | 9 | 1.89 |

## 2004

Silver knew that he needed to strengthen the Rockets if they were to have a real chance of honours in 2004. He kept Werner and Robson as two of the three heat leaders. Silver had wanted Kennett to stay on, but after his spectacularly brilliant year in both the Premier League and the Conference League, he had decided to go straight for the Elite League and returned to his parent club, Eastbourne. The man to replace him was Davey Watt, who had been offered to Rye House by Poole as he was surplus to their requirements. Chris Neath, who was something of a Rye House track specialist and had guested for the Rockets on a number of occasions the previous year, was also signed up, as was Trelawney's Steve Masters. Swindon's Tommy Allen was given one of the reserve berths and, for the other, Silver decided to give young Raiders' star Steve Boxall a run.

It had all the makings of a team that could challenge for the top and there was certainly a bit more than cautious optimism as the Rockets began their season with home and away wins in a two-leg challenge against King's Lynn. The optimism continued as Rye House put together a string of five wins in the Premier Trophy, with just one loss coming at Reading, 48-45, when they had, at one point, been eight points up, but were victims of a six-point, double-point tactical ride. In that run, there was also a 52-42 home victory over Sheffield in the Premier League. All seven riders were performing well, with the match against Newport on 10 April being a particular highlight as they trounced the Wasps 66-27 with no less than four of the team, Neath, Robson, Werner and Watt, scoring full or paid maximums.

Sadly, their charge for the Premier Trophy hit the skids in a disastrous 67-26 defeat at Exeter. Only Neath seemed able to master the wide open spaces of Exeter's track. Nevertheless, after the Exeter defeat, the Rockets went for the next seven matches without another loss. However, two more away defeats in the Trophy to Somerset and Isle of Wight meant that they just missed out on second place and, therefore, progress through to the semi-final stage. The Isle of Wight

Yet another young Rye House discovery Steve Boxall (left) and Stuart Robson (right) also played a major part in Rye House's 2005 success.

match saw one of the strangest races to take place in 2004. In heat two, the Isle of Wight's Chris Johnson was moving at the start, so the referee, Chris Durno, delayed putting up the tapes, causing Steve Boxall to run into them and break them. He was given a handicap of fifteen metres and the riders were called back to the start. As they motored up to the tapes again, Isle of Wight's Glen Phillips had a problem with his bike and went back to the pits. He was then excluded under the two-minute rule. The other three started the race just as Phillips, who was unaware that he had been excluded, came out on to the track. Seeing the other three go, he chased after them. As he was riding in red, Durno put on the red exclusion light, but, seeing the red light, the other three riders all thought that the race had been stopped and slowed up. In the end, the referee decided he'd had enough and awarded the race, making Tommy Allen the winner.

On 31 May, the Rockets, without Dave Watt, took on a strong Elite League's Eastbourne side in an inter-league challenge match. Although it was only a narrow victory, 46-45, it was a triumph for Rye House. Werner scored 17 points, showing that he could match the best in the Elite League, while Neath also scored well with paid 16.

With their exit from the Premier Trophy, the Rockets turned their attention to the Premier League. They had already won two away matches earlier in the season, against Newport and Newcastle, and drawn against King's Lynn. However, Masters had badly injured his wrist in the Trophy match against Somerset, while Watt aggravated a foot injury in the match against Isle of Wight, so both were forced to miss several vital matches in the early stages of the Premier League campaign. Jason King was eventually brought in as cover for Masters, but was not really in the same class and the Rye House scores suffered as a result. At home, the Rockets were still a match for anyone, but away there were a couple of heavy defeats during this period as they went down 58-34 at Workington and, even worse, 62-32 at Hull. Even when Watt and Masters returned, the Rockets seemed unable to translate their brilliant home form to away tracks, in particular the bigger tracks. There was to be one more away win at Newcastle on 8 August, but that was the last of the season. Nevertheless, the impregnable home form and their early season successes away meant that the Rockets finished sixth in the league, their highest position since joining the Premier League. It also meant they were through to the Young Shield quarter-final.

The first leg was held at Hoddesdon, with Rye House taking on league champions Hull. With two heats to go, the Rockets led by 11 points and it looked as though they would gain a big lead to take back to the Boulevard, but it all went wrong in heat fourteen. Hull handed Emil Kramer the black and white helmet, but even then the prospect of a big Rye House win still seemed on the cards as, up to this point, Kramer had only scored two points, while the Rye House pair, Allen and Robson, had scored 11 between them. And it was Robson and Allen who got away from the tapes and led going into the back straight. Kramer and Sanchez gained ground and, with Allen, the three of them entered the third bend more or less together. Allen was undaunted and managed to keep the two Hull riders at bay and, as they entered the home straight, it was still Robson and Allen in the lead. With both the Rockets now gradually pulling away, it looked like a certain 5-2 for the Rye House pair and a 14-point lead. But then disaster struck as Robson crashed into the bend, to be followed just seconds later by Allen. Neither Rye House rider finished the race, leaving Hull to pick up an 8-0, cutting the lead to three points. With the final heat ending in a 3-3, the Rockets had just a three-point lead to take with them to Hull.

The return was more or less a foregone conclusion. The three-point lead only lasted until the beginning of the first heat as Hull took a 5-1. From then on, there was no doubt who the winners were going to be and, in spite of some strong resistance from Werner with 14 points and Watt with 13, sure enough, Hull ran out victors, 52-42 and 96-89 on aggregate.

It had been a reasonable season for the Rockets and certainly better than the first two in their return to Premier League racing. It was a little disappointing in the end as they had started so well, but injuries had affected them badly in the middle of the season.

In the Knock-Out Cup, Rye House started well with a first-round victory over Newcastle, 104-80 on aggregate, winning both legs, but they were unable to progress any further as they went down 101-88 to Isle of Wight in the next round. The Rockets reached the final of the Premier League Fours, coming last to Workington, Stoke and Glasgow.

Watt proved to be the best with a final average of 8.43, but perhaps the most satisfying of all was Werner's return to form. He had not had a particularly good 2003 thanks, in the main, to mechanical problems. With those behind him, however, he was back on top form as the Rockets' captain and also put in an 8-plus average. The third heat leader, Chris Neath, started well but faded a little over the course of the season. He was doubling up, also riding for Wolverhampton in the Elite League, and it may have been that he was tiring as the season went on. Nevertheless, he finished up with a very creditable 7.71 average. Robson's form dipped a little but he still maintained a 7-plus average, while Masters did all that was expected of him. It was unfortunate that his wrist injury put him out for some time and then restricted his scoring when he did come back. The two reserves, Allen and Boxall, did all that was required of them in the reserve berths, both finishing with 4-plus averages.

With Kennett and Evans moving on from the successful Raiders side, Silver and team manager John Sampford needed to find two top-class replacements if they were to maintain, or even better, their 2003 performance. However, the only real newcomer was Tommy Allen, who was also, of course, doubling up in the Rockets team. Other than him, there were high hopes for Rye House's own discoveries, Steve Boxall in particular, and also Barry Burchatt and Harland Cook, who had both made a few appearances at the tail end of the previous season. The team that lined up for the first official fixture on 11 April at Mildenhall were Allen, Boxall, Luke Bowen, Joel Parsons, Cook and Burchatt, with Karl White riding at number two. It was this number two spot that was to give most problems during the season and no fewer than nine different riders were given the number two race jacket. It was a team of youngsters in keeping with Rye House and Len Silver's philosophy of bringing on junior riders and preparing them for bigger things.

Although the opening match was lost 53-40, the Raiders put together a string of six wins from their next seven matches, including two away victories over Newport and Newcastle, the only loss coming at Boston. Allen was proving to be a Conference League star while Boxall, Parsons and Burchatt were all putting in mostly double-figure scores as well. Two away losses at Weymouth and Armadale dented the charge for the title, but then came a string of eight consecutive league wins, starting on 17 July and ending on 18 September, with some hefty wins on the way, including 62-33 over Newcastle and 65-26 over Swindon. The run was interrupted by one loss at Oxford on 24 September. This was to be the last loss suffered by the Raiders all season as they finished the year with a further five wins on the bounce, including three away.

It had been a tremendous year for the Raiders, they had won all their home matches and lost just five away, but sadly for them, Mildenhall were having an even better season, losing just three matches. It meant that, for the second year running, Rye House lost out to Mildenhall in the final reckoning as they finished runners-up again.

Amazingly, Rye House got no further than the first round in the Knock-Out Cup, losing both legs to Boston, 48-42 away and 51-44 at home, to suffer their only home reverse of the season.

By the end of the year, Allen had proved himself nigh on unbeatable both home and away. From 18 July to 24 October, in the last thirteen matches of the season, he scored double figures in all but one, which he missed altogether. Out of those twelve matches he did ride in, there were seven maximums. He finished the season with an average of 10.10. Both Boxall and Parsons were not far behind him, Boxall finishing on 9.91 and Parsons on 9.56. Reserves Barry Burchatt and Harland Cook were arguably the two strongest reserves in the league, Burchatt ending with 7.00 and Cook with 6.68.

As Rye House's seventieth anniversary year came to an end, Len Silver could be very pleased with what he had achieved. He was now owner of the stadium and running two highly successful teams. The public were returning to watch in large numbers and the Rye House tradition of turning out top-class youngsters was continuing. The racing was always first class and, although Rye House had never competed in the top flight of British speedway, they didn't need to to prove they were one of the top tracks in the country.

## *2004 Premier League*

| Date | H/A | Opponent | W/L | Score |
|------|-----|----------|-----|-------|
| 12 April | H | Sheffield | W | 52-42 |
| 9 May | A | Newport | W | 47-42 |
| 22 May | H | Workington | W | 56-39 |
| 28 May | A | Edinburgh | W | 46-44 |
| 29 May | A | Berwick | L | 42-53 |
| 5 June | H | Hull | L | 44-51 |
| 7 June | A | Reading | L | 43-49 |
| 13 June | H | Berwick | W | 48-42 |
| 19 June | H | Exeter | W | 45-44 |
| 2 July | A | Workington | L | 34-58 |
| 3 July | H | Somerset | W | 49-41 |
| 16 July | A | Somerset | L | 40-52 |
| 17 July | H | Edinburgh | W | 50-40 |
| 4 August | A | Hull | L | 32-62 |
| 6 August | H | Reading | W | 49-44 |
| 8 August | A | Newcastle | W | 48-45 |
| 14 August | H | Newcastle | W | 56-36 |
| 19 August | A | Sheffield | L | 25-69 |
| 20 August | H | King's Lynn | W | 58-35 |
| 22 August | A | Glasgow | L | 47-48 |
| 28 August | A | Stoke | L | 40-56 |
| 30 August | H | Stoke | W | 50-45 |
| 1 September | A | King's Lynn | L | 38-57 |
| 4 September | H | Glasgow | W | 51-41 |
| 7 September | A | Isle of Wight | L | 32-63 |
| 11 September | H | Isle of Wight | W | 52-41 |
| 13 September | A | Exeter | L | 18-75 |
| 18 September | H | Newport | W | 51-39 |

P28 W16 D0 L12

For 1,243 Against 1,353

Position: sixth (out of fifteen)

## Premier Trophy (South)

| Date | H/A | Opponent | W/L | Score |
|------|-----|----------|-----|-------|
| 20 March | H | Reading | W | 56-37 |
| 22 March | A | Reading | L | 45-48 |
| 27 March | H | Exeter | W | 51-42 |
| 10 April | H | Newport | W | 66-27 |
| 17 April | H | Isle of Wight | W | 47-42 |
| 18 April | A | Newport | W | 47-43 |
| 24 April | H | King's Lynn | W | 58-37 |
| 26 April | A | Exeter | L | 26-67 |
| 2 May | A | King's Lynn | D | 45-45 |
| 8 May | H | Somerset | W | 49-44 |
| 4 June | A | Somerset | L | 37-56 |
| 8 June | A | Isle of Wight | L | 42-54 |

P12 W7 D1 L4
For 569 Against 542
Position: third (out of seven)

## Knock-Out Cup

First Round

| Date | H/A | Opponent | W/L | Score |
|------|-----|----------|-----|-------|
| 15 May | H | Newcastle | W | 55-39 |
| 16 May | A | Newcastle | W | 49-41 |

Won 104-80 on aggregate

Second Round

| Date | H/A | Opponent | W/L | Score |
|------|-----|----------|-----|-------|
| 6 July | A | Isle of Wight | L | 36-59 |
| 31 July | H | Isle of Wight | W | 52-42 |

Lost 88-101 on aggregate

## Young Shield

Quarter-Final

| Date | H/A | Opponent | W/L | Score |
|------|-----|----------|-----|-------|
| 25 September | H | Hull | W | 47-44 |
| 29 September | A | Hull | L | 42-52 |

Lost 89-96 on aggregate

## 2004 Premier League, Premier Trophy, Knock-Out Cup and Young Shield

| Name | M | R | Pts | BP | Total | CMA |
|------|---|---|-----|-----|-------|-----|
| Davey Watt | 40 | 186 | 370 | 22 | 392 | 8.43 |
| Brent Werner | 45 | 220 | 422 | 28 | 450 | 8.18 |
| Chris Neath | 41 | 190 | 336 | 30 | 366 | 7.71 |
| Scott Robson | 44 | 195 | 299 | 43 | 342 | 7.02 |
| Steve Masters | 32 | 125 | 172 | 30 | 202 | 6.46 |
| Tommy Allen | 44 | 197 | 200 | 27 | 227 | 4.61 |
| Steve Boxall | 39 | 173 | 146 | 30 | 176 | 4.07 |
| Jason King | 6 | 19 | 10 | 6 | 16 | 3.37 |
| Luke Bowen | 8 | 28 | 9 | 2 | 11 | 1.57 |

## 2004 Conference League

| Date | H/A | Opponent | W/L | Score |
|------|-----|----------|-----|-------|
| 11 April | A | Mildenhall | L | 40-53 |
| 12 April | H | Boston | W | 55-38 |
| 18 April | A | Newport | W | 52-41 |
| 2 May | A | Boston | L | 36-57 |
| 16 May | A | Newcastle | W | 53-42 |
| 29 May | H | Carmarthen | W | 50-42 |
| 31 May | H | Wimbledon | W | 52-41 |
| 13 June | H | Weymouth | W | 61-30 |
| 18 June | A | Weymouth | L | 34-59 |
| 9 July | A | Armadale | L | 31-59 |
| 17 July | H | Armadale | W | 54-39 |
| 18 July | A | Buxton | W | 54-36 |
| 7 August | H | Mildenhall | W | 56-36 |
| 14 August | H | Newcastle | W | 62-33 |
| 21 August | H | Swindon | W | 65-26 |
| 30 August | H | Stoke | W | 51-38 |
| 5 September | A | Carmarthen | W | 54-40 |
| 18 September | H | Newport | W | 64-31 |
| 24 September | A | Oxford | L | 42-48 |
| 2 October | H | Oxford | W | 47-46 |
| 8 October | A | Stoke | W | 49-41 |
| 16 October | H | Buxton | W | 42-33★ |
| 21 October | A | Swindon | W | 49-39† |
| 24 October | A | Wimbledon | W | 54-43‡ |

★ Match abandoned after heat twelve. Result stands
† Match abandoned after heat fourteen. Result stands
‡ Raced at Rye House
P24 W19 D0 L5
For 1206 Against 991
Position: second (out of thirteen)

## Knock-Out Cup

First Round
Bye
Second Round

| Date | H/A | Opponent | W/L | Score |
|------|-----|----------|-----|-------|
| 25 June | A | Boston | L | 42-48 |
| 24 July | H | Boston | L | 44-51 |

Lost 86-99 on aggregate

## 2004 Conference League and Knock-Out Cup

| Name | M | R | Pts | BP | T | CMA |
|------|---|---|-----|----|----|-----|
| Tommy Allen | 22 | 101 | 251 | 4 | 255 | 10.10 |
| Steve Boxall | 15 | 67 | 163 | 3 | 166 | 9.91 |
| Joel Parsons | 21 | 100 | 224 | 15 | 239 | 9.56 |
| Luke Bowen | 23 | 107 | 162 | 27 | 189 | 7.07 |
| Barry Burchatt | 26 | 148 | 220 | 39 | 259 | 7.00 |
| Harland Cook | 26 | 130 | 186 | 31 | 217 | 6.68 |
| Gary Cottham | 7 | 22 | 16 | 2 | 18 | 3.27 |
| Mark Baseby | 16 | 54 | 24 | 9 | 33 | 2.44 |

## EPILOGUE — 2005

Although the original idea of this book was to celebrate the first seventy years of Rye House's history, 1934-2004, it would be unforgivable to leave out perhaps the most successful season in Rye House's history, 2005.

At the end of 2004, the Rockets had finished in sixth place in the league and had got through to the Young Shield quarter-finals. If it hadn't been for some injuries, they may have done even better. Silver and Sampford were able to keep hold of two heat leaders and two reserves from the 2004 team, Werner and Neath, and Allen and Boxall. Watt had moved on to try his luck with Elite League Eastbourne, Scott Robson had been signed up by Workington and Steve Masters went off to double up for Belle Vue and Reading. To take their places, 2003 hero Edward Kennett returned and Silver signed up Stuart Robson from Coventry and Daniel King, who was also riding for Ipswich in the Elite League. On paper, it was a stronger team than the year before so there were high hopes right from the start that 2005 could be the year. Before the season started, Silver took the riders away skiing in France for a team-building exercise. On their return, however, Allen broke his ankle before the season had started and it was obvious he would miss the first few matches.

Without Allen, the team used rider replacement and began the season with a run of six Premier Trophy matches without defeat, although it has to be said that five of these matches were at home. Nevertheless, the size of the victories, 61-32 over Isle of Wight and 59-33 over Exeter, for example, showed the rest of the Premier League what Rye House were made of. Even the away victory, at Newport, was by a large margin, 52-38. Both Robson and Neath started off like express trains, banging in double-figure score after double-figure score, while the rest of the team were not far behind, with the first maximum of the season coming from Kennett on 9 April in the victory over Exeter.

The first defeat of the season came at Exeter's County Ground on 11 April, ironically, Allen's first match of the season when the team were at full strength, but, as had been the case in previous seasons, the Rye House riders found the totally different Exeter track a difficult proposition. Another away loss followed on 27 April, this time to King's Lynn, but this was followed by another superb run of seven matches without defeat, three of them away. The last of these was on 10 May at Isle of Wight and left the Rockets runaway winners of the Premier Trophy South table. Having lost just two matches in the Trophy, they topped the table with 26 points. Their nearest rivals, Exeter and King's Lynn, were both 10 points behind on 16. The semi-final was due to be held on 12 June.

In the meantime, the Rockets had the serious business of winning the league to get on with. They had already won two home matches in the league and now went on to win two more, against Glasgow, 55-40, and Workington, 57-36. A brief respite from the league came on 3 June as the Rockets travelled to Edinburgh for the KO Cup first round first leg. It was a close run affair, but Edinburgh just managed to win, 47-43. In the return leg the next day, the Rockets overcame all resistance and put up a brilliant display, winning 57-33 to take the tie 100-80 on aggregate.

Next up was the Premier Trophy semi-final against Sheffield. The home leg was first with the Rockets hammering the Tigers, 66-26. Werner and King, who had been promoted to the team proper in place of Allen, who had dropped down to reserve, both scored maximums. After a score like that, the return leg was more or less a formality, but there were some nervous moments as Rye House went down 50-39, winning the semi-final 105-76 on aggregate.

Back in the league, there were some mixed fortunes as they won one, lost one and drew one of their next three away matches. However, at home, the Rockets remained rock solid, taking on and beating Newcastle, 54-41, Reading, 57-36, and King's Lynn by the very impressive score of 61-34. The next round of the cup followed and again Rye House had drawn a Scottish team: Glasgow. With the Rockets only overcoming Glasgow by six points, 48-42, at home, the team were a little apprehensive as they set out north. However, the need to preserve a slender lead away from home seemed to spur the riders on and they set about the Tigers in no uncertain manner, pulling off a magnificent 57-33 win, with Robson, Neath, Werner and Kennett all recording paid double-figure scores.

After five more league matches, four away from home and three victories, the Rockets had their first final of the season as they met Workington in the Premier Trophy final. The first leg was held at Derwent Park on 6 August. At this point in the season, Rye House had four riders in the top twenty-five Premier League averages: Neath, Robson, Werner and Kennett. Glasgow had three and no other team had more than two. Workington had just one, Carl Stonehewer, and he missed the final through injury. Rye House started the final as the obvious favourites, but after just one heat they were reduced to six riders as Kennett fell on the first bend of the second lap, injuring his arm and putting himself out for the rest of the meeting. It was a big blow to overcome but the rest of the Rockets rose to the challenge magnificently. Only the Workington guest, Magnus Zetterstrom, was able to put up any sort of show and Robson and Werner, in particular, rode as though the Workington track was their own. Boxall, given seven rides, scored a brilliant paid 13 points from the reserve position and that included one race where he had had to start fifteen metres behind after delaying the start. His tally included one incredible wheel-to-wheel race in which he became the only Rocket to beat Zetterstrom and stop him from getting a maximum. It was a close match, but the Rockets took the lead in heat twelve, with a 5-1 from Boxall and Werner, and never relinquished it, running out victors, 46-44.

With a two-point lead from the away leg, there was little doubt that Rye House would bring home their first trophy the following day. And with the match starting with a 5-1 thanks to Robson and Kennett, there was even less doubt. The final was all over at the end of heat eleven. With the score standing at 48-21, it was mathematically impossible for Workington to win, even if they'd won all four remaining heats 5-0. In the end, the score was 61-32 to Rye House, giving them the Premier Trophy 107-76 on aggregate. It had been a runaway victory for the Rockets. Once again, four of the team, Kennett, Werner, Neath and Allen, had scored double figures, with Kennett and Allen both recording paid maximums. It was an unbelievable moment for the team and the supporters as they took their first major title since winning the National League a quarter of a century earlier. But it was the league that they all really wanted and the league they now went after.

The pursuit of the league title didn't get off to a good start as they proceeded to lose their next two away matches, 64-30 to Sheffield and 54-40 to Isle of Wight. At home, they continued to flatten all before them, beating Isle of Wight, 59-37, and Edinburgh, 58-37. An important double over Stoke followed: 56-36 away and 63-27 at home. One more loss away at Workington and then a home win over Exeter and it was time for the Knock-Out Cup semi-final away at Reading. A 47-43 win at Smallmead set the Rockets up nicely for the end-of-season battle for the remaining three trophies: the league itself, the Knock-Out Cup and the Young Shield. There were thirteen matches left in the season and all had their part to play in the destiny of those trophies. After the Knock-Out Cup semi-final, Rye House had three more league matches to race before the second leg. Two of those matches were away from home, including one at their nemesis track, Exeter. To be sure of the league title, the Rockets needed to win them all.

First up was an away match at Newport. Oliver Allen came in as a guest for the injured Chris Neath. It was an inspired choice as Allen turned in a paid maximum. With Kennett, Werner and Tommy Allen all recording paid double-figure scores as well, it ended up as an easy 58-34 victory for the Rockets. The next day, Rye House were at their least favourite track, Exeter. As it happened, it was a very sad occasion for the Falcons. It was their last ever league match on the County Ground as they had been given notice to quit for 2006. Although, like the rest of the speedway world, the Rockets were very sympathetic to the plight of Exeter's loyal fans, there was no time for sentimentality as they had a league to win. And, in what was probably their best ever performance at Exeter, Rye House put on a comprehensive demolition job against the Falcons, running out winners, 53-37. Once again, there was an inspired choice of guest as Shaun Tacey dropped just one point to Seemond Stephens. Robson went one better, scoring a paid maximum, while Daniel King added paid ten. Not only had the Rockets strengthened their grip on the league title but they had done it in a most comprehensive manner, with two very impressive away wins in which no less than five of their regular team had scored double figures. The final league match before the second leg of the cup semi-final was the home match against Newport on 17 September. It was a rout as, for the tenth time that season, the Rockets banged in over 60 points. And this in spite of the fact that Neath was still injured and Kennett and King were away at the World Under-21 Championship final. Oliver Allen guested for Neath again and rider replacement was used for Kennett. It was such an overwhelming victory that Newport only managed to win one heat, heat ten, and that was when Robson fell. Once again, it was a magnificent all-round team effort as Werner scored 16, Robson and Tommy Allen paid 15, Boxall paid 12 and Les Bowen and Oliver Allen paid seven in the crushing 64-28 win. The result meant that Berwick, Rye House's nearest competitor, had to win their next match at Sheffield, otherwise the Rockets would be crowned champions without having to race their last match.

The Berwick match took place the following Thursday, 22 September, and the result all Rye House had been praying for came true, as Sheffield defeated Berwick, 48-41, to give the Rockets their first league title since 1980. A large crowd turned out the following evening to salute the team as they took on Isle of Wight in the first leg of the Young Shield quarter-final. Unfortunately, the celebrations were marred by a serious injury to Robson, though the crash looked far worse than it finally turned out to be as he touched the rear wheel of Kennett's bike in heat six and hurtled in to the fence. At first there was little movement from Robson as he was placed on a stretcher and taken to hospital, but it later turned out that he had escaped with a dislocated shoulder and broken finger. The match itself was another one-sided affair as the Rockets crushed Isle of Wight, 62-30. Neath had returned and scored a 15-point maximum.

The next day, Rye House were in action again in the second leg of the Knock-Out Cup semi-final. Once again, the Rockets put on an awesome display, even without Robson, overwhelming Reading 65-25 to win the tie 112-68 on aggregate. No less than three of the Rye House team, Werner, King and Neath, scored full or paid maximums as every heat was won by a Rye House rider. The Rockets were now in the final and on course for the double. Three days later, they also found themselves on course for the Young Shield as they disposed of Isle of Wight in the quarter-finals. Although they lost the second leg 54-41, their lead from the first leg was good enough to give them a 103-84 winning scoreline.

The following Saturday saw the Rockets' final match in the league, which they duly won 60-31 over Somerset. It was a night of joyous celebrations at Hoddesdon as, although they had already won the league title, it was the night the trophy was actually presented to them.

With the league and Conference Trophy already won, the Rockets were now trying to land the Knock-Out Cup and the Young Shield. In the Young Shield, Rye House disposed of Sheffield in the semi-finals and then found themselves up against King's Lynn in both the finals. The season finished, therefore, with four matches against the Stars.

Sadly, Rye House were unable to add another trophy to their tally as they lost both finals to King's Lynn. After the elation of winning the league, the team seemed to lose a bit of their edge and, without Robson for all four matches, they just failed to overcome the on-form King's Lynn outfit, who seemed to have reserved their best for the two finals.

Although it was a slight disappointment, there is no getting away from the fact that the 2005 Rye House team was, in many people's minds, the greatest to have worn the Rockets' colours. Of course, much of the credit must go to the riders themselves. Robson was absolutely superb until his late season injury, while Werner played a real captain's role, and the two of them, together with Neath and Kennett, all finished the season with eight-plus averages. King was only just behind on 7.57, while Allen and Boxall proved to be all that could be asked for from reserves. Every single member of the regular team scored at least three full or paid maximums during the year.

As well as the riders, though, a lot of the credit had to go to the team manager John Sampford and to the man who had been associated with Rye House for over fifty years, Len Silver himself.

Len Silver, the man himself.

Silver had been a Rye House discovery himself as a rider back in the early 1950s. In 1974, he saved the track from possible closure when he brought senior league racing to Hoddesdon. He was the man who had guided them to their last league win back in 1980 and in 1999 and 2000 he played a crucial role in first resurrecting the Rockets team after their closure at the end of 1993 and then in their return to their home. He also had the courage and foresight to buy the stadium for speedway and had then taken the further step of running clubs in two leagues. There had been many disappointments along the way as the teams suffered from injuries and other problems, just when it seemed they were in with a chance of taking a title, but Len had never given up and now all his hopes and dreams for the club had come to fruition in 2005. During it all, he had never forgotten that Rye House had been, throughout its history, one of the country's leading producers of talented youngsters, a tradition Len is keen to continue today. He also continues the tradition of providing wonderful family entertainment at the track by the river. The names Rye House and Len Silver are now inseparable. Long may that continue!

### 2005 Premier League

| Date | H/A | Opponent | W/L | Score |
|---|---|---|---|---|
| 2 May | H | Hull | W | 50-44 |
| 7 May | H | Sheffield | W | 61-32 |
| 14 May | H | Glasgow | W | 55-40 |
| 28 May | H | Workington | W | 57-36 |
| 22 June | A | Hull | L | 33-57 |
| 25 June | H | Newcastle | W | 54-41 |
| 27 June | A | Newcastle | D | 45-45 |
| 2 July | H | Reading | W | 57-36 |
| 8 July | A | Edinburgh | W | 52-40 |

| 9 July | H | King's Lynn | W | 61-34 |
|---|---|---|---|---|
| 13 July | A | King' Lynn | L | 38-53 |
| 25 July | A | Reading | W | 46-44 |
| 29 July | H | Berwick | W | 65-25 |
| 30 July | A | Berwick | L | 35-57 |
| 31 July | A | Glasgow | W | 47-43 |
| 5 August | A | Somerset | L | 42-48 |
| 11 August | A | Sheffield | L | 30-64 |
| 21 August | H | Isle of Wight | W | 59-37 |
| 21 August | H | Edinburgh | W | 58-37 |
| 23 August | A | Isle of Wight | L | 40-54 |
| 27 August | A | Stoke | W | 56-36 |
| 29 August | H | Stoke | W | 63-27 |
| 3 September | A | Workington | L | 43-47 |
| 4 September | H | Exeter | W | 66-26 |
| 11 September | A | Newport | W | 58-34 |
| 12 September | A | Exeter | W | 53-37 |
| 17 September | H | Newport | W | 64-28 |
| 1 October | H | Somerset | W | 60-31 |

P 28 W20 D1 L7
For 1,448 Against 1,133
Position: first (out of fifteen)

## Premier Trophy (South)

| Date | H/A | Opponent | W/L | Score |
|---|---|---|---|---|
| 12 March | H | Somerset | W | 50-43 |
| 19 March | H | Newport | W | 50-40 |
| 27 March | A | Newport | W | 52-38 |
| 28 March | H | Isle of Wight | W | 61-32 |
| 2 April | H | Reading | W | 55-40 |
| 9 April | H | Exeter | W | 59-33 |
| 11 April | A | Exeter | L | 41-54 |
| 23 April | H | King's Lynn | W | 59-34 |
| 27 April | A | King's Lynn | L | 41-52 |
| 29 April | A | Somerset | W | 48-44 |
| 9 May | A | Reading | W | 48-40 |
| 10 May | A | Isle of Wight | W | 46-44 |

P12 W10 D0 L2
For 610 Against 494
Position: first (out of seven)
Semi-Final

| Date | H/A | Opponent | W/L | Score |
|---|---|---|---|---|
| 12 June | H | Sheffield | W | 66-26 |
| 16 June | A | Sheffield | L | 39-50 |

Won 105-76 on aggregate
Final

| Date | H/A | Opponent | W/L | Score |
|---|---|---|---|---|
| 6 August | A | Workington | W | 46-44 |
| 7 August | H | Workington | W | 61-32 |

Won 107-76 on aggregate

## Knock-Out Cup

First Round

| Date | H/A | Opponent | W/L | Score |
|---|---|---|---|---|
| 3 June | A | Edinburgh | L | 43-47 |
| 4 June | H | Edinburgh | W | 57-33 |

Won 100-80 on aggregate

Second Round

| Date | H/A | Opponent | W/L | Score |
|---|---|---|---|---|
| 16 July | H | Glasgow | W | 48-42 |
| 24 July | A | Glasgow | W | 57-33 |

Won 105-75 on aggregate

Semi-Final

| Date | H/A | Opponent | W/L | Score |
|---|---|---|---|---|
| 5 September | A | Reading | W | 47-43 |
| 24 September | H | Reading | W | 65-25 |

Won 112-68 on aggregate

Final

| Date | H/A | Opponent | W/L | Score |
|---|---|---|---|---|
| 21 October | A | King's Lynn | L | 27-63 |
| 22 October | H | King's Lynn | W | 56-34 |

Lost 83-97 on aggregate

## Young Shield

First Round

| Date | H/A | Opponent | W/L | Score |
|---|---|---|---|---|
| 23 September | H | Isle of Wight | W | 62-30 |
| 27 September | A | Isle of Wight | L | 41-54 |

Won 103-84 on aggregate

Semi-Final

| Date | H/A | Opponent | W/L | Score |
|---|---|---|---|---|
| 13 October | A | Sheffield | L | 36-59 |
| 15 October | H | Sheffield | W | 62-30 |

Won 98-89 on aggregate

Final

| Date | H/A | Opponent | W/L | Score |
|---|---|---|---|---|
| 26 October | A | King's Lynn | L | 34-59 |
| 29 October | H | King's Lynn | W | 51-42 |

Lost 85-102 on aggregate

## 2005 Premier League (includes League, Premier Trophy, Knock-Out Cup and Young Shield)

| Name | M | R | Pts | BP | Total | CMA |
|---|---|---|---|---|---|---|
| Stuart Robson | 48 | 225 | 443 | 65 | 508 | 9.03 |
| Chris Neath | 55 | 264 | 555 | 26 | 581 | 8.80 |
| Brent Werner | 57 | 264 | 491 | 53 | 544 | 8.24 |
| Edward Kennett | 57 | 252 | 454 | 51 | 505 | 8.02 |
| Daniel King | 53 | 253 | 425 | 54 | 479 | 7.57 |
| Tommy Allen | 52 | 233 | 308 | 60 | 368 | 6.32 |
| Steve Boxall | 44 | 180 | 176 | 40 | 216 | 4.80 |
| Luke Bowen | 7 | 22 | 17 | 4 | 21 | 3.82 |